Queen Victoria's Grandsons

(1859-1918)

Christina Croft

© Christina Croft 2014

A Hilliard & Croft Book

Contents

Queen Victoria's Children and Their Sons & Daughters-In-Law

Victoria (Vicky)
=
Frederick William (Fritz) Crown Prince of Prussia/ German Emperor Friedrich III

Wilhelm/William (Willy)
=
Augusta Victoria of Schleswig-Holstein-Sonderburg-Augustenburg (Dona)

Henry
=
Irene of Hesse

Sigismund

Waldemar

Albert Edward (Bertie) Prince of Wales/King Edward VII
=
Alexandra of Denmark

Albert Victor (Eddy)

George
=
Mary of Teck (May)

Alexander John

Alice
=
Louis, Prince/Grand Duke of Hesse-Darmstadt

Ernst Ludwig (Ernie)
=
1) Victoria Melita of Edinburgh/Coburg (Ducky)
2) Eleonore of Solms-Hohensolms-Lich

Frederick (Frittie)

Alfred (Affie) Duke of Edinburgh & Coburg
=
Marie of Russia

Young Affie

Helena (Lenchen)
=
Christian of Schleswig-Holstein

Christian Victor (Christle)

Albert (Abbie)

Harald

Louise
=
John, Marquis of Lorne
No issue

Arthur, Duke of Connaught

=

Louise (Louischen) of Prussia

Young Arthur

=

Alexandra, Duchess of Fife

Leopold, Duke of Albany

=

Helen of Waldeck-Pyrmont

Charles Edward (Charlie)

=

Victoria Adelaide of Schleswig-Holstein-Sonderburg-Glücksburg
(Dick)

Beatrice

=

Henry of Battenberg (Liko)

Alexander (Drino)

=

Lady Irene Denison

Leopold

Maurice

The Grandsons in Birth Order

Wilhelm/William (Willy) (1859-1941) – Eldest son of Queen Victoria's daughter, Vicky

Henry (1862-1929) – Second son of Queen Victoria's daughter, Vicky

Albert Victor (Eddy) (1864-1892) – Eldest son of Queen Victoria's son, Bertie

Sigismund (1864-1866) – Third son of Queen Victoria's daughter, Vicky

George (1865-1936) – Second son of Queen Victoria's son, Bertie

Christian Victor (Christle) (1867-1900) – Elder son of Queen Victoria's daughter, Lenchen

Waldemar (1868-1879) – Fourth son of Queen Victoria's daughter, Vicky

Ernst Ludwig (Ernie) (1868-1937) – Eldest son of Queen Victoria's daughter, Alice

Albert (Abbie) (1869-1931) – Second son of Queen Victoria's daughter, Lenchen

Frederick (Frittie) (1870-1873) – Younger son of Queen Victoria's daughter, Alice

Alexander John (1871-1871) – Youngest son of Queen Victoria's son, Bertie

Alfred (Young Affie) (1874-1899) – Son of Queen Victoria's son, Affie

Harald (1876-1876) – Youngest son of Queen Victoria's daughter, Lenchen

Arthur (Young Arthur) (1883-1938) – Son of Queen Victoria's son, Arthur

Charles Edward (Charlie) (1884-1954) – Son of Queen Victoria's son, Leopold

Alexander (Drino) (1886-1960) – Eldest son of Queen Victoria's daughter, Beatrice

Leopold (1889-1922) – Second son of Queen Victoria's daughter, Beatrice

Maurice (1891-1914) – Youngest son of Queen Victoria's daughter, Beatrice

Prologue

On a dark winter's evening in January 1859, the manager of a London theatre interrupted a performance of a Shakespearean tragedy to announce the birth of a future king. The auditorium erupted in rapturous applause and the audience spontaneously rose to its feet with a hearty rendition of *God Save the Queen.*

Soon afterwards, the London Opera performed an additional verse to the anthem:

"Hail the auspicious morn,
To Prussia's throne is born
A Royal Heir.
May he defend its laws,
Joined with old England's cause,
And win all men's applause!
God save the Queen!"

Half a century later, London theatres erupted again with impromptu performances of the national anthem but this time they would be a war-cry, and, Kaiser Wilhelm II, the man whose birth had aroused such excitement fifty-five years earlier, had become the object of anger, condemnation and scorn.

To the end of his life, however, the Kaiser would remember his grandmother, Queen Victoria, with the deepest affection. He was proud to have been the eldest of her eighteen grandsons, some of whom played a major role on the world stage while others lived and died in relative obscurity. Born into eight very different families – the Hohenzollerns (or Prussians); the Waleses; the Hessians; the Edinburghs; the Christians (or Schleswig-Holsteins); the Connaughts; the Albanys; and the Battenbergs – their upbringing and their fortunes varied widely. Some died in childhood, some were killed in action, and others lived to see grandchildren of their own. There were heroes and villains, valiant soldiers and dissipated youths, but their lives were interconnected through the tiny Queen for whom their welfare and happiness was a constant preoccupation.

As part of a wide, extended family, they lived through the halcyon days of the late nineteenth century European monarchies, witnessing the most spectacular and the most tragic events of the age. Their lives, their status and their relationships would be dramatically torn apart by the bloody battles raging in France and Flanders, but, winners or losers, all were united in reverence, respect and devotion to 'dearest grandmamma.'

Part I – 'By No Means a Commonplace Child'

Royal Childhood

Chapter 1 – A Want of Give & Take on Both Sides

Vicky (Victoria) – Eldest child of Queen Victoria; wife of Fritz, Prince of Prussia
Fritz (Frederick William/Friedrich Wilhelm) – Son of the Crown Prince/Prince Regent of Prussia; Vicky's husband
The Crown Prince (Wilhelm/William) – Fritz's father
The Crown Princess (Augusta) – Fritz' mother
Willy (William/Wilhelm) – Fritz & Vicky's eldest son

Queen Victoria's eldest daughter, Princess Victoria Adelaide Mary Louisa, known to her family as Vicky, had much to celebrate at the dawn of 1859. Married ten months earlier to the dashing and devoted, Frederick William (Fritz) of Prussia, she had recently moved into her new home on Berlin's beautiful *Unter den Linden*, and, in the midst of a particularly mild winter, she could look forward to the imminent birth of her first child.

Intellectually brilliant, pretty and charming, eighteen-year-old Vicky had won the hearts of the British people at a time when the Royal Family was at a peak of popularity. So loved was she by her mother's subjects that when she married the only son of the heir to the Prussian throne, the crowds who gathered to witness her departure for Berlin, called out to her husband,

"Treat her well or send her back home!"

No matter where she might live, nor by what foreign title she might be known, to her mother and to her mother's people, Vicky would ever remain first and foremost their *English* Princess Royal.

The crowds need not have worried about how well the young groom would treat his bride, for Fritz was as in love with Vicky as she was with him. With similar political ideals and interests, they were ready to work together to fulfil Vicky's father's dream of a peaceful and cultured

Prussia heading a united Germany, and maintaining strong ties to Britain.

To all outward appearances, ten months after her wedding Vicky appeared to have all that any young woman could desire – a loving husband; a beautiful home; financial security; the expectation of a child; the support of her parents; and a noble purpose which would engage her considerable intellectual faculties to the full. During her first Christmas season away from home, however, Vicky was not quite as content as many might have imagined.

Throughout her childhood, Christmases at Windsor had been so magical that now she looked back nostalgically to those halcyon days, missing her family and, above all, the father whom she adored. Even the distance between Prussia and England could not weaken the bond between Prince Albert of Saxe-Coburg-Gotha and his eldest daughter, for the Prince had doted upon the girl who, 'gifted to the point of genius', was one of very few people who could match his intellectual brilliance and in whom he could invest such hope for the future of his native Germany. Her eagerness to learn and the speed with which she grasped new concepts delighted him. By the age of ten she had mastered several languages and, the following year, her governess was convinced that, thanks to her extensive general knowledge, linguistic talents and scintillating conversation, she could pass for a girl of eighteen. Unsurprisingly, when the shy Prussian Prince Fritz made his first visit to England, he was deeply impressed by the precocious little girl who exuded enthusiasm and confidence.

Prince Albert was thrilled to witness the blossoming friendship between his daughter and the son of the heir to the Prussian throne, and he saw, at once, the possibility of their fulfilling a long-held dream. Germany was not yet a unified nation but a compilation of independent kingdoms and duchies, including Prince Albert's native Saxe-Coburg, and Fritz's native Prussia. Like many of his countrymen, Prince

Albert was a firm advocate of unification and had produced a lengthy treatise on the subject. A united Germany, he believed, would bring many advantages to the separate states as well as playing a major role in maintaining a peaceful Europe. Since Prussia was by far the most dominant kingdom, it was vital to Prince Albert's dream that the Prussian King should be an open-minded man, who would not only maintain friendly relations with Queen Victoria's rapidly-expanding Empire, but would also govern his country with liberal values.

To Prince Albert's great delight, Fritz, a reticent young man of nineteen, shared his vision for the future of Germany. Like Albert, he was something of a romantic, seeing his homeland as 'a continuation of the mediaeval, the Emperor the successor of Charlemagne'[1]; and, the longer they discussed their ideas, the greater became their conviction that they could bring their dream to fruition. Moreover, Fritz was intrigued by the British Royal Family whose home life was a pleasant contrast to that in which he had been raised. Used to the more formal and increasingly militaristic atmosphere of the Prussian court, he was happily surprised by the informality of Queen Victoria's household; and was particularly impressed by the mutual devotion of Vicky's parents, when his own parents, Crown Prince Wilhelm and Crown Princess Augusta, were constantly at loggerheads.

To Albert, it was clear that Fritz would require a supportive wife who could assist him in the cultural and political development of the new nation; and who better, he thought, was suited for that role than his own eldest daughter, Vicky?

Determined to conceal his aspirations to avoid placing pressure on his child, Albert nurtured his dream in silence but several times he invited Fritz back to England in the hope that the young couple might fall in love. The plan worked to perfection, for the next time that Fritz met fourteen-year-old Vicky, their pleasure in each other's company was apparent to everyone.

When, sooner than anticipated, Fritz proposed, Vicky accepted him; and, painful as it would be to be parted from their daughter, Queen Victoria and Prince Albert were elated. In the months between the betrothal and the wedding in January 1858, Albert devised an intensive course of study to guide his eldest daughter through the intricacies of the German political system, encouraging her to form opinions based on a wide variety of historical and contemporary writings.

Aware of her father's dream, seventeen-year-old Vicky arrived in Berlin filled with high hopes and good intentions. It did not take long, however, for her to discover that her studious, sensitive and liberal-minded husband was an atypical prince in a court where royal brides were viewed primarily as brood mares to produce heirs to the throne. Shocked to discover that the majority of German princesses were educated solely for marriage, she quickly learned that women had no place in Prussian politics and her opinions were of no consequence to her husband's family.

At the time of her marriage, Fritz's father, Crown Prince Wilhelm, had been appointed as Regent for his brother, the childless King Friedrich Wilhelm IV, who had suffered a stroke the previous year and was incapable of carrying out his duties. A patriot and veteran of the Napoleonic Wars, the Crown Prince treated Vicky with a measure of affection and initially embraced some of her liberal views but, as time passed, he fell under the influence of the formidable Otto von Bismarck, whose reactionary and militaristic approach to politics was the exact opposite of all that Vicky and Fritz believed.

Bismarck shared the Crown Prince's view that women had no place in politics, and he so resented the outspoken foreigner that he was quick to spread rumours through the gossip-ridden court that she was trying to impose her English ways on the taciturn husband whom she dominated.

In fairness to the Prussians, Vicky did little to help her own cause. Although she attempted to adjust to the mores of Berlin, her frequent tactless comparison between Germany and England were taken as insults. Matters were not helped by her mother's regular exhortations to remember that, although she was now Fritz' wife, she would forever remain, first and foremost, an English princess.

"If I was to lose sight of my English title and dignity," Vicky wrote to her reassuringly, "I should do myself and my husband much harm, besides be forgetting my duty to you and England."[2]

Attempting to reconcile such apparently divided loyalties did not come easily to a seventeen-year-old girl, who at so early an age had gone from the security of a close-knit family to a foreign country where she was expected to forget all she had learned and behave like a typical Prussian princess.

"There was a want of give-and-take on both sides," her eldest son would later recall. "Her qualities were inadequately appreciated; her contrariety remained."[3]

Shocked as she was by the political system, Vicky was even more stunned by the situation within her own home. Having been raised by loving parents, it was alarming and embarrassing for her to witness the deepening antipathy between her father- and mother-in-law. Fritz's hypochondriacal mother was a cultured and well-educated woman, whose attempts to intervene in politics had been utterly crushed by her husband, whose antipathy towards her was rapidly deteriorating into outright hostility. Their very public rows were excruciating for Vicky; and the demanding Crown Princess' mood-swings rapidly became intolerable as she ceaselessly poured out her problems to Vicky, expecting her to come and comfort her at any hour of the day or night, regardless of the inconvenience.

Homesick to the point where she wept at the thought of her family's life continuing without her, Vicky became pregnant at a time when she was still trying to adapt to a new way of life. Her parents-in-law repeatedly emphasised the importance of producing a male heir, and expected her to adopt the customs of pregnant princesses in Prussia, while her mother was simultaneously urging her to adhere to English traditions. When, for example, an astonished Queen Victoria heard that in Germany pregnant women were not permitted to act as godmothers, she responded by encouraging Vicky to ignore such an 'absurd' and ludicrous rule. She was equally adamant that her daughter should avoid the 'indecorous' German custom of entertaining guests while lying on a sofa in a dressing gown. Such behaviour, said the Queen, might be acceptable in Germany but it would shock the people at home, and Vicky must always remember that she was still England's Princess Royal.

"Let the German ladies do what they like but the English Princess must not."[4]

Along with the stress of attempting to keep everyone happy, by Christmas 1858, Vicky was faced with the frightening prospect of an imminent confinement. Rank and wealth were no protection from the dangers of childbirth during which as many as one in five mothers died. The Queen, convinced that British doctors and midwives were superior to any in Europe, was eager to ensure that her daughter had the best possible care, and so, in the autumn of 1858, she dispatched a monthly nurse[a], Mrs Innocent, and her own doctor, Sir James Clark, to Berlin. The Prussian obstetricians, Doctors Schönlein, Wegner and Martin, were unimpressed by the arrival of the foreigners, and viewed Clark's presence as an implication of their own incompetence.

---

[a] 'Monthly nurses' were appointed to assist 'lying-in' women through the first four weeks after the birth of their babies.

Clark, however, was the eternal optimist when it came to dealing with the Queen, and, the moment he arrived in Prussia, he sent word back to England that the princess was well and in excellent spirits. He was equally cheerful a few weeks later when, on 27th January 1859, he blithely announced that the princess was safely delivered of a son.

"God be praised and thanked," wrote an ecstatic Prince Albert, "that He has ordered all things so graciously, and may He continue to shield the mother and the child!"[5]

All over England, Queen Victoria noted excitedly, people were 'in ecstasies – such pleasure, such delight as if it was their own prince and so it is, too'.

In Berlin, as soon as the 101-gun salute sounded to announce the birth of an heir, Fritz's father, the Crown Prince, excitedly ran from a meeting in the Foreign Office and hailed an ordinary cab to take him to see his grandson as quickly as possible. The celebrations that followed had, according to one observer, the air of a great family party; and the public was even more delighted when the proud father responded to the congratulations he received from the Chamber of Deputies, with the promise that:

"If God should preserve my son's life, it shall be my chief endeavour to educate him in the opinion and sentiments that bind me to the Fatherland."

In the midst of the toasts and telegrams, however, few were aware of the trauma that Vicky and the baby had endured. During the thirteen hour labour, the child was discovered to be in the breech position, which, in normal circumstances, would necessitate a caesarean. At the time, though, such an operation almost invariably resulted in the mother's death, and none of the doctors was prepared to accept responsibility for killing the English princess. Fearing for the life of both mother and child, Doctor Martin eventually opted to use forceps, and, by the time the baby was dragged from the womb, he appeared so lifeless that he was believed to be dead.

"The moment the little one was born," a German midwife recounted many years later, "a despairing moan [came] from the mother...'The Princess is dying — she is paying dearly for her son,' whispered the doctors, while working with blanched faces over the prostrate body. Of course, I had to abandon the child momentarily to help them, and when — [Vicky] having revived after a little while — I knelt down before the couch on which our heir rested, imagine my fright: he had not yet uttered a cry, nor did he move a muscle. 'Still-born, by Heaven!' I thought."[6]

The midwife gestured to Dr Martin who immediately seized the baby and rubbed him so vigorously that the nerves of his shoulder, already weakened by the forceps, were irreparably damaged leaving him with a disability which would plague him throughout his life.

When a horrified Queen Victoria eventually learned the extent of Vicky's sufferings, she was determined to travel to see her at the first opportunity. Although, with idiosyncratic candour, she made no secret of the fact that she found small babies extremely unattractive, her excitement at being a grandmother overcame her usual revulsion. 'Your child would delight me at any age,' she gushed to Vicky, while bemoaning the numerous duties which prevented her from leaving at once for Berlin. In the meantime, she would have to make do with receiving descriptions and sketches of the little boy, who, she observed with amusement, bore a striking resemblance to his mother at the same age.

According to Prussian law, a royal baby had to be christened as soon as possible, which, to Queen Victoria's great disappointment meant that she and Prince Albert could not be present for the ceremony. Instead, she dispatched Lord Raglan and Captain Ross to act as her representatives at the service in the Crown Prince's palace, during which the baby was named Frederick William Victor Albert – although he would always be known as Wilhelm or William, shortened to Willy within the family.

Vicky's delight in little Willy far outweighed the agonies she had experienced bringing him into the world. So absorbed was she by the joys of motherhood that Queen Victoria, who had specifically asked her to write every detail of Willy's progress, warned her against 'baby-worship' which was unbecoming in any woman but particularly so in a princess, who had so many other duties to perform.

Fritz was no less enamoured of his 'large and attractive' son, whom he proudly showed him off to visitors at every opportunity.

"They say all babies are alike," wrote one German lady. "I do not think so: this one has a beautiful complexion, pink and white, and the most lovely little hand ever seen! The nose rather large; the eyes were shut, which was as well, as the light was so strong. His happy father was holding him in his arms."[7]

Vicky and Fritz's did not have long to enjoy the novelty of being new parents, for, within a few days of Willy's birth, it was made patently clear that the child belonged not to them but to the country. It would not do for a Prussian prince to be overly influenced by an English mother, and therefore, the Crown Prince and his wife would take overall responsibility for his upbringing. Contrary to Vicky's wishes, her mother-in-law forbade her to breast-feed him; and in the nursery there was a good deal of friction between English monthly nurse, Mrs Innocent, and the German Doctor Wenger, who had very different ideas about how best to care for small infants.

Far more distressing for Vicky, was the growing awareness that the damage to Willy's shoulder was worse than initially realised. Although he was able to move his fingers, his left arm was weak and failed to grow, while the trauma to the nerves led to spasmodic torticollis – a painful condition of the neck, in which the head jerks involuntarily, particularly when the sufferer is stressed or agitated. Later, there would be a suggestion that his brain had been starved of oxygen, leading to permanent damage that manifested in erratic behaviour and dramatic mood-swings[b].

Vicky refused to believe that the disability could not be corrected and, though buoyed by Sir James Clark's typically optimistic prognosis that in time Willy would outgrow the problem, she reluctantly accepted the experimental treatments suggested by other doctors. When Willy was only a few months old, Dr Wenger suggested binding his right arm to his side, in the hope that he would then be obliged to use the left one, in much the same way as a 'lazy eye' is corrected by placing a patch over the 'good' eye. The experiment proved futile and, even as Willy approached his first birthday, he seemed unaware that he had a left arm since it was quite useless and he had no feeling in it. Although Vicky, with characteristic pessimism, was rapidly becoming disillusioned by the treatments, those around her continued to assure her that there would be a cure. Willy's English nurse was convinced that his inability to crawl would lead to his learning to walk more quickly, and various medical men, whom Queen Victoria consulted, repeatedly stated that the problem was not insurmountable.

In an age where disability was viewed as weakness, every attempt was made to conceal the problem, but within fourteen months exaggerated rumours began to appear in the newspapers, and Vicky heard whispers that 'a one-armed man can never be king.' Increasingly desperate, she watched helplessly as the doctors continued their bizarre experiments, attempting to straighten his neck by strapping him into a

---

[b] While it is possible that some of Willy's more erratic behaviour was due to brain-damage at birth, it is worth remembering that his paternal grandmother was equally erratic; his father was prone to depression; and his great uncle, King Friedrich Wilhelm IV, was also afflicted by depression, eventually became insane.

24

machine, while a rod was pressed to his spine, and his head was turned by means of a screw. Weights were tied to his left arm in an effort to make it grow; and the most outlandish treatment of all involved tying the damaged limb to a recently-slaughtered hare!

The humiliating 'cures' were exhausting and painful but totally ineffective; and, as Willy developed, his difficulties with balance became more obvious and were exacerbated by his susceptibility to painful ear infections. Running, he could not keep pace with smaller boys; he could not jump easily or climb trees; and he found it difficult to learn to swim or to remain in the saddle when learning to ride.

Unsurprisingly, the little boy's frustration sometimes exploded in tantrums, the most public of which occurred when he was four years old. On the way to the wedding of his uncle, the Prince of Wales, Willy seized the muffler of his six-year-old Aunt Beatrice and hurled it from the carriage. Once inside the chapel, he threw his ceremonial dirk across the aisle and, when his young uncles attempted to restrain him, his kicked them and bit their legs. His father, with remarkable psychological insight, found an ideal method of dealing with the little boy's tantrums. On hearing from his nurses that Willy caused a commotion whenever they tried to bathe him, Fritz sent an order to the sentries, telling them not to present arms to his son when he passed the following day. When Willy complained that the guards had failed to acknowledge him, Fritz told him calmly,

"The sentries are not allowed to present arms to an unwashed prince."

That evening, there were no more tantrums at bath time.

Gradually, though, Willy's deformity began to undermine his confidence and he became so shy that his aloofness was often mistaken for arrogance – a misunderstanding which would tarnish his image to the end of his life. In time, he learned to overcompensate for his shyness by creating a mask of self-assurance, concealing his fear of rejection by laughing and talking too loudly, making jokes and dominating conversations, which he had prepared in advance.

"After being with [him] for some time," an observer wrote many years later, "one began to see that his brilliance was mostly superficial and all his conversation studied beforehand. It seemed to me that he anticipated what subjects of conversation would crop up and then got his staff to look up statistics, which he afterwards brought out in conversation, with the result that people were astounded at his knowledge."[8]

By the time that he was ten years old, his mother had accepted that the arm could never be healed and the only solution was to help him to adapt to the situation and, as far as possible, conceal the deformity. Extra raised pockets were sewn into his clothes, allowing him to disguise the shortness of his arm, while his little hand was usually hidden by a glove. Later portraits often show him standing with one hand pressed to his side in an apparently arrogant pose, which was, in reality, merely an attempt to distract from the deformity. As he was unable to hold a knife and fork, a footman stood behind him to cut up his food, and a spoon with a serrated edge was designed specifically for him, although similar implements were later used by guests at his banquets.

As the future Kaiser, it was vital that Willy should become a competent rider but his lessons were painful and traumatic as he frequently fell from his pony. Again and again, amid many tears, he was forced to remount but, eventually, the seemingly tyrannical regime proved successful as he became so skilled a horseman that he could take the reins in his 'useless' left hand, leaving his right hand free to hold a sword or acknowledge the crowds. An inspirational military gymnastics instructor, Captain von Dresky, helped him to master shooting and swimming, and, despite his handicap he became a remarkably proficient rower.

His father, who, as Willy wrote later, 'had the most genuine sympathy with any and every form of suffering', calmly accompanied him to medical consultations and stayed unflinchingly by his side as surgeons cut his neck in the hope of releasing the tension on the nerves. His mother, however, continued to fret 'night and day' about him. She dreaded his treatments and cringed to see him suffer but the more anxious she was, the more convinced he became that she found his deformity repulsive and consequently could not love him. The developing tension between mother and son could not have suited the vulture-like Bismarck better, and the wily statesman was already preparing to use the situation to his own ends.

Chapter 2 – Joyless the Youth

Vicky (Victoria) – Eldest child of Queen Victoria; wife of Fritz, Crown Prince of Prussia

Fritz (Friedrich Wilhelm) – Crown Prince of Prussia; son of King Wilhelm I; Vicky's husband

The King of Prussia – Wilhelm I; Fritz's father

The Queen of Prussia – Fritz's mother

Willy (William/Wilhelm) – Fritz & Vicky's eldest son

Charlotte – Fritz & Vicky's eldest daughter

Henry – Fritz & Vicky's second son

Three weeks before Willy's second birthday, his great uncle, King Friedrich Wilhelm IV, died, and his grandfather ascended the throne as Wilhelm I. The following year, 1862, the new King appointed Otto von Bismarck as Minister President – the Chief Minister, who would preside over the legislature and act as a senior advisor to the monarch.

Ambitious for himself and for the country, Bismarck was determined to bring about a Prussian-led German unification, but, while Fritz and Vicky – now Crown Prince and Crown Princess – shared the dream of a peaceful and co-operative union, they were alarmed by Bismarck's methods and the ruthlessness with which he was prepared to bring the plan to fruition.

Fiercely anti-socialist, anti-Catholic and anti-democratic, Bismarck was such an ardent monarchist that he quickly gained the King's confidence, and throughout the 1860s provoked a series of wars to establish Prussia's dominance over the other German states[c]. While his foreign policy combined calculated diplomacy with military might, his control of domestic affairs was equally cunning and brutal. Taking charge of the press, he was able to publicise

---

[c] See Chapter 4

real and invented scandals to destroy the reputation of his enemies; and he gradually introduced legislation to curb the power of any group which opposed him. Since Vicky and Fritz were opposed to his underhand dealings and dictatorial manner, the Minister President took every opportunity to denigrate the English princess and to alienate her husband from the King and his court, using their eldest son as a pawn.

Willy's disability and the humiliating treatments he had endured left him with abhorrence of weakness in himself or in others; and, to mask his shyness and shame he had developed an arrogant bravado, which the master manipulator, Bismarck, would use to the full. Flattering the susceptible boy and instilling in him a sense of his own importance, he filled his imagination with stories of Prussian strength and superiority. Next to Bismarck's powerful rhetoric, the liberal opinions of Willy's parents sounded weak and effete; and, while the Minister President massaged his frail ego with blandishments, his mother appeared hypercritical in her attempts to correct his increasingly haughty behaviour.

Bismarck was happy to encourage the little boy in his belief that his mother did not love him, but in reality nothing could have been further from the truth. Vicky regularly praised him, describing him as handsome with beautiful bright eyes; and telling Queen Victoria that:

"He is by no means a commonplace child; if one can root out – or keep down – pride, conceitedness, selfishness and laziness he may be a fine character some day; he takes an interest in everything he sees and is very quick of understanding besides having a will of his own, which is a great thing."[9]

Repeatedly she made excuses for him, stressing that his selfishness had been 'more encouraged than checked' by his overindulgent grandparents; and stressing that, despite his bravado, his was truly 'a dear promising child – lively and sweet-tempered and intelligent.'

When Willy was eighteen months old, Vicky gave birth to a daughter, Charlotte, known in the family as 'Ditta' from Willy's childish attempts to say 'sister'; and two years later, August 14th 1860, a second son, Henry, was born. A rather delicate child who, while still very young, suffered an inflammation of the lungs and was afterward regularly taken to spas in the hope of strengthening his constitution, Henry became Willy's closest companion, supporting him through his medical treatments and empathising with him in the face of their mother's criticism.

For all her intellectual genius, tact was not Vicky's forte, and – like her mother who had candidly described her offspring as 'backward' or 'ugly' – she readily and frequently expressed her honest opinions about the appearance and progress of her children. Willy was handsome, but Charlotte was unfortunately 'plain' with such thin hair that it had to be cropped like a boy's; and 'poor' Henry, who was quite simply 'ugly', 'mortified' his mother's feelings by his physical resemblance to the apparently unattractive Princess Marie of the Netherlands.

Fortunately the children did not know of these harsh descriptions since the comments were made in private to Queen Victoria, but they were aware of their mother's frustration at their lack of progress in the schoolroom, and her failure to understand why they were neither as intelligent nor as studious as she had always been. She recognised that Willy was a clever boy, whose progress was hindered by his exhausting and painful medical treatments, but the same excuse could not be made for his siblings. Both Charlotte and Henry were 'backward' and 'lazy' and she became so determined to force them to learn that Queen Victoria felt a need to intervene:

"Don't press poor dear Henry too much; it will not do any good and he will learn none the better for it...more harm than good is done by forcing delicate and backward children."[10]

The constraints of the court and their numerous duties prevented Fritz and Vicky from participating as fully as they would have liked in their sons' education, but they were nonetheless able to ensure that their curriculum encompassed a wide variety of practical and academic subjects, rather than being based on solely on the military training that was customary for Prussian princes. To that end, they appointed various nurses, governesses and tutors, the first of whom, Mrs. Hobbs ('Hobbsy') was an affectionate English woman, who was soon replaced by a governess, Fraulein Dobeneek – known to the children as 'Dokka' – who had no qualms about caning the young princes for their misbehaviour. On one occasion, while giving Willy a thrashing, she told him,

"Believe me, Your Highness, what I have just done, pains me as much as it pains you."

The quick-witted boy immediately replied, "Ah! In the same place I suppose?"

In 1867, eight-year-old Willy and five-year-old Henry were removed from Dokka's care, and placed under the supervision of a thirty-eight-year-old tutor, George Hinzpeter, who came on the highest recommendation from the English diplomat, Sir Robert Mourier. Ascetic in appearance and uncouth in his table manners, Hintzpeter was quick to impose his own Calvinistic austerity on his pupils. He did not believe in praise but expected the highest standards from the princes, particularly from Willy, since, as he said, a future king must be in every way be superior to his people.

Despite his severity, Hintztpeter was well-intentioned and sufficiently observant to notice how easily-led and susceptible Willy was to Bismarck's flattery. In an attempt to combat Bismarck's influence, Hinztpeter encouraged the boy to form his own opinions, and to think for himself, disregarding the advice of others. Unfortunately, the lesson backfired as it served only to make Willy less inclined to heed his mother's admonishments, and matters were made worse when the tutor openly stated that the Crown Princess was too wrapped up in her husband to show much affection to her children.

Hintzpeter's regime was as austere as his character. The boys' lessons began at dawn and continued into the evening, interspersed with 'recreational' rides or walks during which the princes were expected to recite aloud from the Classics. It was he who insisted that, no matter how frequent and painful his falls from his pony, Willy must remount and continue remounting until he could ride unaided; and, although, in the long run, his harshness proved beneficial, at the time it was so excruciating for Henry to witness that he frequently burst into tears at his brother's suffering.

Within the schoolroom, Hintzpeter's methods were equally uninspiring:

> "Joyless as the personality of this dry, pedantic man, with his gaunt meagre figure and parchment face, grown up in the shadows of Calvinism, was his educational system;" Willy later recalled, "joyless the youth through which I was guided by the 'hard hand' of the Spartan idealist."[11]

The dullness of the lessons did not, however, dampen Willy's enthusiasm for his favourite subjects: history and languages, at which he excelled. The appointment of specific language tutors, relieved the boredom of Hintzpeter's lessons, as the boys enjoyed learning English from the 'lively' Miss Archer, and the 'charming' Miss Byng; and being taught French by the 'delightful elderly' Mlle Darcourt.

Whenever possible, their parents participated in their education. Vicky spoke with them in English and French, and encouraged them to experiment in painting and drawing. Fritz often read to them and told them exciting tales of German history. One of Willy's happiest memories was of sitting on the floor beside his father as he explained the pictures in a giant book about the treasures of the Holy Roman Empire.

Henry, though less academically gifted, was adept at practical skills and from his earliest years showed a marked enthusiasm for mechanical devices and engines. While Willy looked back to Germany's past and absorbed himself in tales of mythical heroes, Henry had an eye to the future and was keen to learn all he could about the latest inventions, particularly those related to transport. Like his mother's brother, Alfred, Duke of Edinburgh, he quickly developed a passion for the sea, and he and his elder brother spent many hours sketching battleships and dreaming of a great Prussian navy.

In accordance with their own liberal views, Vicky and Fritz were keen to ensure that the boys would come regularly into contact with ordinary people. Twice a week they were taken to factories or workshops to learn about trade and different manufacturing processes, and also to recognise the necessity of showing respect to people of all classes. On leaving any business, the boys doffed their caps and thanked the proprietors and workmen for their time.

Although, under Hintzpeter's tutelage, many hours were taken up with study, there was still plenty of time for recreation. German cousins and the children of their parents' friends often came to play with the boys in the gardens of Frederick the Great's summer palace, the Sanssouci. There, they ran freely in noisy games of 'robbers and soldiers, Red Indians, or military drill'. There were family outings, to the Zoological and Botanical Gardens; and visits to the circus, the theatre and the opera. Some of the foremost musicians of the day were invited to perform in the Crown Prince's palace, where Henry developed a love of military music and enjoyed writing his own compositions. Willy had a particular passion for folk dances, and despite his disability, his fingers were supple enough to enable him to become a competent pianist. In the holidays, the young princes enjoyed long morning rides with their mother, and afternoon walks with their father, with whom they went rowing or swimming.

Eager to remove them from the influence of the court, where their grandparents flattered and spoiled them, and Bismarck continued to fill Willy's head with grandiose notions, Vicky had been searching for a family home away from the intrigues of Berlin, when, in 1863, she and Fritz acquired a rundown estate in the village of Bornstedt near Potsdam. There, like Marie Antoinette at the Petit Trianon, the Crown Princess discarded her royal status to sit spinning at a wheel, while her husband worked the land, and her children played around her. At Bornstedt, Willy was always far more amenable as he revelled in his mother's undivided attention and, for a short while at least, he saw her as far less distant and cold than he had imagined.

Holidays were spent at the seaside in Belgium, or visiting their relations in Coburg, Baden, and Darmstadt, but, far and away, they most enjoyed their visits to England, where Willy and Henry revelled in the affection of their fond grandmother, Queen Victoria, and spent many happy hours at her seaside home, Osborne House, on the Isle of Wight.

Chapter 3 – Frail and Fairy-Like

The Hohenzollerns (Prussians)

Vicky (Victoria) – Eldest child of Queen Victoria; wife of
Fritz, Prince of Prussia
Fritz (Frederick William) – Son of the Crown Prince/Prince
Regent of Prussia; Vicky's husband
Willy (William/Wilhelm) – Fritz & Vicky's eldest son
Henry – Fritz & Vicky's second son

The Waleses

Bertie – (Albert Edward) Queen Victoria's eldest son; Prince
of Wales
Alexandra – Bertie's Danish wife; Princess of Wales
Eddy – (Albert Victor) – Bertie's eldest son
George – Bertie's second son
Louise – Bertie's eldest daughter
Victoria – Bertie's second daughter
Maud – Bertie's youngest daughter

Other English relations

Affie – Queen Victoria's second son
Lenchen – Queen Victoria's third daughter
Louise – Queen Victoria's fourth daughter
Arthur – Queen Victoria's third son
Leopold – Queen Victoria's youngest son
Beatrice – Queen Victoria's youngest child

"Osborne," wrote Willy, echoing the sentiments of
several of his cousins who were equally enamoured of the
place, "is the scene of my earliest distinct recollections."[12]

Designed by Prince Albert as a private family home,
Osborne House was filled with delights that appealed to the

hearts of the young Prussian princes. From the private beach, where they swam and collected fossils and shells, they could gaze across the Solent to the Royal Naval base at Portsmouth, and watch the endless stream of merchant vessels heading out to the farthest reaches of their grandmother's Empire. With an eye for the details of rigging and gun ports, Willy sketched the battleships and sail boats, firing his imagination with thoughts of a mighty Germany navy, equalling that with which Britannia ruled the waves; while Henry dreamed of embarking on thrilling round-the-world voyages.

Sometimes the boys boarded their grandmother's yacht, *Alberta,* as it sailed to the mainland to collect various uncles and aunts; and at the naval dockyard, they were given a tour of Nelson's flagship, *Victory*, and permitted to take part in the cadets' training session by loading and firing a gun.

In the grounds of the Italianesque house, they enjoyed mock battles and staged re-enactments in the miniature fort and barracks built by their uncles when they were young; and for Willy, who soon developed a passion for archaeology, the children's Natural History museum created by their grandfather, Prince Albert, was filled with fascinating treasures gathered by his mother and aunts and uncles when they were young. There were games of tennis and skittles; pony rides and walks; teas and treats and a constant supply of companions.

Osborne was but one of their grandmother's homes, each of which was filled with its own delights. At Buckingham Palace, the children could play with the toys that their mother had outgrown; and at remote Balmoral they enjoyed stalking and pony rides, and mixing freely with the local people, enjoying the 'good mountain air' in which delicate Henry thrived.

Relations constantly came and went, including the Queen's youngest daughter, Beatrice, who was only two years older than Willy, but had taken her role as aunt with amusing seriousness, insisting that she was far too busy to play since she had to write to her nephew.

Four years older than Beatrice, the haemophiliac Uncle Leopold was a cheerful companion; and his elder brother, Arthur, who was preparing to enter the Royal Military Academy at Woolwich, soon became Willy's great favourite. As a serving naval officer, the Queen's second son, Alfred ('Uncle Affie') was often away on his travels but, on the rare occasions when he met his young nephews, Henry found they had much in common, with their love of mechanical devices and their passion for the sea and sailing. During Willy and Henry's formative years, shy Aunt Lenchen and artistic Aunt Louise were almost constantly with the Queen, and Willy, who often joined them on their morning rides, spent many happy hours playing in Aunt Louise's room:

> "...and many a sweetmeat was hidden there for me. She was of a joyous, sunny temperament, and had as keen a sense of humour as her mother, the Queen, the very sort that wins the heart of a child at once. I always loved and admired her, and for me my whole life long, she remained 'the indulgent auntie.'"

There were numerous cousins to whom Willy could boast about recent Prussian victories, and, if they grew tired of his overbearing nature or were so irked by his dramatic changes of mind that they called him 'William the Sudden', he could always find solace in the company of his doting grandmother, whom he loved deeply. She was, he wrote later, a remarkable combination of the perfect monarch and the perfect wife, mother and grandmother; and few things brought him more pleasure than when she addressed him as 'my boy,' or better yet, 'my dear boy.' More indulgent with her grandchildren than she had been with her own children, she was sure to make their holidays fun, giving them a shilling for every baby tooth they lost; and, when Willy had a tooth extracted she gave him five shillings – a crown. There were raffles and treasure hunts with cakes as prizes; and now and again she would join them to watch a circus or theatre troop perform a children's show at the palace.

Despite her formidable reputation and her insistence upon good manners, Queen Victoria was ever ready to praise her grandsons and to defend them from their parents' criticism. Vicky might have thought Henry an unattractive child, but to Queen Victoria, he was 'a great darling' whom everyone admired; and Willy held a special place in her heart not only as her eldest grandchild but also because: 'that beloved and promising child was adored Papa's great favourite.'

Queen Victoria and Prince Albert had been delighted when Willy was born, and from the first moment they saw him, both were utterly enchanted. During the first eighteen months of his life, he brightened an otherwise difficult period for his grandparents as they faced various international and political crises, and several family bereavements. In the autumn of 1860, for example, a family reunion in Coburg was marred by the sudden death of Prince Albert's stepmother, but in the midst of sorrow and mourning, Willy's arrival alleviated the gloom.

"…Then our darling grandchild was brought," wrote the Queen. "Such a little love! He came walking in on Mrs Hobbs' hand, in a little white dress with black bows. He is a fine fat child, with beautiful white soft skin, fine shoulders and limbs, and a very dear face like Vicky and Fritz and also Louise of Baden[d]. He has Vicky's eyes and Fritz' mouth, and very fair curly hair. We felt so happy to see him at last!"

Unlike his mother, his grandparents paid little attention to his disability; and, while the Queen regularly consulted her own doctors about treatments and potential cures, she was more concerned about the possibility of his

---

[d] Fritz's sister

38

picking up the cockney accent of his nurse, Mrs Hobbs, than she was about his arm. To Prince Albert, Willy was the hope of the future – a child who would one day fulfil his dream of leading a cultured and unified Germany into the new century.

Sadly, Albert did not have long to enjoy the pleasures of being a grandfather, nor did he have time to share his ideals with the future Kaiser. On 14th December 1861, six weeks before Willy's second birthday, he died at Windsor at the age of only forty-two, plunging the entire country into mourning and bringing devastation to his family.

Queen Victoria was so grief-stricken that, for almost six years, she withdrew from the public gaze, creating speculation that she was about to abdicate in favour of the Prince of Wales. In reality, nothing could have been further from her mind, for she had little faith in her eldest son whom she held partially responsible for the death of 'beloved Albert.'

Prince Albert Edward, known to his family as Bertie, could not have contrasted more sharply with his elder sister, Vicky. Never a scholarly boy, his laziness and shocking behaviour in the schoolroom caused his parents endless consternation, and all his father's attempts to interest him in learning met with outright failure. Prince Albert eventually realised that Bertie's forte was his ability to charm other people, and he began to arrange for him the kind of experiences that would appeal to his gregarious nature. He organised domestic and foreign tours, including a successful visit to the United States and Canada; and, against the advice of Bertie's university tutors who feared that the prince would be led astray by his fellow officers, he granted his wish by allowing him to spend the summer of 1861 attached to a regiment of Guards in Ireland.

During Bertie's absence in Ireland, his mother, suspecting that he had inherited the wayward traits of her promiscuous Hanoverian uncles, was busily seeking a suitable bride for him in the hope that an early marriage would prevent him from erring. With Vicky's help, she had discovered 'a perfect pearl' in Alexandra, the sixteen-year-old daughter of the heir to the Danish throne, who, being innocent and beautiful but hardly a scholar, appeared to be all that Bertie could desire. In early autumn 1861, a 'chance' meeting was arranged for the couple in the German town of Speyer, and, although Bertie was not as enthusiastic as his mother had hoped, he was not averse to meeting Alexandra again.

Negotiations between the two families continued when Bertie returned to university at Cambridge and it seemed that an engagement was imminent, when suddenly, in mid-November, Prince Albert received some shocking news. As his tutors had warned, Bertie had been led astray by his companions, who had successfully smuggled an actress, Nellie Clifden, into his rooms, launching him on a womanising career that would continue to the end of his life.

The discovery of the affair horrified Prince Albert. Not only had Bertie betrayed his trust and risked the reputation of the Royal Family, but he had also jeopardised the possibility of marriage with Alexandra. In an effort to limit the damage, Prince Albert set out to Cambridge where he and Bertie walked for hours in the pouring rain – Albert assuring his son that he wished only to help him, and Bertie, duly repentant, promising never to be so foolish again.

The matter appeared to have been resolved but, by the time Albert returned to Windsor, he was shivering and exhausted to the point of collapse. Over the next three weeks his condition continued to deteriorate until, eleven days before Christmas, he breathed his last.

Distraught beyond measure, Queen Victoria sought explanations for her husband's untimely demise, and, in her desperation, she could not avoid making the link between Bertie's 'fall' and his father's last illness. She tried to forgive him for his weakness but, as she told his elder sister, she could not look at him 'without a shudder.'

"She is very kind about the P. of Wales," wrote a lady-in-waiting, in January 1862, "and He is doing His best, but all that is full of difficulties."[13]

Fortunately for them both, before his death, Prince Albert had made arrangements for Bertie to embark on a tour of the Near East, which would keep him away from home for four months, giving mother and son time to adjust to what had happened. He departed in February 1862, and, during his absence, the ever-candid Queen felt it her duty to inform Alexandra's parents about his affair with the actress. While the Danes expressed gratitude for her honesty, they were rather taken aback by the Queen's apologies, since to them it seemed perfectly normal for young princes to have several affairs before marriage, and consequently it was no impediment to an engagement with Alexandra.

In June 1862, within a month of Bertie's return from his tour, he had had further meetings with Alexandra and was speaking openly and happily of his future bride. He finally proposed in early autumn, and, to the satisfaction of both Britain and Denmark, the betrothal was formally announced.

The wedding took place in March 1863, and, following a brief honeymoon at Osborne, the couple settled into Sandringham House, Bertie's country estate in Norfolk, which soon became the social centre of 'the fast set' of aristocrats, politicians, diplomats, businessmen and the nouveaux riche. Visitors to Sandringham and to the Wales' London residence, Marlborough House, were struck by the contrast with the Queen's sombre court. Through the heady fog of cigar smoke and the echo of laughter, drinking, dining, card games and dancing often continued until dawn.

"The Princess always charming and lovely to look at;" one visitor wrote, "and the Prince, the model host, so courteous and ready to talk about anything,"

The only drawback for visitors was that Bertie, whose girth was rapidly expanding, had the curious habit of insisting that all of his guests should have their weight recorded in a visitors' book!

From her seclusion in Windsor Castle, Queen Victoria was far from amused by the tales of the goings-on at Marlborough House, and her once high opinion of Alexandra rapidly deteriorated. Where she had formerly found her warm and supportive, now she considered her stiff and cold and nothing more than 'a distinguished lady of society'. Her conversation was limited; her inability to understand her duties was frustrating; she was chronically unpunctual; and the childlike qualities which had once seemed so endearing, now appeared rather foolish.

"I am sorry too for Bertie;" Queen Victoria wrote. "I don't think she makes his home comfortable; she is never ready for breakfast – not being out of her room till 11 often, and Bertie breakfasts alone and then she alone."

Bertie's younger sisters were equally disillusioned, as Alexandra very rarely invited them to visit Marlborough House, preferring to entertain her own relations.

In fact, the apparent stiffness and preference for entertaining the Danes was probably due to Alexandra's otosclerosis – a progressive condition of the ear, leading to deafness. It was far easier to lip-read in her native language than to struggle to hear what was being said in English, although she eventually succeeded in teaching sign-language to the Queen. Moreover, Alexandra did not enjoy the endless entertaining that so appealed to Bertie; and, for the most part, she was merely trying to please her husband.

In spite of her criticism, Queen Victoria could not deny Alexandra had endeared herself to the British people, who appreciated her beauty and sought to emulate her style. To conceal a small scar on her neck, she tended to wear high collars which soon became the height of fashion; and when rheumatic fever left her with a slight limp, aristocratic ladies adopted the same gait in an attempt to appear à la mode!

Her popularity soared within a few months of the wedding when it became known that she was expecting a child but, while the country rejoiced, the Queen worried that her lifestyle would have a detrimental effect on her health and that of the baby. Her anxieties appeared to be justified when, two months sooner than expected, Alexandra went into labour.

On the afternoon of 8th January 1864, the expectant princess was watching her husband playing ice-hockey on Virginia Water at Windsor, when she suddenly felt unwell and asked to be taken home. Her lady-in-waiting, Lady Macclesfield, recognised the onset of labour, and realising that there was no time to take her back to Marlborough House, arranged instead to take her to nearby Frogmore, the former home of Bertie's late grandmother, the Duchess of Kent. Of course, nothing had been prepared and, with neither obstetricians nor midwives on hand, the local physician Doctor Brown was sent for as Lady Macclesfield prepared for the birth as best she could. Eventually at two minutes to nine in the evening, Brown and Lady Macclesfield safely delivered a tiny premature boy, weighing less than four pounds.

In spite of his size and prematurity the baby, who was named Albert Victor but known to the family as Eddy, appeared to be perfectly healthy:

> "A nice thriving-looking plump baby, with bright blue eyes, delicate features and pointed chin; a nose that will be aquiline, I shd think, and a likeness to both parents," wrote one of the Queen's ladies-in-waiting. "A very intelligent way of looking at one."[14]

Other observers disagreed about his 'plumpness', concurring that, although he looked well, he was very thin and puny. 'A perfect bijou – very fairy-like but quite healthy,' Vicky thought, and Queen Victoria agreed that despite his frail appearance and his being a 'rather fidgety' baby, he was very pretty and bore a strong resemblance to his mother.

In the first few weeks of his life, he was praised for his wise appearance and his serenity, but, as he grew, it became clear that his apparent placidity was actually lethargy and a complete lack of interest in what was happening around him. Often he seemed so oblivious of everything that observers assumed that he was either extremely lazy or – in the parlance of the era – 'backward'. In fact, it is likely that Eddy had inherited his mother's otosclerosis, and his apathy might have been due to his inability to understand what was being said.

Fortunately, he soon found a perfect companion, when a baby brother, George, was born on June 2nd 1865. Although, unlike Eddy, George was 'hardly pretty', he was brighter and stronger than his elder brother and the two soon became inseparable. Three younger sisters – Louise, Victoria and Maud – followed in quick succession, and with the birth of a younger brother, Alexander John, the close-knit family was complete. Sadly, though, baby Alexander, who had been born prematurely in the early hours of the morning of 6th April 1871, was clearly unable to thrive. That evening he was christened but survived only a few more hours, dying on 7th April.

Alexandra was distraught at her baby's death for she so loved being a mother that she virtually smothered all her children with affection. Often she kept guests waiting for dinner while she coddled and bathed her babies, and discussed their progress with their nurses.

"She was in her glory," wrote one of the nurses, "when she could run up to the nursery, put on a flannel apron, wash the children herself and see them asleep in their little beds."[15]

So attached was she to her babies that she longed to keep them as children forever. Even when they grew older and George was serving in the Royal Navy , she wrote to him as though he were a small child, sending 'great big kisses' for 'Georgie's lovely little face'; and when Eddy was sixteen she cheerfully told a friend:

"I do wish to keep them children as a long as I can, and they do so want to be men all at once."

The comfort she took in her children's affection undoubtedly sprang from her need of attention which her husband often failed to provide. Despite his assurances to his father after the Nellie Clifden affair, the attractions of a beautiful wife and a growing family, could not satisfy Bertie's voracious appetites, and his philandering increased rather than diminished after his marriage. He shocked his sister, Vicky, by frequenting some of the most notorious clubs in London; and, renowned for his flirtations and affairs with the wives of his guests, he regularly flouted propriety by making prolonged visits to married women when their husbands were not at home.

Alexandra endured his infidelities with a dignified silence, and even the Queen had to admit that she was a 'pattern of self-denial' and had a lot to endure. The British public, however, were far less tolerant and, as Alexandra's popularity rose, her husband's decreased to the point where a series of misdemeanours led to his being hissed in the street and jeered when he attended the theatre.

In the winter of 1866-1867, Alexandra, pregnant with her third child, contracted rheumatic fever and for several weeks lay in a critical condition. While the Queen and country anxiously followed her progress, Bertie delayed his return from the Windsor Races until a public outcry compelled him to go home to his ailing wife. Even then, despite the token gesture of moving his desk into her room, he continued to entertain his friends and enjoy his flirtations while Alexandra lay on her sick bed upstairs.

Two years later, a more serious event led to an even greater outcry when, as a result of his philandering, he became the first member of the Royal Family to appear in a court of law. Sir Charles Mordaunt and his young wife, Harriet, had been regular guests at the Marlborough House parties, and Bertie had often visited their Warwickshire home while Sir Charles was away. In February 1869, Harriet gave birth to a daughter and, in the throes of post-natal depression, confessed to her husband that the child could have been fathered by any one of a number of men, including the Prince of Wales. An outraged Sir Charles immediately instigated divorce proceedings and, when the case came to court, Bertie was summoned as a witness. He acquitted himself well, admitting that he had frequently visited Harriet and had written her some rather injudicious letters, but insisting that their relationship had been entirely proper and innocent. Eventually, to quell the scandal, Harriet's father declared the unfortunate young woman insane and had her committed to the Chiswick House Asylum but it was widely rumoured that her incarceration was simply a cover-up to protect the Prince of Wales.

Bertie's reputation plummeted and it was not until he suffered a near-fatal bout of typhoid in 1871 that he regained public sympathy and his popularity was restored. The Queen hoped that his brush with death might have taught him a lesson and that in future he would curb his promiscuity, but no sooner had he recovered than he returned to his former ways.

Alexandra chose to ignore Bertie's infidelities, and ensured that her children were unaware of any discord between their parents. She encouraged them to participate in family gatherings, honouring their father by writing and reciting poems for his birthdays, and giving them free run of the house rather than confining them to the nurseries. Lenient to the point of indulgence, rather than correcting her sons, Alexandra encouraged their high-spirits by participating in the practical jokes which her Danish family so enjoyed. Sliding downstairs on tea trays was a favourite pastime, and the boys threw themselves into boisterous games, charging around wildly even when important guests were staying in the house.

Queen Victoria was ever ready to defend her Prussian grandsons but her opinion of their Wales cousins frequently fluctuated. One moment they were 'dear, darling children' despite being inordinately thin and frail, and the next they were so ill-bred and ill-mannered that she confessed that she could not 'take to them at all.' She was happy that their mother insisted on a simple upbringing – teaching them to respect their servants, and to share their toys with the children of the Windsor Lodge Keeper and of other families on their estates – but she had no doubt that their unruly behaviour was entirely due to Bertie's bad example, and Alexandra's being 'most unreasonable and injudicious' in their upbringing.

Even the Queen, though, was sometimes left helpless with laughter at their antics. On one occasion, while they were dining with her, Eddy and George's manners were appalling and, when they eventually climbed under the table, their grandmother told them to stay there until they had learned to behave. As the dinner continued, the miscreants remained silently in their hiding place until the Queen, wondering what further mischief they were planning, ordered them to come out. At once both boys sprang up stark narked and charged around the room bellowing a war chant much to the Queen's amusement.

Naughtiness was one thing but the lack of a good education was quite another and, having taken such care over the schooling of her own children, Queen Victoria was troubled to see that neither Bertie nor Alexandra paid much attention to their sons' studies. Although Alexandra often read to them, she had no real interest in their performance in the schoolroom; while Bertie, who had pointedly rebelled against his own tutors, saw no reason to insist on the importance of an academic education.

Initially under the care of a gentle nursery supervisor named Mrs Blackburn, the boys had graduated to the care of a 'nursery governess', but, by the time that Eddy was seven years old, the Queen was so alarmed by his lack of progress that she decided to take matters into her own hands. During her stays at Osborne House, she had been impressed by a young curate, John Neale Dalton, of the neighbouring Whippingham Church. At twenty-nine-years-old he had lived an exemplary life and, being a Cambridge graduate, appeared ideally suited to tutor the young princes. He willingly accepted the appointment and set out for Windsor, to remain in the family's service for the next fourteen years.

Although not unduly concerned about the content of his sons' lessons, Bertie had definite ideas about the purpose of their education. Dalton was to prepare Eddy to attend Wellington College, which had been opened ten years earlier as a lasting monument to the recently-deceased Arthur Wellesley, Duke of Wellington. The school, of which Bertie was a governor, was originally founded to provide a good education to the orphaned sons of army officers and middle-class boys who wished to pursue a military career, and would therefore, Bertie believed, be an ideal environment in which his son could mix freely with his peers and prepare for a period of service with the army. George, on the other hand, had often expressed a desire to go to sea, and so Dalton was to prepare him for a cadetship in the Royal Navy. Despite the Queen's misgivings about his lack of interest in the boys' education, Bertie insisted that Dalton should provide him with daily reports about their progress.

Apart from following his brief from the Prince of Wales, Dalton, of his own volition, decided to take full responsibility for the princes' moral education. Aware of their father's reputation for womanising, the tutor hoped to prevent the boys from following his example by imposing on them an authoritarian regime, which George quickly came to respect and would later impose to a harsher degree on his own children[e]. Interestingly, Bertie's devout father, Prince Albert, had opposed appointing a clergyman as tutor to his sons for fear that he would be too dogmatic and place his responsibilities to the church above his duties to his pupils. Bertie, however was happy with Dalton's methods, and raised no objection to his insistence on daily bible readings and extensive religious education.

For all his good intentions, it did not take long for the highly-academic Dalton to discover that his was no easy task. Neither of the boys enjoyed reading, although as the Royal Librarian recalled, George liked books about ships and travel and:

> "He liked to paint the engravings...giving the covering of a horse a green tint, and painting a cow red and an elephant yellow."[16]

While far from being an intellectual, George was enthusiastic and made steady progress, but Eddy was noticeably apathetic and, in the tutor's opinion, lazy. In his daily reports to the Prince of Wales and the Queen, Dalton observed that George could be sly and arrogant, while Eddy was agreeable and docile, but the two were so dependent on one another that it would prove disastrous – particularly for Eddy – if they were to be separated. Such was the force of Dalton's personality that he was prepared to take on not only the Prince of Wales but also the whole of Parliament to ensure that the boys stayed together for as long as possible.

At their father's insistence, the princes' curriculum included plenty of physical and outdoor activities. Fencing masters and gymnastic coaches were employed at Marlborough House, and every morning the boys spent time in the riding school. There was plenty of leisure time, too, and children of their own age were invited to play with them in the gardens of Sandringham, where they built dens, went fishing and played with bows and arrows. Apart from regular visits from their Danish relations, they were often joined by

---

[e] See Chapter 17

the children of Queen Victoria's popular cousin, Princess Mary Adelaide, and her husband, Prince Francis of Teck.

While staying with the Queen, they sometimes came into contact with their Prussian cousins, Willy and Henry, who adored the beautiful Alexandra but found Bertie aloof and patronising. Willy was so struck by his Aunt Alexandra's beauty that he kept a photograph of her on his desk for most of his life. Unfortunately, his feelings were not reciprocated, for since the Prussian seizure of Schleswig-Holstein from the Danes, Alexandra hated all things German and could not take to her 'arrogant' nephew at all.

Interestingly though, Alexandra made an exception for Willy's mother, since Vicky had been one of her staunchest supporters before and after her marriage; and despite her dislike of Germans, the Princess of Wales was equally fond of Queen Victoria's second daughter, Alice, the wife of the heir to the German Grand Duchy of Hesse-Darmstadt.

Chapter 4 – Seldom a Mother and Child So Understood One Another

The Hohenzollerns (Prussians)

Vicky (Victoria) – Eldest child of Queen Victoria; wife of Fritz, Crown Prince of Prussia
Fritz (Frederick William) – Vicky's husband; Crown Prince of Prussia
Willy (William/Wilhelm) – Fritz & Vicky's eldest son
Henry – Fritz & Vicky's second son
Charlotte – Fritz & Vicky's eldest daughter
Sigi (Sigismund) – Fritz & Vicky's third son
Moretta (Victoria) – Fritz & Vicky's second daughter

The Hessians

Alice – Queen Victoria's second daughter
Louis – Alice's husband; Prince of Hesse-Darmstadt
Victoria – Alice & Louis' eldest daughter
Ella – Alice & Louis' second daughter
Irene – Alice & Louis' third daughter
Ernie (Ernst Ludwig) – Alice & Louis' elder son
Frittie (Frederick) – Alice & Louis' younger son
Alix – Alice & Louis' fourth daughter
May – Alice & Louis' youngest daughter

When Queen Victoria's second daughter, Alice, gave birth to her own second daughter in November 1864, she confessed to being 'momentarily disappointed'. In the German states, as in Russia, Salic Law precluded girls from inheriting thrones and the first duty of any princess was to provide her husband with an heir. As the wife of Prince Louis, heir to the German Grand Duchy of Hesse-Darmstadt (or Hesse-and-by-Rhine) Alice recognised the importance of producing a son but when, two years later, in 1866, she gave birth to a third girl, she had far more on her mind than her baby's gender.

Four years earlier, nineteen-year-old Alice had arrived in Darmstadt in a combination of conflicting emotions. In love with her devoted and accommodating husband, she could not have been more content in her marriage, but the death of her father seven months earlier cast a long a shadow over her happiness. Alice had adored Prince Albert, and had bravely sat by his bed as he lay dying, struggling to remain cheerful as she listened to his instructions for what should be done when he was gone. The Prince Consort knew only too well that Queen Victoria, who had been on the verge of a nervous breakdown since the recent death of her mother, would require immense support in the early weeks of her widowhood, and, although he wished Alice's wedding to go ahead as planned, he urged her to do all she could to help her mother to cope with her loss.

True to her promise, Alice, with a strength beyond her years, assumed all the Queen's duties, dealing with ministers, working through the 'red boxes', making all necessary arrangements, and bearing the immense weight of her mother's grief. So occupied was she in caring for the Queen that there was little time to deal with her own profound sorrow at her father's death; and by the time of her wedding in July 1862, many observers noted how quickly she had aged and how emaciated she had become.

Fortunately for Alice, marriage would provide an escape from the gloom and perpetual mourning of her mother's court, and would, she hoped, enable her to build a more cheerful life of her own. It did not take long, though, for the first flush of romance to dwindle away, leaving her with the sad realisation that she and Louis were far less compatible than she had originally imagined.

Like her father, Alice was a profound thinker and spiritual seeker, prone to melancholic moods, and deeply moved by aesthetics, music and art. Louis was somewhat bluff but well-meaning, a soldier by profession and more a man of action than one of contemplation. The musical evenings which Alice arranged often bored him. He had little interest in art, and, while Alice was happy that he allowed her to make all the decisions regarding the decoration of their home and the upbringing of their children, she longed for a soul-mate but found instead a husband who, in her opinion, she had to care for as though he were a child.

Matters were not helped by their difficult financial situation, for Louis was not a wealthy man as he waited to come into his inheritance, and the couple began their married life in a few cramped rooms of his parents' house until their home, the New Palace, for which Queen Victoria provided most of the funds, was completed. Even then, financial restraints placed a strain on their relationship, as Alice could not travel as freely as her siblings did, and was frequently reduced to begging her mother for assistance.

"We must live so economically," she told Queen Victoria, "– not going anywhere, or seeing many people, so as to be able to spare as much a year as we can. England cost us a great deal, as the visit was short last time. We have sold four carriage horses and only have six to drive with now, two of which the ladies constantly want for theatre visits etc.; so we are rather badly off in some things."[17]

To save the expense of tutors, Alice and Louis taught their daughters themselves, according to a curriculum which Alice devised, including the practical skills of housekeeping, accountancy, needlework, cookery and gardening; and, to avoid paying dressmakers, Alice made the children's clothes, which were handed down from one to the next as they grew.

Notwithstanding her pecuniary difficulties, Alice had taken to heart her father's maxim that with privilege comes responsibility, and was consequently involved in countless philanthropic – and often costly – activities. She interested herself in the care of the sick, orphans and the mentally ill; she promoted the arts and invited unorthodox theologians to her home; she organised meetings for women workers and she sought to improve education for girls. Soon after her arrival in Darmstadt, the Hessians were amazed to see an English princess carrying slop buckets in the hospitals or scrubbing the floors of a sick person's home, but she gradually won their affection and admiration by her tireless efforts to improve the lot of the poor.

Normally, Queen Victoria would have been impressed by such philanthropy, and, having always spoken highly of 'dear good Alice', she recognised her invaluable service after her father's death. Since her marriage, however, Alice had fallen foul of her mother, who objected to her regular requests for more money, and who now accused her of having 'done herself much harm' and 'become so sharp and bitter that no one wants her in the house.'

The root cause of the Queen's annoyance was Alice's willingness to state openly what others only dared think: it was time for Queen Victoria to snap out of her self-indulgent seclusion and to resume her public duties, seeing and being seen by her people. To make matters worse, Alice had dared to criticise the brusque John Brown, her mother's favourite Highland Servant whose rudeness to other members of the family and household had provoked a great deal of resentment. According to Alice, Brown coddled her mother in a way that Prince Albert would never have done, and rather than helping her to overcome her grief, he was allowing her to prolong it.

The Queen was incensed by Alice's outspokenness and, accusing her of being 'dissatisfied and disagreeable', she wasted no time in telling her relatives across Europe that Alice had acquired so many airs and graces that she was now 'vain and conceited'.

"When [she] came the last two times she grumbled about everything – and Louis also sometimes – the rooms, the hours, wanting to make me do this and that…If Alice wishes to come she should accommodate herself to my habits."[18]

The situation was not helped by the Queen's inability to understand her unconventional daughter's 'unseemly' interest in human biology and medicine. Hospital visiting and caring for the sick was one thing, but Alice's studies of anatomy were unsuitable for a woman, and the ease with which she spoke of indelicate matters made her mother reluctant to allow her younger daughters to visit Darmstadt for fear of what they might hear!

As so often happened in disagreements between her mother and her siblings, Vicky sought to restore harmony by reminding her mother of Alice's 'many excellent qualities' and explaining away her outspokenness as nothing but 'nerves.' Her efforts were sincere and genuine, for, since childhood she and Alice had been exceptionally close, and their bond had been strengthened by their shared experiences of marriage and life in Germany.

In 1864, the same year as Alice's second daughter, Ella, was born, Vicky had given birth to a third son, Sigismund. By now, she had gained enough confidence to stand up to her in-laws and Bismarck regarding her children's upbringing and she was determined that this little boy would be kept free of the Prussian influence that she felt had so tainted his elder brothers.

"Oh *how* I loved that little thing," she wrote frankly, "from the first moment of its birth, it was more to me than its brothers and sisters, it was so fair, so loving, so bright and merry how proud I was of my little one…Fritz and I idolised him – he had such dear winning ways, and was like a little sunbeam in the house."[19]

'Sigi' thrived on his parents' affection and soon they were convinced that he was far more intelligent than his brothers, leading Vicky to the conclusion that he would grow up to be like her 'beloved Papa'.

Alice was equally effusive, telling Queen Victoria that Sigismund was 'lovely and pretty' and:

"The greatest darling I have ever seen – so wonderfully strong and advanced for his age – with such fine colour, always laughing and so lively he nearly jumps out of our arms."[20]

What she failed to mention was the fact that she knew the child so well because, when she and Vicky were together, they breast-fed each other's babies.

The strength of the bond between the two sisters, and the solace they found in each other's company, made the events of 1866 even more difficult to bear, for in June that year they found themselves on opposing sides in a war.

While most of the German states supported the idea of unification, two opposing factions had developed with very different ideas about the nature of a united Germany. The German Federation, comprising mainly the southern states, including Hanover, Bavaria and Alice's Hesse-Darmstadt, favoured a union of all German-speaking peoples under the leadership of Austria. The majority of the northern states, on the other hand, wished to distance themselves from Austria, favouring instead a 'lesser Germany' headed by Prussia.

Naturally, Bismarck was determined to see Prussia in a position of superiority, and he was willing to go to any lengths to achieve his aim. Seizing upon the dispute over the territories of Schleswig-Holstein, he provoked a war against Austria, knowing that the German Federation would side with the Austrians, and their almost inevitable defeat would enable him to take a step closer to creating the unified Germany of which he dreamed.

Although the war lasted only seven weeks, it could not have come at a worse time for Vicky and Alice. Both feared for the safety of their husbands, who were leading their troops into battle; and while Vicky had recently given birth to a fifth child, Victoria (Moretta), Alice was in the later stages of her third pregnancy. Typically in war time, diseases were rife and, as Alice feared for the health of her unborn baby, Vicky faced an even more tragic situation.

Hardly had Fritz departed with the army than twenty-one-month-old Sigi fell ill. As most of the doctors had left with the troops, it was several days before meningitis was diagnosed by which time there was no hope of saving him. His death on 18th June broke Vicky's heart, and, according to Willy, she never recovered from the loss.

> "What I suffer, none can know, few knew how I loved," she wrote to Queen Victoria. "It was my own happy secret; the long cry of agony which rises from the innermost depth of my soul reaches Heaven alone!"[21]

To add to her sorrow, Fritz could not – or would not – abandon his troops to return home for the funeral, and Vicky was left to deal with her grief alone. Queen Victoria arranged for a memorial to the little boy to be erected in the church at Whippingham, and Vicky consoled herself by having an effigy of Sigismund placed in his cot, which she regularly visited, to the consternation of the court.

Three weeks later, as the Prussians marched towards Darmstadt, Alice gave birth to a third daughter, Irene, named after the goddess of peace. Within a fortnight, the Prussian victory was sealed. Fritz's triumphal return to Berlin was tinged with sorrow for the death of little Sigismund, and, as the rest of his family went out to greet the returning army, Willy was asked to recite a poem in memory of his dead brother.

Louis, too, returned home safely from the war but, while the Hessians greeted him as a hero for his courage in battle, he and Alice were left to deal with the consequences of defeat. Unlike many of the surrounding states, Hesse was allowed to retain its independence but the reparation payments demanded by Prussia virtually bankrupted the Grand Duchy and left Alice and Louis in greater financial straits than ever.

"We are almost ruined," Alice wrote to the Queen, "and must devote all our energies to the reconstruction of our suffering country."[22]

Fortunately, the war had not damaged the relationship between the sisters, and in the calm that followed, they regularly spent time together, sharing reminiscences of their childhood, and discussing their experiences of pregnancy and motherhood.

Eighteen months after the war, Vicky gave birth to a fourth son, Waldemar, on whom she lavished the same affection she had shown little Sigismund. Having so recently lost one son, she anxiously watched over her new baby, alert to any sign of illness. His proneness to croup and chesty coughs caused her endless worry but 'Waldie' soon outgrow his ailments and became a 'big healthy' child, filled with fun and mischief, and bringing endless delight to his parents.

To Willy it seemed that Sigismund's death had brought about a transformation in his mother's attitude to her children. He, Charlotte and Henry often viewed her as 'stern' and sometimes cold, but, he realised later, 'the younger ones, who knew her as a tender mother, idolised her.'[23]

Nothing could erase the heartbreak that Vicky and Fritz felt at Sigismund's death, but Waldemar's cheerfulness and affectionate nature went some way to compensate for their loss. Like Sigismund, Waldie was, in Vicky's opinion, 'so much more gifted than his brothers'; and so enthusiastic that he was a pleasure to teach.

"He is such a dear child," she told the Queen. "Although rather more spirited than is easy to manage, he is so trustworthy and honest and has such an open, fine, manly disposition."[24]

The Queen witnessed Waldie's high spirits when, during a visit to England, he released a pet crocodile under her desk!

When it came to appointing a tutor for the little boy, Vicky and Fritz chose a man who was quite the opposite of his brothers' rather narrow-minded tutor, Hinztpeter. Hans Delbriik was an outspoken philosopher and historian whose views often differed so sharply with Vicky's that they enjoyed many a spirited debate.

"Fearlessness is Delbriick's distinguishing characteristic," wrote an observer in 1913. "He remains an intrepid disciple of the Hegel philosophy, despite modern views of its heresy. No publicist reared in such intimate contact with the ...Imperial household in the capacity of a teacher sails so close as Delbriick to the wind of frank expression."[25]

Such outspokenness and sincerity appealed to Vicky's intellect, and Waldie made excellent academic progress under his inspirational tutelage.

Waldemar was nine months old when, following a particularly difficult labour, his Aunt Alice finally gave birth to a son. Much as she loved her three daughters, nothing could exceed her joy at the birth of an heir on 25th November 1868, and her happiness was echoed throughout the whole of Hesse-Darmstadt.

'My heart is indeed overflowing with gratitude for all God's blessings,' she told her mother, who sent a hamper of food from England to congratulate her on the birth of little Ernst Ludwig, known to his family as Ernie.

Unlike his English cousins, Ernie was a particularly big baby who developed so quickly that, by the time of his christening, three days after Christmas, he had already outgrown many of his clothes; and, when he was just eight months old, his mother proudly boasted that he was already taller and bigger than his seventeen-month-old cousin, Louise of Wales.

Like Waldemar, Ernie was, for a while, particularly prone to chest infections, but he soon overcame his childhood ailments and became such a rowdy 'rough boy', who played so wildly with his sisters, that Queen Victoria commented that it was no surprise that Alice was often exhausted with so many 'big' children to care for.

Educated at home, Ernie was taught by both parents, speaking German to his father and English to his mother; and though noticeably lazier and less studious than his sisters, he quickly developed a passion for art, which would remain with him to the end of his life. Like his parents, he took a keen interest in nature and gardening, and by the age of two was familiar with the names of many plants and flowers. He was equally fond of the numerous animals who lived in and out of the New Palace – guinea pigs, ponies, dogs and pet birds, including a little bull finch which was sadly killed by an owl.

Determined that her children should be able to live independently, Alice included practical skills in Ernie's curriculum. His father taught him basic masonry and woodwork, and how to grow vegetables; but it was equally necessary for a future Grand Duke to master the accomplishments of a prince. He was introduced to as many people as possible so that he might learn the art of making polite conversation; and Alice often introduced him to the poor and sick so that he would develop a spirit of compassion and responsibility. Music had a special place in the New Palace in Darmstadt, for Alice was an accomplished pianist, and Ernie often listened to her play, or accompanied her, or his sister, Irene, in duets. With Irene, too, he practised dancing; although both were rather less appreciative of the singers and musicians whom their mother invited to perform in their home.

As the only boy, Ernie was doted upon by his elder sisters; and, in Queen Victoria's opinion, a little spoiled. With the birth of a brother, Frederick ('Frittie') in October 1870, however, twenty-three-month-old Ernie found his first true companion and playmate.

"Baby is so nice and fat now, and thrives very well," Alice wrote of Frittie. "I think you would admire him, his features are so pretty, and he is so pink and looks so wide awake and intelligent."[26]

Ironically in the light of subsequent events, in the same letter, she inquired about the health of her younger brother, Leopold – who was a haemophiliac and had recently suffered a serious bout of bleeding – and asked if he would stand as godfather to the baby.

Ernie and Frittie were virtually inseparable, and, despite being a 'big rough boy', Ernie treated his little brother with remarkable tenderness, particularly when, as often happened, Frittie became unwell. For the first six months of his life, he had thrived, and Alice had regularly described his strength and healthy appearance, but in June 1871, he felt ill and mysterious bruises appeared on his skin. He recovered quite quickly but when, within a fortnight, he had 'a very slight return of his illness,' his mother was struck by the similarity of his symptoms to those of her haemophiliac brother, Leopold.

Although haemophilia was not well understood at the time, Alice was well aware of the suffering endured by her brother. The blood of the haemophiliac fails to clot, so a minor wound can bleed profusely, and a small knock or bump can lead to internal haemorrhages, sometimes in the joints, causing intense pain and deformity, and, ultimately, even death. Alice had often tended Leopold during his episodes of bleeding but she had no reason to suspect that his condition was hereditary or that she was a carrier, which made the realisation that Frittie, too, was a haemophiliac, all the more distressing.

61

At first, she remained hopeful. Ten months after his initial illness, Frittie had 'endless bumps and bruises as Leo used to have', but his mother added iron to his diet to strengthen his blood and trusted that he would soon outgrow the condition. By the beginning of 1873, however, she could no longer close her eyes to the evidence. Frittie's regular episodes of bleeding confirmed that he, too, was a haemophiliac.

"I was much upset," she wrote after one persistent episode when he bled so profusely from his ear that it had to be treated with caustic, "when I saw that he had this tendency to bleed, and the anxiety for the future, even if he gets well over this, will remain for years to come."[27]

Sadly, for Frittie there were no 'years to come.'

One morning in May 1873, while his father was away on business, Frittie was playing with Ernie in their mother's room as she worked through her papers. Shortly before nine o'clock, Alice went out to call for the boys' nurse and, in those few brief moments of her absence, Frittie somehow fell through the open window onto the terrace twenty feet below.

Frantically, Alice ran down the stairs and found him lying on his side, unconscious but with no visible signs of injury; and, when the doctors arrived, they confirmed that he had no broken bones but they could not dismiss the likelihood of internal bleeding.

Throughout the day, there was little change but towards the evening the side of his head began to swell suggesting a haemorrhage. All evening, Alice held him in her arms, praying that Louis, who had been urgently telegraphed, would arrive in time to say goodbye to his son. Her prayers were in vain for, at eleven o'clock, Frittie stopped breathing, and by time Louis arrived he had been pronounced dead.

Three days later, he was laid to rest in 'quiet spot amid trees and flowers', to which his family would return each year on his birthday and the anniversary of his death.

Alice, already prone to melancholy, never fully recovered from the sorrow the loss. For months after the accident, everything reminded her of him – wayside flowers that he had loved, the springtime, the silence that came from his room – and her only consolation was Leopold's assurance that, in many ways, his death was a blessing for, had he lived, he would have had a lifetime of suffering.

Alice was not alone in her grief. Ernie was not yet five-years-old, when he witnessed the tragic event, and the trauma was compounded by the loss of his playmate and a misguided sense of guilt for what had happened. Each evening he prayed for his little brother, and talked of him often when he and Alice were alone. Death preyed on his mind to the extent that, almost a year after the accident, Alice told the Queen:

> "He said the other day – for the recollection of death has left such a deep impression and he cannot reconcile it with life, it pains him – 'When I die, you must die, too, and all the others; why can't all die together? I don't like to die alone like Frittie.'"[28]

Queen Victoria commissioned a statue of the little boy, which was kept at Frogmore on the Windsor estate.

Shared sorrow over Frittie's death brought the Hessian children even closer to one another. In June 1872, a fourth daughter, Alix, had been born; and almost a year to the day after Frittie's accident, the family was complete with the birth of a fifth little girl, May. With the same tenderness with which he had once watched over his brother, Ernie now cared for his younger sisters, who felt that 'a kinder, dearer brother there never was.'

His relationship with his sisters was, though, surpassed by that which he shared with his mother to whom he was 'inexpressively precious'.

"…Seldom a mother and child so understood each other, and loved each other as we two do," Alice told the Queen. "It requires no words; he reads in my eyes as I do what is in his little heart."[29]

Despite the tragedy of losing his brother and his own early preoccupation with death, Ernie enjoyed a happy childhood, for, even though money was often scarce, his sisters were cheerful companions, and his parents did their utmost to provide their children with happy experiences. Often they went to the seaside in Belgium, and occasionally to Cannes; there were many English holidays with their grandmother, and visits to their Prussian cousins in Berlin. Often, too, they entertained their mother's siblings, and became particularly close to the children of her younger sister, Lenchen, with whom they had much in common.

Chapter 5 – A Happy, Ordinary, Little Family

The English Families

Lenchen – Queen Victoria's third daughter
Christian – Prince of Schleswig-Holstein; Lenchen's husband
Christle – Christian Victor; Lenchen's eldest son
Abbie – Albert; Lenchen's second son
Thora – Helena Victoria; Lenchen's first daughter
Marie Louise – Lenchen's second daughter

Bertie – Queen Victoria's eldest son; Prince of Wales
Alexandra – Bertie's Danish wife; Princess of Wales
Eddy – Bertie's eldest son
George – Bertie's second son

The German Families

Vicky – Crown Princess of Prussia; Queen Victoria's eldest child
Fritz – Crown Prince of Prussia; Vicky's husband

Alice – Princess of Hesse; Queen Victoria's second daughter

In 1866, while Vicky and Alice were dealing with the fallout of the Austro-Prussian War, rumblings of discontent were being heard across Britain, and the once-popular Queen Victoria was rapidly becoming an object of criticism and scorn.

In the immediate aftermath of Prince Albert's death, the nation had sympathised deeply with the widow's grief. Flags at half-mast had hung limply above the Manchester Infirmary; the tolling of the bell of the Parish Church echoed over the cobbled streets of Leeds; in Edinburgh and Dublin, prelates chanted prayers for the dead and the bereaved; and in London, curtains covered the doorways of closed theatres and music halls. Concerts and sporting events were postponed; and Charles Dickens cancelled a week of sell-out performances in Liverpool and Chester.

Sympathy for the widow and her fatherless children was genuine, but as her mourning continued for days and weeks and months, the public began to lose patience with the absent monarch who, by 1866, had been virtually invisible to her people for over five years. Republican newspapers openly questioned the purpose of a monarch who was never seen, and even less critical journalists were beginning to write disparagingly of the cost of maintaining a Royal Family which served no obvious purpose.

Criticism of the monarchy was nothing new, and royal marriages in particular had always provided churlish editors with the opportunities for complaints about the ever-lengthening civil list and the number of foreign princes expecting to be kept from British coffers. Even at the time of Queen Victoria's wedding, Albert had been described as an impoverished gold-digger; Vicky's marriage had led to complaints that the Princess Royal could have made a more advantageous match than that with a Prince of Prussia; and the same objection was repeated four years later when Alice, married the heir to the 'paltry' Grand Duchy of Hesse-Darmstadt.

By the time that the engagement of Queen Victoria's third daughter, Helena (Lenchen), was announced, however, the Queen's popularity had reached its nadir, and newspapers columns were filled with all kinds of tales about another 'German beggar', who was being foisted on the British taxpayer. Lenchen might have brushed off the criticism but what was more wounding was the tension and discord her engagement caused within her own family.

Since Alice's departure for Hesse, her younger sister, Lenchen, had assumed the role of their mother's private secretary and constant companion. As a child, she had been the tomboy of the family – an adventurous little girl who showed great equestrian skill and enjoyed the rough and tumble of her brothers' boisterous games. Her father had encouraged her boyish pursuits and, as she told a friend, she had 'loved him more than anything on earth', but in the atmosphere of silent mourning that followed his death, there was no place for high spirits, and all she could do was try her best to comfort her mother and behave as a suitable replacement for Alice.

"Her manner," wrote Lady Frederick Cavendish when Lenchen was nineteen-years-old, "is like one who has thought and done too much for her age, and been a comforter when others are only thinking of being merry-makers."[30]

Stifled in Windsor, Lenchen longed to escape to a husband, a family and a life of her own, but, while Queen Victoria understood her desire to marry, she was sure that finding a suitable *parti* would be no easy task. Less graceful and, in her mother's frank opinion, less attractive than her elder sisters, 'poor dear Lenchen' was merely the third daughter of the monarch and so there was little hope of a great dynastic match. At the time, the idea of a princess marrying a commoner seemed out of the question,[f] and, to make matters worse, Queen Victoria, having already lost two daughters to foreign courts, insisted that whomever Lenchen married must be willing to settle in England.

In spite of the difficulties, Queen Victoria remained hopeful that, with Vicky's help, an appropriate suitor could be found. After all, Lenchen had many positive traits; she was 'affectionate and good-hearted'; she was a brilliant

---

[f] Later, with the Queen's blessing, Lenchen's younger sister, Louise, married a 'commoner' – the Marquis of Lorne. At the time, despite Queen Victoria's support, the marriage provoked a good deal of criticism from foreign courts, and even Louise's brother, the Prince of Wales, was initially dubious about the wisdom of such a 'mésailliance'.

pianist; and, if she were not regularly pretty, she had beautiful hair and striking amber eyes.

It did not take long for Vicky to unearth a potential partner: her husband's cousin, the prematurely aged Prince Christian of Schleswig-Holstein, who was, according to Vicky, amusing, intelligent, very fond of children, fluent in English and, all in all, 'the best creature in the world.'

Not everyone shared Vicky's enthusiasm, for, at first sight, Christian appeared far from an ideal prince. Fifteen years older than Lenchen, with bad teeth, little hair and a persistent irritating cough, he came from a family whose lands had been lost in the seizure of Schleswig-Holstein. Queen Victoria, though, saw only the potential of an impoverished bachelor being willing to settle in a home which she would provide for him in England, and having made further inquiries into his good character, she was eager to arrange a meeting between him and Lenchen. Surprisingly, perhaps, the couple were instantly attracted to one another, and, in early autumn 1865, Queen Victoria told Alice and Vicky, in the strictest confidence, to expect an imminent engagement. By November, everything was settled, and, if the Queen was a little disappointed with her future son-in-law's appearance, she convinced herself that with the help of a good dentist, and a doctor to deal with his cough, his looks would improve and the good English air would quickly rejuvenate his aged features. Such was her fondness of Christian that she even made allowance for his smoking – a habit which she despised.

> "It was not so bad as if he drank, but still it was a distinct blemish on his otherwise impeccable character. The Queen decided to be broad-minded and actually to give him a room where he could indulge in this habit…She looked upon this room as a sort of opium-den."[31]

When, therefore, the betrothal was officially announced in early December 1865, both the Queen and

Lenchen were horrified by the furore which ensued. The press produced a plethora of ridiculous tales about the German beggar who was, they claimed, already married with a brood of children whom Lenchen intended to adopt; he was insane; he was a drunkard; and, typically, he was marrying solely for prestige and the hope of receiving a steady income from Britain. Matters were not helped when the Queen agreed to open Parliament for the first time since Prince Albert's death, for it was widely – and correctly! – reported that she had only emerged from her seclusion in order to secure a dowry for her daughter.

The press could be ignored, but the tensions within the family were far more pressing and distressing. Alexandra, Princess of Wales, objected so strongly to the part that Christian's family had played in the seizure of Schleswig-Holstein from her native Denmark that she declared categorically that she would not attend the wedding – a decision supported by Bertie in an uncharacteristic show of marital loyalty. Alice was equally unsupportive, letting it be known that her unfortunate sister was being all but forced into a loveless marriage so that the Queen could keep her service forever; and complaining that Lenchen's dowry and annuity were equal to her own, when her sister was also receiving a free home in England.

Bismarck, meanwhile was furious. Christian's elder brother, the pretender to the disputed duchies of Schleswig-Holstein, had gained a good deal of support from the smaller German states, who opposed Prussia's increasing dominance over them. The fact that Queen Victoria had sanctioned the marriage was viewed as an insult to the Prussians, and Vicky's part in bringing the couple together further alienated her from the intimidating Minister President.

Typically, the Queen flew to Christian's defence. Bismarck could be ignored; Alexandra was unreasonable; but that Alice and Bertie should take sides against their Queen and mother was too shocking:

"...when your parent and sovereign settles a thing for her good, which interferes with none of your rights and comforts, opposition for mere selfish and personal objects – indeed out of jealousy – is monstrous! I cannot tell you what I have suffered."[32]

Fortunately, by Christmas, the family feud had subsided and, seven months later, in July 1866, the wedding took place in Windsor. As though to emphasise her support for the couple, the Queen took the unusual step of giving her daughter away, explaining that, although it was contrary to tradition, in the absence of Lenchen's father, it was most appropriate for one who 'sits on a throne and does many things wh. a man does.'[33]

The newly-weds had hoped to spend their honeymoon in Christian's family castle in Augustenburg, but the King of Prussia, on Bismarck's insistence, forbad them from doing so, on the grounds that the castle occupied a strategic position in the midst of the Austro-Prussian War. An indignant Queen Victoria protested violently in an angry letter to the Prussian king, but her efforts served only to exacerbate the divisions between Vicky and Fritz, and Bismarck; and Lenchen and Christian settled instead for a few days at Osborne, followed by a honeymoon in Paris.

After the honeymoon, the couple moved into Cumberland Lodge – a grand house of 'warm red-brick, covered with Virginia creeper and honeysuckle'[34] – on the Windsor estate, sufficiently close to the Queen to enable Lenchen to continue her duties. The arrangement suited Lenchen, too, since her mother was on hand to assist her through the birth of her first child in the spring of 1867.

As her confinement approached, Lenchen and Christian moved into Windsor Castle, and there, at four in the morning on Sunday April 14th, the Queen was woken with the news that her daughter had gone into labour. Throughout the day Queen Victoria remained at her side, comforting her and assuring her that everything was going smoothly until at last, at five in the evening, a 'fine, healthy' boy was born.

Lenchen recovered quickly from her confinement, and on 21st May appeared looking well and happy at the christening, which was performed by the Archbishop of Canterbury, and during which the Prince of Wales, all past disagreements forgotten, acted as godfather. The baby was named Christian Victor, and among his more unusual christening gifts was a silver brandy saucepan from Queen Victoria.

In spite of the Princess of Wales' continued grudge against the Schleswig-Holsteins, the rest of the family was delighted by 'Lenchen's boy' – 'a pretty attractive dot' – whom the family called Christle, shortened to Kicky by his siblings.

By the time of her second confinement two years later, Lenchen had begun to show signs of the hypochondria that would later manifest more clearly. She worried intensely about the approaching birth, and desperately wanted her mother to be again at her side. In spite of the agonies she endured watching her daughters' suffering, Queen Victoria had every intention of returning from Osborne to Windsor for the event, but the baby – another 'fine healthy boy' – was born prematurely in February 1869, before the Queen had time to make the crossing. Her disappointment at being absent for the birth was amply compensated by the news that the child was to be named Albert ('Abbie') in honour of his grandfather; and consequently, she commissioned a bronze bust of the Prince Consort to be given to him for his christening.

Christle and Abbie could not have differed more starkly from their 'puny' and naughty Wales cousins. 'Nothing can beat Lenchen's boy – who one really sees grow daily,' wrote the Queen when Christle was two years old; and repeatedly over the next few years she expressed her astonishment at the healthy appearance and rapid growth of

71

the 'splendid fellows'. She was still more impressed by their excellent behaviour, for, unlike their Wales cousins, they were always 'so cheerful and so good,' and their excellent table manners impressed their eagle-eyed grandmother.

Raised with a lack of pretension, they mixed freely with the children on the Windsor estate, and, dressed in simple clothes, they enjoyed the simple pleasures of picnics and pony rides around Virginia Water. Spending a good deal of time outdoors in the beautiful gardens around Cumberland Lodge, the boys followed their father's passion for gardening and riding, and learned to play cricket by participating in matches organised by a sports-loving footman.

From their mother, who was an excellent pianist, they gained an appreciation of music, and learned to play the violin and piano; and both enjoyed theatrical performances, often appearing in plays to entertain their parents and guests.

Like her elder sisters, Lenchen had a particular interest in nursing, and she encouraged her children to accompany her on hospital visits, and to assist her in preparations for the care of wounded soldiers. From an early age, Christle showed himself to be a particularly compassionate child, with:

"...the keenest interest in everything to do with the care of the sick as well as the wounded horses."[35]

Following the Queen's seasonal migrations between Windsor, Balmoral and the Isle of Wight, the boys enjoyed stalking and trekking in the Scottish mountains, and playing in the toy fort created by their uncles at Osborne. There, they both developed a fascination with the military which, in Christle's case, was so pronounced that for his fifth birthday his grandmother presented him with the uniform of the Scotch Fusiliers.

Before Christle was six years old, two younger sisters – Thora, or 'Mousie' to her brothers, and Marie Louise – were born; and, on 12th May 1876, they were joined by a baby brother, Harald. Sadly, the baby did not thrive, and,

72

within a few days of his birth, his jaundiced appearance so alarmed the doctors that it was decided to have him christened immediately. Over the next twenty-four hours, he suffered repeated convulsions before dying early in the morning of 20th May.

Harald's death affected Lenchen deeply and exacerbated her hypochondria, which, Queen Victoria believed, was not helped by Christians excessive coddling. Her pregnancies had not been easy; and the suppression of her emotions after her father's death resulted in a series of real and imaginary ailments, for which her doctors prescribed laudanum. Gradually she became so addicted to the opium in the concoction that her mother anxiously persuaded the doctors to give her placebos instead. The ruse worked and on several occasions she recommended medications to the Queen, which were actually nothing more than coloured water.

Despite Lenchen's difficulties, the Christians were, according to Marie Louise:

"...very happy, ordinary, little family devoted to each other, though we did not always see eye-to-eye and many were the free fights with pillows, cushions or whatever else came to hand."[36]

Although nannies and tutors were appointed, Lenchen herself taught her sons to read and write, while Christian taught them German by recounting fairy tales. When Christle was nine years old, however, his parents believed he would benefit from the company of his peers, and arranged for him to join a class of twenty-one pupils at the recently established Lambrook Preparatory School in Berkshire.

Robert Burnside, the headmaster and founder of the school, was so impressed by his royal pupil that he tended to show favouritism to him, which, although it did not affect his relationship with his peers, left him, according to Lady Frederick Cavendish, 'terribly ill-grounded and inattentive.'

His grandmother, however, was so impressed by Burnside that he was invited to Scotland when the family was staying at Balmoral, so that Christle could stay with him in a house on the estate and continue his lessons.

Three years later, Abbie, too, was enrolled at Lambrook, where both brothers participated in school plays, and displayed their cricketing skills during inter-school matches, some of which, to the excitement of the pupils, were unexpectedly attended by Queen Victoria and her suite.

From Lambrook, Christle progressed to Wellington College, where, at his parents' insistence, he was to be given no preferential treatment except that he must never be flogged. Despite his tutor's consternation at this stipulation, it had no detrimental effect on Christle, for he progressed well in his studies, enjoyed the camaraderie of his fellow students and, again, excelled on the cricket pitch, captaining the First XI, and making such an impression that, to this day, the Prince Christian Victor prize is awarded to the most competent bowler.

Abbie, meanwhile, progressed to Charterhouse School, which had recently been rebuilt in a new location in Godalming under the headmastership of Reverend William Haig-Brown, and, by the mid-1870s, accommodated approximately five hundred pupils. Haig-Brown was a forward-thinking man who, according to one of his contemporaries, knew 'how to lubricate the wheels of discipline with the oil of humour, to the immense benefit of the whole.'[37]

The school was ideally suited to Abbie's love of sports, since it already had a great reputation for:
"...the zeal with which all games, especially cricket and football, were pursued. It contributed more than one captain to University elevens, and was the first school in England to institute a public sports day."[38]

The boys were not forced to participate in one sport rather than another, for the headmaster encouraged them to pursue their own interests and choose for themselves whether they preferred, cricket, football, tennis, rowing or taking long walks by the river. Abbie's first choice was always cricket, and, like his elder brother, he impressed his peers with his aptitude for the game. Like his elder brother, too, he was popular with his classmates, who described him as 'a good sort' with no sense of entitlement or superiority.

During the school holidays, between visits to Ascot and yachting at Cowes, there were occasional trips to Germany where their mother toured the spas in the hope of finding a cure. The Princess of Wales' continued resentment over the seizure of Schleswig-Holstein, meant visits to Marlborough House or Sandringham were rare, but there were stays at their paternal relations' estates in Augustenburg, where they spent time with their cousins, Calma; Ernst Gunther, who would eventually inherit the duchy, naming Abbie as his heir; and Augusta Victoria (Dona), who would go on to marry their maternal cousin, Willy of Prussia. There were visits, too, to Darmstadt where Christle and Abbie's sisters became great friends of Aunt Alice's children. The 'happy, ordinary, little family' might have been simple and unpretentious in their habits, but, as Marie Louise later wrote, they were 'related to the whole Almanac de Gotha'.

Chapter 6 – The Pain Is Beyond Words

The Hohenzollerns (Prussians)

Vicky (Victoria) – Eldest child of Queen Victoria; wife of Fritz, Crown Prince of Prussia

Fritz (Frederick William) – Vicky's husband; Crown Prince of Prussia

Willy (William/Wilhelm) – Fritz & Vicky's eldest son

Henry – Fritz & Vicky's second son

Charlotte – Fritz & Vicky's eldest daughter

Sigi (Sigismund) – Fritz & Vicky's third son

Moretta (Victoria) – Fritz & Vicky's second daughter

The Hessians

Alice – Queen Victoria's second daughter

Louis – Alice's husband; Prince of Hesse-Darmstadt

Victoria – Alice & Louis' eldest daughter

Ella – Alice & Louis' second daughter

Irene – Alice & Louis' third daughter

Ernie (Ernst Ludwig) – Alice & Louis' elder son

Alix – Alice & Louis' fourth daughter

May – Alice & Louis' youngest daughter

The Prussian victory over Austria in 1866 had taken Germany one step closer to unification and, within four years, Bismarck was ready to complete the process. Convinced that nothing could unite the states so well as a common enemy, the Minister-President remained alert to any opportunity to provoke a war, and, in 1870, the perfect situation arose out of a dispute over the successor of the recently deposed Queen of Spain.

Following a disjointed and troubled reign, Queen Isabella had abdicated in favour of her son, but powerful factions wanted an entirely new dynasty and were open to suggestions of candidates from other European royal families. The names of various princes were put forward but when the Prussians proposed Prince Leopold of Hohenzollern-Sigmaringen, a cousin of King Wilhelm I, the French Emperor, Napoleon III, was aghast. Already wary of Bismarck's militaristic designs along his eastern border, Napoleon could not countenance the idea of being encircled by the Hohenzollerns, and demanded that Prince Leopold's name be withdrawn.

On Bismarck's advice, King Wilhelm accepted the demand, but, as the Minister-President had hoped, the French went further and sent their ambassador to the King at the spa town of Ems to obtain his assurance that he would never put forward any other Prussian candidate. Although Wilhelm politely stated that he could not give such an assurance, the meeting was so cordial that, when the King sent a full transcript of the proceedings to Bismarck, he gave him permission to publish it. The arch-manipulator seized his chance, carefully doctoring the account to create the impression that the meeting had been far more hostile than was the case, and that insults had been traded on both sides.

The French were so incensed by the false reports and perceived insults that they issued a declaration of war, in response to which, to Bismarck's satisfaction, virtually all of the German states rose up in indignation to offer Prussia their support. Bismarck had found the common enemy and, once again, Vicky and Alice saw their husbands riding out at the head of their armies. This time, at least, the sisters were on the same side.

Eleven-year-old Willy and nine-year-old Henry followed the course of the Franco-Prussian War with boyish fascination. Each morning they marked the progress of the German armies on a map, and, after their tutor had retired for the night, they celebrated their father's victories with pillow fights. This, though, was a longer and bloodier conflict than the Austro-Prussian War had been, and, as the number of casualties increased, the boys saw, too, something of the darker side of battle when they joined their mother, visiting the wounded in the hospitals that she had founded at Homburg and Frankfurt.

Even at the height of the hostilities, while Vicky was doing her utmost to ameliorate conditions for the casualties, Bismarck continued his vendetta against her, spreading rumours that both she and Alice were passing military secrets to the French via their mother in England. The fabricated reports led to such suspicion in Berlin that Vicky's offer to assist in improving the facilities for the wounded was met with a firm rebuttal.

> "What an effort it costs me [to visit the hospitals]," she wrote to the Queen, "as I have nothing to do in them and I can see how badly managed they are without being able to improve them. The stifling atmosphere is enough to knock one down – and the dirt too repulsive."[39]

The combined German forces moved swiftly and effectively and, within two months, Napoleon III had been captured and deposed. Four months later, the Prussians march triumphantly through Paris and there, on 18th January 1871, in the Hall of Mirrors at Versailles, King Wilhelm I was pronounced Emperor of the newly-unified Germany.

'It is difficult to describe the tumult of emotions I underwent on that great day,' wrote Willy; but the war was not yet over and it would be a further four months before hostilities were finally concluded with the Treaty of Frankfurt.

In the meantime, on 27th January 1871, as Willy celebrated his twelfth birthday, his father's thoughts turned to the enormity of the task that lay ahead of him. Now he would not only eventually inherit the Prussian throne but would also become German Emperor, it was clear to his father that the easily-led boy required even greater protection from the flatterers and intriguers who surrounded him in Berlin.

"It is truly a disquieting thought," Fritz wrote in his diary, "to realise how many hopes are even now set on this boy's head and how great a responsibility to the Fatherland we have to bear in the conduct of his education, while outside consideration of family and rank, court life in Berlin and many other things make his upbringing so much harder."[40]

Back at home, relations between Willy and his mother had temporarily improved. Bismarck's preoccupation with the unification left him little time to flatter the impressionable prince, and, free of his interference, Vicky was beginning to see Willy in a far more positive light. The day after his birthday, she wrote to Queen Victoria, expressing her satisfaction with his excellent tutor and the progress he was making in his studies. In a rare compliment, she assured her mother that Willy was very popular, lively and intelligent; and, for once, there was 'a bond of love and confidence' between them, which nothing could destroy. Like Fritz, though, she recognised that this was a crucial time in her son's development, and she planned to play a greater role in every aspect of his upbringing.

Willy's thoughts, meanwhile, were dominated by the dream of a glorious military career. In March, when the victorious armies returned home, he threw himself 'in an ecstasy' into his father's arms, before joining a procession through the streets of Berlin where:

"The reception...was deafening and could be heard from the Crown Prince's Palace breaking out again and again for many hours after, until at length my father stepped out on to the balcony surrounded by his family and showed himself to the enthusiastic Berlin multitude."[41]

79

It was an image that would remain with Willy into adulthood, and one which he would dream of repeating for many years to come.

The conclusion of the Franco-Prussian War heralded a period of peace and prosperity for the newly-unified Germany, and while, thanks to Bismarck's domination of domestic politics, Fritz and Vicky became increasingly isolated from the court, they were freer to spend more time with their growing family.

In Hesse, meanwhile, Alice and Louis' financial situation improved when, on the death of his uncle in 1877, Louis inherited the Grand Duchy. With greater financial freedom, however, came an increase in responsibilities, and Alice typically devoted herself with even greater fervour to her numerous and varied charities. Frittie's death, though, still weighed heavily upon her and, while still in her early thirties, she became prone to a myriad of ailments.

"Dear Mama," she had told the Queen in 1876, "I don't think you know how far from well I am."

A year later, plagued by neuralgia, rheumatic pains, eye problems and insomnia, she wrote even more plaintively:

"Too much is demanded of one; and I have to do with so many things. It is more than my strength can stand in the long run..."[42]

Exhausted and depressed, her thoughts returned constantly to her late father and to Frittie, and, by the age of thirty-five, she was contemplating the briefness of life and the prospect of her own imminent death.

One evening, in autumn 1878, her eldest daughter, Victoria, became hoarse while reading to her younger siblings. A headache and general malaise soon developed and it did not take long for the doctor to diagnose diphtheria. The horrific and highly-infectious disease attacks the lymph nodes and causes the membranes of the throat to swell – sometimes to the point of asphyxiating the sufferer – before attacking the internal organs resulting in a complete physical breakdown and, ultimately, death. Victoria was immediately isolated, but, within two days, her younger sister, Alix, showed symptoms of the disease, and, by the end of the week, Irene, May and their father were similarly afflicted.

Ernie and his elder sister, Ella, appeared to have escaped the infection and, for their own protection they were hastily dispatched to their paternal grandmother in nearby Bessungen. Barely had they arrived, however, when Ernie, too, showed signs of the disease and was immediately sent back to the New Palace in Darmstadt.

Over the next fortnight, Alice barely slept as she took charge of the care of her family. On the doctors' instructions she covered herself in protective clothing and wore a mask when approaching their beds to administer the only available treatment: inhalations of potassium chloride. Before leaving their rooms, she sprayed herself with disinfectant and adhered to the doctor's orders that she must refrain from hugging or kissing her sick children.

Gradually, the elder girls began to recover, but Ernie and his youngest sister, May, remained in a dangerous condition until 15th November when May appeared to be recovering. Towards midnight, convinced that May was past the worst, Alice left her room to attend to her other patients when suddenly the child sat up and choked. By the time Alice returned she had died.

'The pain is beyond words,' Alice hastily telegrammed to her mother before breaking the news to Louis, who was still too ill to rise from his bed.

To prevent further spread of the infection, it was vital that the coffin should be closed and the body buried as soon as possible. Alice hastily made all the necessary arrangements, but, just two days after May's death, she could not bear to see her youngest child's departure, and could only watch through a mirror as the little coffin was carried from the house.

The following day, Ernie appeared to be sinking rapidly:

"This is quite agonising to me," Alice told the Queen, "*how* I pray that he may be spared to me! His voice is so thick; new membranes have just appeared. He cries at times so bitterly..."[43]

In view of the severity of his illness, his mother did not tell him of his sister's death, and when, two days later he had improved sufficiently to ask her to take a book to May, she felt 'almost sick to smile at the dear boy.'

The stress was unbearable and unrelenting throughout the early days of December but when, at last, Ernie began to recover, Alice finally told him that May had died. Ernie burst into tears and was so distressed that Alice, unable to restrain herself, took him in her arms and kissed him to bring him comfort.

Whether this was, as Disraeli told the British Parliament, the 'kiss of death', or whether, as her sister, Lenchen, believed, she had contracted the illness by resting her head on a pillow beside Louis, on 7th December, Alice, too, developed the horrendous symptoms of diphtheria.

Perhaps she had had a premonition of her own imminent death, for the day before her symptoms developed, Alice had written a series of lengthy instructions for Ernie's future education, urging his tutor, Herr Muther, to:

"...encourage in him fear of God and submission to His will, a high sense of duty, a feeling of honour and truth."[44]

For a week she suffered dreadfully, choking on the inflamed membranes of her throat, as the toxins spread through her entire body. For some days she drifted in and out of consciousness until, on 14th December, seventeen years to the day since her father's death, she died, murmuring, "Dear Papa..."

The loss of their mother was a tragedy for the united and happy family but for Ernie, with whom she had shared a particular bond, the grief was indescribable. Recollections of his sense of responsibility for Frittie's death were exacerbated by the thought that it was his kiss which had killed his mother.

Meanwhile, the fear of the contagion was so great that Vicky's father-in-law, the German Emperor, forbade her from attending her sister's funeral in Hesse, lest she should bring the disease back to Prussia. His precautions were in vain, for, within a few months, the epidemic had spread to Berlin, claiming Vicky's youngest son, ten-year-old Waldemar, among its victims.

Just as Alice had insisted on nursing her own sick children, so Vicky insisted on tending Waldie, but, for all her tender ministrations, he died of paralysis of the heart caused by the diphtheria toxins, at half-past-three in the morning on 27th March 1879.

For the rest of her life, Vicky often wrote of her longing to see 'little Waldie' again, and even twelve years after his death she told her daughter:

"Yesterday was my own Waldie's [anniversary] and my heart ached bitterly."[45]

Unlike in Hesse, where the entire population had come out in sympathy with the bereaved parents, the Prussian press used the tragedy to make another vindictive attack on the heartbroken mother. God, wrote one journalist, had taken her child as punishment for her hardness of heart and she should, therefore, accept his death as a lesson in compassion. Fortunately, though, her often disunited family was, for once, united in sorrow. Henry hurried home from a voyage to Hawaii; and Willy, concealing the extent of his own grief, showed nothing but respect and consideration for his parents.

In fact, Waldemar's horrific death had a far more profound effect on Willy than was initially apparent, for he quickly developed a horror of infections in general, and diphtheria in particular. Almost a decade later, while he was staying at the Marble Palace, he was told that one of his neighbours had died of the disease and immediately ordered all his belongings to be packed so that he could move away from a place where the air was 'so unhealthy.' His fear of illness did not ease with age. When a lady at court informed him that her son was unwell, he was angry that she had dared to come into his presence; and when he heard that his wife had visited the home of a child who died of an infectious disease, he insisted that all her dresses should be immediately disinfected.

In England, meanwhile, as soon as she heard of the death of 'dear good Alice', Queen Victoria's thoughts turned to Louis and the 'poor, motherless children'. Within a few weeks of Alice's passing, she invited the family to Osborne in the hope that the fresh sea air would aid their recuperation, and that she would have an opportunity to discuss the children's future. It was not a happy reunion, for, after such an ordeal, they were pale and thin, and the now bespectacled Ernie was noticeably tearful. Within a few weeks, however, the colour began to return to his cheeks and, though he continued his lessons with Herr Muther, who had travelled from Hesse with the family, there was also plenty of time for relaxation, and for the Queen to assure him of her affection.

Much as she loved Louis, the Queen doubted his ability to raise his family unaided, and, for the sake of the children, she felt it was imperative that he should remarry as soon as possible. Naturally, his bride must be willing to build on Alice's foundations, and there was, in the Queen's opinion, no more suitable person for that role than her own youngest daughter, Beatrice. Neither Louis nor Beatrice was attracted to the other and they were both relieved when they discovered that the Church of England forbade prohibited marriage between brothers- and sisters-in-law. The disgruntled Queen suggested that the rule should be changed in this instance but her hopes were dashed and nothing came of the plan.

At the end of February 1879, the Hessians returned home but the Queen continued to monitor their progress, writing frequently, offering advice and adhering to a promise she had made to 'try to be a mother' to them. It was with some consternation that she discovered that Ernie was far less studious than he had formerly been; and he was so easily distracted and lazy that his tutor was exasperated by him. The Queen quickly offered a stern rebuke, reminding Ernie that he must always try to live up to the example of, and standards set by, his saintly mother.

Despite her reprimand, Queen Victoria's affection for Ernie was unfailing, and, in late September 1879, when he and Louis arrived for a holiday at Balmoral, she was delighted by how well he looked, and how he thrived in the 'good highland air'. Already, she was thinking of suitable matches for his elder sisters, and it would not be long before she formed the disastrous notion that Ernie would do well to marry his cousin, a daughter of her own third son, Alfred (Affie) Duke of Edinburgh.

Chapter 7 - A Stripling with Want of Balance

The Edinburghs

Affie (Alfred) – Duke of Edinburgh; Queen Victoria's second son
Marie – Duchess of Edinburgh; Affie's Russian wife
Young Affie (Alfred) – Only son of Affie & Marie
Missy (Marie) – Eldest daughter of Affie & Marie
Ducky (Victoria Melita) – Second daughter of Affie & Marie
Alexandra – Third daughter of Affie & Marie
Beatrice (Baby Bee) – Youngest daughter of Affie & Marie

The Connaughts

Arthur – Duke of Connaught; Queen Victoria's third son
Louischen (Louise Margaret) – Duchess of Connaught; Arthur's wife
Daisy (Margaret) – Eldest child of the Duke & Duchess of Connaught
Young Arthur – Only son of the Duke & Duchess of Connaught
Patsy (Patricia) – Youngest child of the Duke & Duchess of Connaught

The Albanys

Leopold – Duke of Albany; Queen Victoria's youngest son
Helen – Duchess of Albany; Leopold's wife
Alice – Daughter of Leopold
Charlie (Charles Edward) – Duke of Albany; Son of Leopold

By the early 1870s, Affie, Duke of Edinburgh, had fallen from the pinnacle of his mother's admiration to the depths of her disfavour. Throughout his childhood, she had repeatedly praised his enthusiasm, his industry, his cheerfulness and, above all, his physical resemblance to his father; and when, at his own request, he had joined the Royal Navy at the age of fourteen, she was proudly impressed by his achievements and the speed with which he earned his promotions.

Since Prince Albert's death in 1861, however, the once-cheerful boy had grown into such an impatient and bad-tempered young man that members of the household dreaded him coming home on leave; and even his mother felt that she could no longer trust him.

"His presence in my house during the last year," she wrote, "was a source of no satisfaction or comfort. He came only for moments and, when he did, displeased high and low and made mischief. In short he was quite a stranger to me."[46]

Her displeasure temporarily abated when, during a visit to Australia in 1867, he was shot in the back by a deranged Irishman, but, as he recovered, the attention he received only increased his arrogance to the point where his mother told Vicky that she was, 'not as proud of Affie as you might think, for he is so conceited himself.'

Most irksome of all, though, for the Queen, was the fact that her handsome son enjoyed several affairs and soon developed an unnerving infatuation with his sister-in-law, the Princess of Wales, with whom he danced virtually every dance at the Marlborough House balls, before falling 'violently in love' with the wife of the Duke of Westminster.

"He is indeed in many things wonderfully like adored Papa – and his figure is a miniature of that angel," sighed his mother. "Oh! that he were as pure!"[47]

Despite Bertie's continual philandering, Queen Victoria remained convinced that the best solution to the problem of errant princes was marriage, and so, undaunted by the knowledge that Affie's irascibility would be off-putting to many a princess, she embarked on the difficult quest of finding him a suitable bride. Her efforts were repeatedly thwarted, for Affie rejected outright every suggestion that she made, as he was already busily pursuing a Russian Grand Duchess, whom he had met during a family gathering in Denmark.

Queen Victoria was not amused. Since the Crimean War she had disliked the Russians; and the opulent decadence of the Romanov Court filled her with disdain. Although she had never met Marie Alexandrovna, the eighteen-year-old daughter of Tsar Alexander II, she convinced herself that all Russian princesses ostentatiously paraded their wealth, and the prospect of her palaces being filled with chanting priests was more than she could tolerate. Affie, however, as stubborn as his mother was, refused to be dissuaded; and eventually, taking comfort from Alice's assurance that, far from being flamboyant, Marie had simple tastes, and was very fond of children, the Queen relented sufficiently to invite the prospective bride to England.

To her intense indignation, Queen Victoria soon learned that the Russians were no more enthralled by the idea of the match than she had been. In St. Petersburg, it was widely believed that the only daughter of the most powerful autocrat in the world could do better than a younger son of the English monarch; and the Tsar himself was hesitant about handing over his beloved child to a rough-spoken sailor with a reputation for womanising and short-temperedness. He adamantly refused to send Marie to England to be vetted by the Queen; and when, eventually, it was agreed that the couple could marry, he insisted that the wedding should take place in Russia.

Queen Victoria did not attend the lavish ceremony in the Winter Palace in January 1874, but she received a full report from Vicky, who told her that, despite her 'tasteless and unbecoming' dress, Marie looked very pretty. Three months later, when the couple arrived in London, the Queen was pleasantly surprised by both the appearance and the manner of her new daughter-in-law. Although she could not describe her as 'regularly pretty', Marie had, in her mother-in-law's opinion, 'a pretty bust' and a pleasant smile; and, more impressively, she was not in the least afraid of her irritable husband but was so easy to talk to that she made 'a most agreeable companion.'

Assuming that all Britons shared her dislike and mistrust of Russians, the Queen remained anxious about a pre-arranged wedding procession through London, but her fears were quickly allayed as the crowds received the new Duchess of Edinburgh with nothing but warmth and admiration.

"The Grand Duchess speaks English better than most English girls; she has a most pleasing manner, and a presence singularly ladylike and distinguished,"[48] the *Ladies Treasury* reported; while the Poet Laureate, Tennyson, observed that the crowds were very enthusiastic in welcoming the 'large and Imperial' Marie. His somewhat rambling poem, written to mark the occasion, expressed the hope that the marriage would heal the old wounds of the Crimean War and create better relations between Russia and Britain:

'Shall fears and jealous hatreds flame again?
Or at thy coming, Princess, everywhere,
The blue heaven break, and some diviner air
Breathe thro' the world and change the hearts of men,
    Alexandrovna?
But hearts that change not, love that cannot cease,
And peace be yours, the peace of soul in soul!
And howsoever this wide world may roll,
Between your peoples truth and manful peace,
    Alfred—Alexandrovna!'[49]

In the weeks that followed, the Queen's admiration for her new daughter-in-law increased. She was pleased to observe that Marie practised her Orthodox religion privately; and, despite the huge dowry and annuity provided by her father, she lived very simply, preferring studious pursuits to idling her time away in society. Although her armoires were filled with priceless jewels, at home she paid so little attention to her dress that members of her household were shocked by her appearance; and yet, in public she knew how to shine, demonstrating that she was every inch the daughter of a Tsar. In fact, she was so convinced of her superiority that she was most put out to discover that her sisters-in-law would appear ahead of her in the order of precedence and, only when the Queen intervened, did she grudgingly accept the compromise of appearing second only to the Princess of Wales.

For Marie, the question of precedence was but one of many minor irritations that made life in England disagreeable. Her London home, Clarence House, was small and uninteresting compared to the palaces of her childhood; and the Queen's court was bourgeois and dull compared to the glittering court of the Tsar. In England, the late hours were tiring; the food was bland; and when, within weeks of the wedding, Marie discovered that she was expecting a child, her mother-in-law sought to control every aspect of her pregnancy.

Affie, meanwhile, had quickly recovered from the first rush of wedded bliss, and returned to his former habits of being rude to the staff and drinking to excess. Fortunately for Marie, much of the time he was away at sea, although he made a point of being present for her confinement, and had even taken the trouble to invite her mother to come over from Russia to help her through her ordeal.

On 15th October 1874 – almost nine months to the day since her wedding and two days before her twenty-first birthday –Marie gave birth to a son in Buckingham Palace. Her mother, the Tsarina, who was racing across the continent, arrived too late for the event, and, by the time she reached London, she was so exhausted and ill[g] that Marie and Affie felt it necessary to summon her doctors from

---

[g] Tsarina Marie Alexandrovna was suffering from tuberculosis.

Russia. No sooner had they arrived that they warned that the Tsarina's condition was serious and consequently she should return home as soon as possible.

Queen Victoria, who had been at Balmoral at the time of the birth, felt deeply for the unfortunate Tsarina and suggested that the baby's christening should be brought forward to enable her to attend before leaving the country. The Queen's advice was accept, and a private ceremony took place in Buckingham Palace on 23rd November, during which the baby was christened Alfred Alexander William Ernest Albert, although in the family he would be known as 'Young Affie'.

Shortly after the christening, the Edinburghs moved into Eastwell House in Kent – a 'great grey house' surrounded by a 'magnificent park, with its herds of deer and picturesque Highland cattle, its lake, its woods, its garden...' – where, the following year, Marie gave birth to a second child, also named Marie (Missy); and over the next decade three more daughters, Victoria Melita (Ducky), Alexandra and Beatrice (Baby Bee) were born.

Life at Eastwell, with its glorious gardens, was filled with enchantment for the Edinburgh children. Building dens in the trees, they revelled in their imaginative games:

"...We were Robinson Crusoe; we were Robin Hood and his followers; we were Red Indians or pirates, and goodness knows what else."[50]

In the winter there was skating on the lake, tobogganing, huge candle-lit Christmas trees, plum puddings, and tables filled with gifts for the entire household. In the summer there were visits to Osborne, where, like their cousins, they played in the Victoria Fort and Albert Barracks, Young Affie, as the only boy, taking the lead and dominating most of the games.

Beyond this Arcadian façade, however, the children were aware that their lives were not quite as secure or idyllic as they might have appeared. It was common knowledge that their grandfather, the Tsar, was conducting an affair with a younger woman, who had born him three children, all of whom he had installed in the palace while his wife lay on her sickbed. In 1880, the unfortunate Tsarina died to the sound of her husband's illegitimate children romping through the rooms upstairs. Soon afterwards, to the chagrin of his family, the Tsar married his young mistress but their happiness was short-lived. Only a few months later, in March 1881, Young Affie and his sisters heard that their grandfather, Tsar Alexander II, had died horrifically as a result of a terrorist's bomb.

Even within their own home, life was often tense for the Edinburgh children as they witnessed the rapid deterioration of their parents' marriage. Their father was a distant figure, frequently away at sea and although, on his return, he would occasionally play with them, the game he most enjoyed involved hiding in a dark corner and springing out on them pretending to be an ogre. Even at Christmas they witnessed his temper when 'he was excessively meticulous and could get very angry if the smallest detail he had planned was not religiously adhered to.'[51]

In their father's absence, their mother took complete charge of their upbringing, and she had very definite opinions about how young princes and princesses should behave. The children were not allowed to be ill; they must never complain; they must eat whatever was set before them; they must be able to hold a sensible conversation; and their mother:

> "...never admitted any mixing of generations; she was never comrade or companion, but always very definitely the parent; the one who represented authority as well as love, the ruling sovereign of her household, the one who held the sceptre and let you feel that the power over good and evil was hers."[52]

While the girls grew closer to one another, Young Affie was gradually becoming alienated from the rest of the family. As the only boy, he discovered he had less and less in common with his sisters, and, although on rare occasions boys of his own age were invited to play at Clarence House, his parents already had an eye to his future in Coburg.

Some years earlier, Prince Albert's brother, the childless Ernst, Duke of Coburg, had named Affie as his heir, which meant Young Affie was second in the line to the dukedom. When, therefore, in 1886, Affie was appointed Commander of the Mediterranean Fleet and he and his family moved to Malta, it was decided that his only son should be sent instead to Coburg to receive a German education.

Residing in the recently-built Edinburgh Palace, Young Affie was provided with his own tutors, a loyal valet named Rose, and a carefully planned curriculum, which would prepare him not only for his future role as duke, but also to enter a prestigious Prussian officers' training school, since a military education was deemed necessary for all German princes.

Given such special attention, Young Affie began to develop a sense of his own importance, which, due to the absence of his parents, was rarely checked. Although his mother visited whenever possible, she and the rest of his family were living peripatetically, travelling between England, Malta and Germany, and, as her marriage continued to deteriorate, she took increasingly long holidays in her native Russia. Unavoidably aware of his unique status within the family, the little boy who had once enjoyed playing with his sisters, became something of a stranger to them, treating them with disdain or off-handedness whenever they were together.

"My memories of Alfred are of a stripling, eager, blundering, a little swaggering, always getting into trouble, always being scolded," wrote his sister, Missy. "He was gay but easily offended, had keen intelligence but a want of balance."[53]

Nonetheless, Missy and her sisters remained devoted to him and sought to defend his increasingly wayward behaviour, as their mother, who had held out such high hopes for him, was rapidly beginning to view him with the same disdain with which she viewed his father.

If the Duke of Edinburgh were a disappointment to his mother, his younger brother, Arthur, Duke of Connaught, could not have pleased her more. 'Beloved by everyone', 'an angel of purity', 'so good, so innocent', 'so amiable and so unassuming', there were not enough adjectives to describe Queen Victoria's favourite son. Cheerful and enthusiastic as a child, Arthur had lost none of his charm as he grew into manhood. He had neither strayed nor fallen from grace, but continued to impress his mother by diligently devoting himself to his royal duties and, after graduating from the Royal Military Academy at Woolwich, earning rapid promotions in the army. While most princes experienced some form of military training, Arthur was a professional soldier, who saw active service in various parts of the Empire.

The Queen was not alone in her admiration of her courageous son. His sisters frequently praised him, and his mother's ladies-in-waiting never ceased to take delight in his company: 'Such a gentleman, so courteous and so kind,'[54] wrote Marie Mallett; 'my own darling Prince Arthur,'[55] said Lady Frederick Cavendish; and Lady Augusta Bruce thought him, 'so handsome, so dear, so good and so courteous.'[56] Unsurprisingly, therefore, when he fell in love with Louise Margaret (Louischen) of Prussia, the German princess, ten years his junior, gladly accepted his proposal.

Three months after Alice's death, the wedding took place in St. George's Chapel, Windsor – an event at which, according to the Duke of Cambridge, the Queen was in good spirits and the bride looked 'nice and fresh'.[57]

"It was a most stately and beautiful sight: a day of floods of sunshine..." wrote another observer. "The bride has a very winning countenance, full of character, yet youthful and innocent-looking: nice dark eyes."[58]

The groom's brother-in-law, Fritz of Prussia, dressed in a striking white uniform, made an impression on the crowd; and Vicky was:

"...in good looks, being thinner; their eldest son [Willy], an ugly fellow was with them...The Princess of Wales looked lovely, Prince George at her side with his waggish round face...Prince Eddy is a beautiful boy, nearly as tall as Princess Beatrice, beside whom he walked, supporting the Queen, who took her full part in the ceremonial, and walked as grandly as ever, looking her best in long sweeping black and white, and a diamond coronet...Martial music, trumpets, grand organ marches – all stately."[59]

The couple spent their honeymoon at Claremont in Esher, before returning to live in Buckingham Palace until their own home, the newly-built Bagshot Park in Surrey – 'a pretty place with lovely gardens' – was habitable.

In January 1882, three years after the wedding, Louischen gave birth to their first child, Margaret ('Daisy') and, almost a year to the day later, on 13th January 1883, a son, Young Arthur, was born at Windsor. His father, who arrived home from his military duties too late for the birth, was overjoyed at finding a 'fine healthy boy' and his wife completely recovered from her confinement. Young Arthur was christened with due ceremony in the private chapel at Windsor Castle, in the presence of a vast number of his uncles, aunts and cousins.

As a serving soldier, the Duke of Connaught continued to be posted to far-flung places, and, in late 1885, arrangements were made for him to take up a position as Commander of the Bombay Army the following spring. In the interim, a third child, Patricia (Patsy), was born, and, soon afterwards she and Young Arthur travelled with their parents to Rawalpindi.[h]

Throughout the course of his father's Indian command, and his later position in Ireland, Young Arthur, regularly travelled back and forth between India and England, where, to his father's consternation, he and his sisters were cared for by their grandmother. The Duke doubted Queen Victoria's ability to deal with such high-spirited children and repeatedly expressed his desire to keep them with him, but the Queen equally forcefully insisted that the climate, particularly in the summer months, was too dangerous for 'such nice little things' and so she *expected* them to remain with her in England.

Unwilling to stand up to his mother, the Duke sought the help of his sister, Louise, expressing his fear that, since the Battenberg children of his youngest sister, Beatrice, already lived with the Queen[i], they would be favoured to the detriment of his own children. Unfortunately, Louise, who was known for mischief-making in the family, exacerbated the situation by replying that Beatrice was not ideally suited to care for children and she had already described Young Arthur as 'slow and wanting'. The Duke indignantly flew to his son's defence, telling Louise that:

> "Poor [Young] Arthur, like all boys, is occasionally naughty, but he is a good dispositioned child and I have always found him very intelligent and even thoughtful, of course he is not 6 years old yet, and it is difficult to expect a child to always be obedient at that age."[60]

In reality, he need not have worried, since Louise had probably exaggerated the difficulties, for the Connaught children were fond of Aunt Beatrice and her husband 'Uncle

---

[h] The Indian climate was deemed unsuitable for a child of Daisy's age, so she remained behind with Queen Victoria.
[i] See Chapter 8

Liko' – a fact that provoked slight resentment and jealousy in their father. Moreover, the Queen, who, like many a grandparent, was far more indulgent to her grandchildren than she had been to her own children, was delighted by Arthur's well-behaved brood and greatly amused by their antics.

Ironically, while the Duke was needlessly worrying that the Queen might be too strict with his children, his wife, Louishen, was ruling them with a military-style severity. Her own childhood had been damaged by the vindictiveness of her father, whose cruelty eventually compelled his wife to desert him, and perhaps it was this early experience which created a harsh streak in her character. The household was run with meticulous precision and her daughters were so afraid of her that they trembled in terror if she discovered a minor misdemeanour.

Louischen also had an acute sense of her royal status and insisted that her children should not mix too freely with the 'lower orders'. Consequently, Young Arthur developed an idea of his own superiority which contrasted sharply with his father's 'common touch'. On one occasion, he complained that a sentry had failed to salute him as he walked by. The Duke replied carelessly, "I dare say, my dear," at which Young Arthur asked indignantly, "But papa, won't you put him in the guard room for such a piece of neglect?"[61]

Fortunately, his otherwise uninspiring tutor, Henry Hansell, recognised the danger of his becoming arrogant, and offered a solution. Hansell, a young Oxford graduate, who shared his pupil's interest in shooting, and inspired in him a love of golf, suggested that Young Arthur would benefit from attending school with his peers. He was, therefore, enrolled at Farnborough Preparatory School in Hampshire, before becoming the first royal prince to attend Eton College. Soon afterwards, he was joined at Eton by a younger cousin, Charles Edward of Albany, whose ultimate fate was to be sealed by an encounter with Young Arthur in the corridors of the college.

Queen Victoria's fifteenth grandson, Charles Edward (Charlie), Duke of Albany, came into the world on the 19th July 1884 at a time of deep mourning. Only four months earlier, his father, Queen Victoria's youngest son, Leopold, had died, leaving a twenty-three-year-old widow, Helen, and a fourteen-month-old daughter named Alice.

"My beloved Leopold!" Queen Victoria gasped on hearing the news, but, on reflection, she conceded that death was probably a blessing for Leopold, who had often cried out that he would rather die than continue to suffer such agonies.

That Leopold had survived to the age of thirty was something of a miracle. Diagnosed with haemophilia while still a child, his episodes of bleeding had frequently brought him to the brink of death; and the prolonged periods of recuperation had left him frustrated at being unable to pursue a meaningful career. By far the cleverest of the Queen's sons, he had developed his talents during his enforced periods of rest, and had such a ready understanding of politics that the Queen had come to rely on his advice in the same way as she had once relied on that of his father. To the irritation of his elder brother, Bertie, who had been denied such an honour, the Queen had even given him a key to her 'red boxes', allowing him access to official papers and confidential reports from the government. Unfortunately for Leopold, however, his mother's extreme solicitude and dependence upon him served only to exacerbate his dissatisfaction, as she repeatedly refused him permission to take up various posts across the Empire.

Despite her insistence on keeping him on hand, the Queen was not unaware of Leopold's frustration and she understood his longing for a wife and family of his own. While she feared that his condition would deter potential brides, she remained active in her search for a girl with whom he might find happiness. Her initial attempts came to nothing. The flighty Daisy Brooke – who would later enjoy an affair with the Prince of Wales – was not in the least attracted to Leopold, nor he to her; and the delightful Princess Frederica of Hanover told him sadly that she was already in love with someone else. Still, the Queen scanned the Almanac de Gotha, and scoured the courts of Europe until, in the autumn of 1880, she came across Helen of Waldeck-Pyrmont – the daughter of the Sovereign Prince of the small German principality not far from Darmstadt; and the sister of the Queen Consort of the Netherlands.

Leopold was duly dispatched to Helen's family home in Arolsen where, to the Queen's relief, the couple made an almost immediate impact on one another. Their engagement was announced in December 1881, and four months later, on 27th April 1882, twenty-nine-year-old Leopold and twenty-one-year-old Helen were married in St. George's Chapel at Windsor. As he was still recovering from a recent bout of his illness, Leopold had difficulty walking but even this could not detract from the joy of the occasion:

> "A lovely day for the wedding!" wrote Prince George of Cambridge. "At 10.45 drove to Windsor in full dress…where the ceremony took place at 12 in State, the Queen and all the Court present. Everything went off to perfection and without the slightest hitch, and the Queen did it admirably and looked extremely well and quite happy. The Bride looked nice and Leopold got through the ceremony very well, though still very lame, but he walked with a stick."[62]

The couple moved into the 'warm and comfortable' Claremont House where, ten months after the wedding, a healthy baby girl, Alice, was born.

Leopold and Helen's mutual devotion was obvious to everyone; and the Queen was greatly impressed by her daughter-in-law's down-to-earth good sense, and the serenity with which she cared for her husband during his episodes of bleeding. Helen's kindly ministrations could not, however, prevent the regular flare-ups of his illness and when, a year after Alice's birth, he suffered from an agonising inflammation of his joints, his doctors recommended an escape from the dampness of England to the warmer climes of Cannes.

Helen, by then in the early stages of a second pregnancy, was not well enough to travel with him. She remained at home in Claremont, where, not long after his departure, she received news that Leopold had slipped in his hotel and developed a haemorrhage in his knee. A few days later, he died.

Helen reacted to the news with remarkable serenity and courage; and the Queen, touched by her grief, promised to assist her in any way that she could. She postponed making any arrangements around the time of Helen's expected confinement, and when, on July 19th 1884, she heard that she had gone into labour, she hurried to Claremont where, that evening, a 'strong' baby boy was born.

It was Leopold's express wish that the child should be named Charles Edward after his Stuart ancestor; and from the moment of his birth, he inherited his father's title of Duke of Albany. Five months later, Charlie, as he was known in the family, was christened by the Bishop of Winchester in the Parish Church at Esher, in a ceremony attended by Leopold's family and many of his friends.

"The little fellow seemed a nice looking little baby and appeared in fair health," wrote one of the guests. "We drove thence to Claremont, where we lunched with the Duchess of Albany, who was looking well."[63]

Like her sisters-in-law, Helen was determined to raise her children as simply as possible, and she was so keen to instil in them a sense of responsibility that both Charlie and his sister, Alice, came to hate the word 'duty'. On one occasion, Charlie made a little boat out of a scrubbing brush belonging to a tenant at Balmoral but when he put it into the river, it disappeared downstream. On hearing what had happened, his mother took him at once to a local shop to buy a new brush for the tenant out of his own meagre pocket money.

Already somewhat afraid of his mother, matters were made worse for the little boy by the appointment of a nanny named Creak, who doted on his sister but considered Charlie 'delicate, nervous and tiresome'. Eventually, Nana Creak's disregard for her little charge led to her dismissal, much to the chagrin of Queen Victoria who had first recommended her. The Queen was, though, delighted by Helen's 'good little children' and she was happy to care for them when their mother was away, visiting her relations in Waldeck or busily occupied with her numerous charitable endeavours.

At Claremont, the Albanys enjoyed entertaining their Connaught, Hessian, Wales and Battenberg relations; as well as occasional visits from their cousin, the young Queen Wilhelmina of the Netherlands, whom they also visited in The Hague. Sometimes they joined Queen Victoria for holidays in France, but less pleasurable were the trips to their maternal grandparents' beautiful rococo home in their mother's native Arolsen. The journey, according to Alice, was 'a nightmare of seasickness'; and, despite the kindness of their relations, they were always happy when the holiday was over and they could return to Claremont.

Queen Victoria's respect and admiration for Helen deepened each year, and she was gratified to see the care which she put into her children's education. Each evening she read aloud to them, and encouraged them to make use of their late father's vast collection of books to further their own interests and knowledge. Many celebrated academics and writers were invited to visit, including their father's friend, Charles Ludwig Dodgson – the mathematician and author of *Alice in Wonderland*.

When Charlie was four years old, Dodgson thought him 'entirely fascinating, a perfect little prince, and the picture of good-humour,'[64] and in the course of subsequent visits, he enjoyed reading to 'the charming children' and teaching them how to make paper pistols.

Like his Connaught and Christian cousins, Charlie was soon enrolled in a preparatory school – Park Hill near Lyndhurst in the New Forest, under the headship of Mr William Rawnsley – before progressing to Eton, two months before his fourteenth birthday. From Eton, he and his cousin, Young Arthur of Connaught, often travelled back to London together to spend time with their grandmother, who never ceased to praise their charming manners and good humour. There, they came into regular contact with their Battenberg cousins, whose presence in her household provided the Queen with the brightest pleasure of her later years.

Chapter 8 - Battenbunnies

The Battenburgs

Beatrice – Queen Victoria's youngest child
Liko (Henry) – Prince Henry of Battenberg; Beatrice's husband
Drino (Alexander) – Beatrice and Liko's eldest son
Ena (Victoria Eugenia) – Beatrice and Liko's daughter
Leopold – Beatrice and Liko's second son
Maurice – Beatrice and Liko's youngest son

The Hohenzollerns

Vicky – Queen Victoria's eldest daughter
Willy (Wilhelm) – Queen Victoria's eldest grandson
Moretta – Willy's sister

Others

Christle – Elder son of Queen Victoria's daughter, Lenchen
Arthur – Queen Victoria's third son

Had Queen Victoria had her way, her youngest daughter, Beatrice, known as 'Baby' long after she had left the nursery, would never have married at all. By the time she was twenty-seven-years old, Beatrice and her mother had never been separated for more than a couple of days, and the Queen was so used to her company that she actively discouraged any thoughts of marriage, avoiding discussing the subject, and ensuring that handsome princes were kept well out of her way.

In 1884, however, while attending a family wedding in Darmstadt, Beatrice met and fell in love with the bridegroom's brother – the dashing Prince Henry ('Liko') of

Battenberg. Queen Victoria was horrified. She had no objection to Liko himself, and she could not deny that he was 'excessively good-looking', but the prospect of Beatrice being married was so abhorrent to her that she refused to discuss the matter. When Beatrice persisted with her request, she met with such a stony silence that, for several months, mother and daughter communicated only by note.

Queen Victoria, though, was ever a romantic at heart, and when she grudgingly realised that Beatrice and Liko were truly in love, she knew she could no longer stand in their way. Before agreeing to the match, however, she ascertained that Liko would be willing to resign his commission in the Prussian army to live with her in England. Liko agreed, and when he arrived at Osborne in January 1885, the Queen was delighted by the ease with which he fit into her household.

Not so delighted was Beatrice's nephew, Willy of Prussia, who wasted no time in expressing the Prussian court's attitude to the match. The Battenbergs were products of a morganatic marriage between a Hessian prince and a former lady-in-waiting, and their not-quite-royal blood made them unworthy of a daughter of the British Queen. It had been bad enough that Willy's cousin, Victoria of Hesse, had married Liko's brother, Louis, but the prospect of his grandmother welcoming a Battenberg into the British Royal Family was anathema. At the heart of Willy's objections was the fear that, by sanctioning Beatrice's marriage, the Queen would give impetus to the cause of his sister, Moretta, who was desperate to marry another Battenberg brother, Sandro[j]. As ever when her plans were criticised, the Queen was incensed, and she flew to Liko's defence, telling Willy to go and travel to 'find his level'.

The wedding took place at the small but pretty Whippingham Church on the Isle of Wight, on July 23rd 1885; and that afternoon, following a twenty-course

[j] See Chapter 11

'breakfast' in two grand marquees on the lawns of Osborne House, the couple departed for a brief honeymoon at Quarr Abbey House near Ryde. Two days later, the Queen, as was her custom with newly-married daughters, paid them a visit and, within a week, the couple had returned to take up permanent residence with Beatrice's mother.

Queen Victoria and her ladies-in-waiting were utterly charmed by Liko, whose cheerful presence wafted like a spring breeze through the staid air of Windsor Castle. Beatrice, it was noted, appeared happier than ever and, despite suffering a miscarriage four months after the wedding, marriage clearly suited her perfectly. For Liko, however, the constraints of his life with his mother-in-law proved more difficult than he had anticipated. The transformation from the thrilling lifestyle of a Prussian officer to that of a permanent companion to the rapidly aging Queen was so frustrating that he seized every opportunity to escape. Often he disappeared for weeks at a time, leaving Beatrice bereft in his absence.

"Prince Henry is off tomorrow on a four month yachting trip to Corfu and next to Albania..." wrote one of the Queen's ladies-in-waiting in 1889. "He is in the highest spirits just like a boy going home for the holidays but poor Princess Beatrice appears daily with red and swollen eyes."[65]

Deprived of any meaningful role other than the Governorship of the Isle of Wight, Liko, did, however, have plenty of time to spend with his children, the first of whom, Alexander ('Drino') was born in Windsor Castle at five o'clock in the morning of November 23rd 1886. Since his birth came almost a year to the day since Beatrice's miscarriage, the arrival of a healthy boy was all the more gratifying. Among the guests who gathered for his christening on December 18th were his cousins, Eddy of Wales, Young Arthur of Connaught, and Charlie of Albany, who would become a regular companion throughout his childhood.

The following year, to Drino's chagrin, a baby sister, Victoria Eugenie ('Ena'), was born; but the little boy soon overcame his disgruntlement at no longer being the centre of attention, as he and Ena became happy playmates who spent much of their time together.

"Drino," observed his Aunt Vicky, "is the liveliest and most intelligent boy that I have seen for a long time...He and Ena play little duets together on the piano, and read stories to one another in the evening."[66]

Queen Victoria was greatly amused by their 'impudence' and adventurous spirit, and when she heard that Beatrice was expecting a third child she was uncharacteristically delighted.

Not everyone, however, shared her joy. Truculent journalists complained about the proliferation of Battenbergs, and in satirical and often cruel articles vehemently objected to the number of young princes for whom the taxpayers would have to provide.

"Another Battenberg on the way!" wrote one particularly cruel journalist. "Well!!! Well!!! One cannot help drawing a comparison between the plague of rabbits in Australia and the plague of Battenbergs in Europe..."[k]

He went on to suggest callously how the 'Battenbunnies' could be exterminated.

The 'marvellously flourishing' new baby was born on May 21st 1889, and named after his uncle, Leopold. His 'heaps' of brown hair, his pretty face, and even his 'sweet smell' endeared him to Vicky and his Prussian cousins, who observed that the strength of his cries suggested that he was a

---

[k] Amusingly, Queen Victoria herself had once made a similar comparison, when, explaining her lack of interest in the birth of another grandchild, she complained that it seemed 'to go like the rabbits in Windsor Park.

very robust child. Sadly, though, little Leopold had inherited more than his uncle's name. At seven months old he survived a near-fatal attack of bronchitis; and shortly before his fifth birthday, a severe nosebleed confirmed his mother's suspicions – Leopold Battenberg was also a haemophiliac.

Despite his condition, and his parents' initial reluctance to allow him to follow many of his siblings' more boisterous pursuits, Leopold was far less restricted than his uncle had been and he would go on to gain a military commission and travel as far as Australia, China and Japan. Nonetheless, his childhood was blighted by the condition which often left him confined to a wheelchair or bedridden for several days.

In 1891, when Leopold was two years old, Beatrice's gave birth to Queen Victoria's youngest grandson, Maurice. It has sometimes been suggested that Maurice, too, was a haemophiliac but there is scant evidence to support this claim, and he very much enjoyed the lively games he played with his often unruly siblings. In his quieter moments, Maurice rode around the Windsor estate with his brother, Leopold, in a little pony carriage, paying particular attention to the animals on the farm; more often than not, though, he ran wildly through his grandmother's homes in noisy and adventurous games.

'Gangan', as the Battenbergs called Queen Victoria, was so amused by Beatrice's children that she rarely corrected them; and, while members of her household found them too lively, she thought them 'good little children'. Oblivious of Drino's endless chattering and Ena's strength and wildness, she regularly invited them to dine with her, and never ceased to praise their cleverness, their humour and their lovely manners.

Vicky was equally impressed by the 'dear, amusing, original and quick' children, of whom Leopold was her favourite:

"'I love you, I do,' he said to me yesterday, bringing me a bunch of white violets. 'I picked them for you because I love you.'"[67]

The birth of the Battenberg children coincided with some of the happiest years of their grandmother's widowhood. Coming into daily contact with her, they saw not the formidable Queen and Empress of India, but a fond and frequently amused old lady who thoroughly enjoyed their company and went to great lengths to ensure their happiness. For Drino's eleventh birthday, for example, she organised the entertainment with performing dogs followed by a remarkable new invention – a film show.

Their grandmother's affection compensated to some extent for their mother's apparent coldness; for, the demands of her role as the Queen's unofficial private secretary left Beatrice little time to spend with her sons, and, according to her brother, Arthur, she was 'not good with children.'

Their father, meanwhile, was frequently away on his cruises and adventures, trying to compensate for the tedium of being constantly tied to his mother-in-law, and the unkindness he often received from other members of the extended family, who continued to look disdainfully on his not-so-royal background. On one occasion, while attending a dinner at the Mansion House, he was about to take his allotted place at the table, only to find that his chair had been pushed away by the other guests; and, on another occasion, his intended neighbour-at-table, Prince George of Cambridge, took one look at the seating-plan and declared:

"I'm damned if I'm going to sit there."

By the mid-1890s, Liko desperately longed for a more meaningful purpose and, when he heard of the forthcoming Ashanti Campaign to the African Gold Coast, he requested permission to take part[1]. Initially, the Queen was

---

[1] The Anglo-Ashanti Wars had continued in fits and starts since the beginning of the century, and the campaign of 1895-1896 was the continuation of attempts to make the area a British protectorate.

horrified by his request, knowing that the climate killed more of her soldiers than did enemies in battle. Beatrice, however, understood his desperate desire for adventure, and eventually prevailed upon her mother to grant his wish.

The Queen's grandson, Christle of Schleswig-Holstein, had already been assigned to take part in the campaign as an aide-de-camp to the commander, Sir Francis Scott. As Christle set sail in November, Liko was 'bursting with excitement' at the prospect of following him a couple of weeks later. On December 7th, to the rousing strains of *Auld Lang Syne,* he and his fellow travellers set out by train to the ship, *Coromandel,* which departed for Africa the following day.

Drino, Leopold and Maurice followed their father's journey with interest, as the Queen received daily reports of the campaigns progress. Within two days of the *Coromandel's* departure, Christle had already reached Sierra Leone but it would be a further ten days before Liko set foot on African soil. Nonetheless, all the reports were favourable; the voyage was going well and the British forces, supported by many native troops, were pressing quickly towards their objective.

On Christmas Day, as the boys received cheerful letters and greetings from their father, their cousin Christle was becoming increasingly concerned about his wellbeing. By then, Christle was accustomed to life as a soldier in foreign climes[m], and when, like countless other officers, he contracted malaria, he was able to withstand the recurrences of the illness. He was aware, though, that his uncle had become used to a more sedentary life in England, and feared that the long marches through blistering heat could prove too much for him.

On 10th January, en route to Coomassie, Liko developed a fever and was so unwell that he was taken back to the trading town of Kwisa, and from there transferred to

---

[m] See Chapter 13

Cape Coast, where a British hospital ship, *Blonde,* was due to set sail for Madeira. After only a few days' rest and the attention of the ship's doctor, Hilliard, Liko began to feel better and was able to telegraph home to his family that he had been very ill but was now recovering. When the ship departed Africa on 17th January, he appeared to be out of danger but, suddenly, two days later, he had a relapse, and died at the age of only thirty-six.

It was left to his brother-in-law, Arthur, to break the news to Beatrice and her mother, the latter of whom responded first with disbelief and then with deepest sorrow.

"The sun has gone out of our lives," Queen Victoria told Vicky, who first thoughts were of his 'poor' children.

"How will they ever be cheerful again at home, when poor dear Aunt Beatrice's loneliness is ever before them and no man of the family in the house, to help in a 1000 little ways?"[68]

The children, wrote the Queen, 'wept piteously' on hearing the news; and when, after receiving hundreds of messages of condolence, the Queen wrote an article for Lloyds newspaper to thank the public for their support, the editor noticed that 'the royal letter deploring his loss, bore distinct traces of having been penned with tears.'[69]

Beatrice, though devastated, behaved with remarkable courage, and dignity. When, on a cold January day, Liko's body, preserved in rum, was returned to the Isle of Wight, she and her two elder sons, nine-year-old Drino and six-year-old Leopold, walked behind the coffin as it was carried for burial at Whippingham Church.

The effect on the boys of the loss of their father was probably not fully realised at the time, but, in her efforts to suppress her grief, their mother devoted herself even more thoroughly to her mother's service, leaving her less and less time to spend with her children.

Before his departure for Ashanti, however, Liko had left very clear instructions for his sons' future education.

Already Drino and Maurice had followed their cousins into preparatory schools, which had been carefully selected by both of their parents. Originally, Beatrice and Liko considered enrolling them in Park Hill, where their cousin Charlie of Albany was a pupil, but after further reflection they opted instead to send Drino to Stubbington House School on the Solent, which was far more convenient for travelling to and from Osborne.

Unlike his cousins, Drino found it difficult to adapt to school life. Having been spoiled by his grandmother, he had developed a precociousness that irritated his fellow pupils whom he viewed with disdain. Possibly because of his unhappiness at Stubbington House, or possibly because of a scandal in 1891, when the headmaster sued the parents of a sick child for outstanding fees, Beatrice and Liko opted to send Maurice to Lockers Park in Hemel Hempstead instead.

Drino and Maurice were reunited when, as their father had wished, they progressed to Wellington College, where their Christian cousins, Christle and Abbie, had already won the praise of their tutors. Drino, however, was no happier at Wellington than he had been at Stubbington House. His tutors described him as lazy and self-indulgent, and he was often bullied by his schoolmates who viewed him as excessively arrogant and weak. Nonetheless, the college was intended to ready the boys for a military career – a virtual prerequisite for late nineteenth century princes – and Drino, like several of his cousins, was prepared to devote himself to his duties as a soldier.

Part II – 'Sheer Military Nonsense'

Scholars, Soldiers & Statesmen

Chapter 9 – The Herring & The Sprat

The Waleses

Bertie – (Albert Edward) Queen Victoria's eldest son; Prince of Wales
Alexandra – Bertie's Danish wife; Princess of Wales
Eddy – (Albert Victor) – Bertie's eldest son
George – Bertie's second son

    Since the Crimean War, Queen Victoria had taken a great deal of interest in the lives of ordinary soldiers, and was keen to ease the sufferings of the casualties of war. She had regularly visited military hospitals, learning the names of the patients, collecting their photographs, and discussing with Florence Nightingale the best means of assisting their recuperation. At a time when the British Empire was rapidly expanding, she took her role as Commander-in-Chief of the Armed Forces seriously, following her troops' successes and defeats with maternal concern; and she listened carefully, too, to the accounts of her sons and grandsons, some of whom saw active service in far-flung parts of the Empire.
    The connection between the monarchy and the military was evidenced in numerous photographs and paintings, portraying princes in uniform, complete with the insignia of various chivalric Orders. In Britain, the highest honour was the Order of the Garter, which the Queen conferred on her grandsons around the time of their seventeenth birthdays. The nearest Prussian equivalent, the Order of the Black Eagle, was conferred on the King's grandsons when they were ten years old.
    Never was the military connection quite so in evidence as on state occasions – weddings, funerals and jubilees – when princes invariably appeared in ceremonial dress; and, of all the royal pageants in history, few displayed

such a plethora of royal personages as Queen Victoria's Golden Jubilee procession in 1887.

After so many years in semi-retirement, and never having quite overcome her shyness at appearing in public 'alone', the Queen was not looking forward to the fetes organised by the Prince of Wales in honour of her fifty years on the throne. Nonetheless, she recognised the significance of the occasion and, having agreed to comply with Bertie's plans, she personally began making arrangements to house the numerous guests who would descend on London. More problematic for her was trying to arrange the order of precedence with which the royal visitors would enter Westminster Abbey, since the disparate members of her very large family had different ideas about who was superior to whom.

Willy was so eager to take centre-stage that he seized on the fact that his father had been unwell, and suggested that *he,* not the Crown Prince, should represent the German Emperor. Queen Victoria was so put out by his impudence that she considered not inviting him at all, but eventually, having being prevailed upon by Vicky to do so, she allowed him to come on the understanding that there was no room for him at Buckingham Palace and he would be lodged instead with Bertie at Marlborough House. Other relations were accommodated at Clarence House and Windsor Castle, but, even then, with so many guests arriving, several of the Queen's granddaughters had to share a bed.

Returning from Balmoral on Monday 20th June, Queen Victoria entered London to rapturous applause. As crowds began to gather to secure good vantage points from which to watch the grand procession the following day, the Queen hosted a reception for her numerous guests, whose titles were as impressive as their colourful attire. There were Maharajas; the Queen of Hawaii; the Kings of Belgium, Saxony, Denmark and Greece; together with numerous Crown Princes, Crown Princesses, Grand Dukes, Grand

Duchesses, and the representatives of monarchs from all over the world.

The next morning, the sun shone brightly over London as the guests prepared for the majestic procession to Westminster Abbey where a Thanksgiving Service was to be held. At eleven o'clock, the first carriages left Buckingham Palace and, half an hour later, bugles sounded to herald the arrival at the Abbey of a dazzling display of princesses. As they took their seats to the left of a raised dais prepared for the Queen, the National Anthem was played, and their fathers, husbands and brothers, led by the Crown Prince of Prussia and the Prince of Wales, set out on horseback, to provide the Queen's escort. Spurs and sabres jangling, glittering helmets reflecting the sun, they wound their way to the entrance, dismounted and, to the sound of a second bugle and a second rendition of the National Anthem, took their seats at the right of dais.

At length, the bugles sounded for a third time, as the tiny Queen walked into the Abbey. She was escorted by the Archbishop of Canterbury and four assistant bishops, who led her to the dais where:

"...she advanced to her seat at its very centre, where there was a plain-looking, old-fashioned armchair, said to have once belonged to St. Peter himself. She stood at a spot just opposite to this seat. All the rest of us had risen, and remained standing during her approach. Before seating herself, she made a little courtesy, which salutation was returned by all those who had awaited her coming from the opposite dais or platform. She was simply attired in a neat, black dress, wearing a bonnet very small and unobtrusive, while about her neck she wore a handsome necklace composed of single stone diamonds. After she was in her seat, and the rest of us had followed her example, the religious services were begun, and most impressive they seemed."[70]

115

When the service was over, the princesses approached the dais and kissed the Queen, before her sons and grandson follow suit, kneeling before her to kiss her hand. Then, in reverse order, the whole company returned to Buckingham Palace for a banquet where no fewer than sixty-nine royal guests sat down to dine.

In spite of his grandmother's anxieties, Willy proved to be a charming guest, entertaining his neighbour, the future Queen Liliuokalani of Hawaii with scintillating conversation, and reintroducing her to his brother, Henry, whom she had met in Hawaii, almost ten years before.

That evening, several of the princes were invested with the Order of the Bath, while the princesses were presented with Jubilee medals and brooches, and a great firework display completed the day's celebrations. For all her dislike of appearing in public and the exhaustion she felt Queen thoroughly enjoyed her jubilee.

"I am very happy," she said at the end of the day.

In many cases, the insignia and uniforms worn at the jubilee had little to do with effort or achievement, since the honours were given as a mark of favour from the sovereign, and it was customary practice for young princes to be automatically assigned to a regiment. Most followed some form of military or naval training, but, while some saw active service and were committed to their careers, other simply enjoyed the carefree lives of young officers, having neither interest in, nor aptitude for, life in the army or navy. Such was the case of the second-in-line to the British throne, Eddy of Wales.

In 1876, the Prince of Wales' plans to send his elder son, Eddy, to Wellington College were thrown into disarray by a report from his tutor, John Dalton. The twelve-year-old prince, Dalton observed, was so dependent on his younger brother, George, that separating the two would have a very detrimental effect on his already slow progress. Since

George was already set on a naval career, it would be better, Dalton said, for both princes to enrol as cadets in the hope that the naval discipline might instil in 'indolent' Eddy a sense of responsibility and independence.

Queen Victoria had no objections to George going to sea, but she feared that the rough life of a sailor was inappropriate preparation for a future king. Nonetheless, after much discussion, she came round to Bertie's belief that the boys should commence training together aboard the cadet ship, *Britannia,* which was moored off Dartmouth. It was hoped that when their two year course was completed, Eddy would be better equipped to progress to Wellington College to prepare for a stint in the army.

The following year, 1877, accompanied by Dalton, thirteen-year-old Eddy and twelve-year-old George began their course on the understanding that they were to be treated no differently from their fellow trainees. Although their apartments were separate from those of the other cadets, they were no better furnished, and the princes were expected to participate fully in all the exercises, duties and studies demanded of their peers.

Even in uniform the differences between the two princes were strikingly obvious. A friend of Dalton's, who visited the ship, wrote later:

"I can see them now in the cadet's uniform of which they were so proud, though not yet promoted to the dignity of a dirk. The one, tall and slim with a quiet, thoughtful face, the other, shorter with a round face and laughing eyes, full of mischief – a regular pickle!"[71]

Their contrasting appearance was quickly picked up on by their fellow cadets, who saw a rare opportunity to mock and even bully a future king. Lanky Eddy was nicknamed 'Herring'; and little George, who was frequently provoked into fights, was known as 'Sprat'.

Having grown accustomed to his mother's over-indulgence, George was initially stunned by the blows and shocked by the way that he was treated not as a prince but as any other young sailor. One night, he refused to get up to take his turn on watch, and, when the midshipman whom he was supposed to relieve came to wake him, he swore loudly and punched him in the eye. The midshipman silently returned to his post but the following day, when he told his companions what had happened, they adopted their customary practice of holding an impromptu court-martial at which George was sentenced to a 'spanking'. He was seized by four of the strongest boys and held face down on a table until the midshipman whose eye he had blacked, had meted out the punishment. George flew off in a rage but, some days later, approached his punisher to apologise for his behaviour.

Following the incident, his companions noted a change in him – he no longer assumed the air of a prince as he had done at the outset of his training, but rather viewed himself as one among many serving seamen. From then on, he quickly took to naval life, enjoying the orderliness and routine, and, like Cousin Henry of Prussia, adapted to the ship's discipline.

While George was acquiring new skills, however, Eddy, to his hypercritical tutor's despair, was making no more progress than he had done in the classroom. After two years, Dalton could only report that he was in no danger of overtaxing himself and had failed in every subject he had taken.

In view of this damning report, the possibility of Eddy attending Wellington College became even more remote; after all, would not competition with his peers, expose the intellectual weakness of the heir to the throne? Dalton's solution was to avoid the college altogether and instead Eddy and George should continue their studies and naval training on a round-the-world voyage. This time, however, Dalton believed that the brothers should be separated, each assigned to a different cruiser.

The Admiralty and government supported the plan – after all, even princes were susceptible to the vicissitudes of nature and, in an age when shipwrecks were still quite common, it would be foolish to risk the lives of both the heir and the spare by allowing them to undertake a potentially dangerous voyage in the same ship. Bertie, however, disagreed. While he accepted that the Grand Tour would be beneficial, neither he nor their mother believed that the boys should be separated, and he expected appropriate arrangements to be made to accommodate his wishes. When, therefore, he discovered that the First Lord of the Admiralty had already commission two ships, he was so incensed that he summoned the Prime Minister, Disraeli, and railed at him in such violent language about the Admiralty's unwelcome interference in his domestic affairs, that the ever-diplomatic Disraeli graciously accepted the blame and agreed to ensure that the Prince of Wales' wishes were complied with.

Dalton, meanwhile, continued to argue that the boys should be separated and, when Bertie forbade him to mention the subject again, he tendered his resignation, only to withdraw it a short time before the princes' departure.

The corvette chosen for the expedition was a three-year-old ironclad *Bacchante,* which, on Queen Victoria's insistence, was put through various tests including battling a storm to demonstrate its sea-worthiness. On the evening of Monday 5th August 1879, the corvette was brought from Spithead to Cowes and, the following day, the Connaughts and the Edinburghs, as well as the Wales sisters, were given a guided tour of the vessel which would be home to the princes for the next three years. For three weeks, the ship passed through her paces in the English Channel until, on August 26th, the princes finally bade farewell to their parents and weeping sisters and set out to sea.

In the first few days of the voyage, the boys were terribly homesick and, just hours after their departure, George wrote in gushing terms to his mother:

"My darling Motherdear, I miss you so very much & felt so so sorry when I had to say goodbye to you and sisters & it was dreadfully hard saying goodbye to dear Papa...I felt so miserable yesterday saying goodbye. I shall think of you all going to Scotland tonight & I only wish we were going too...So goodbye once more my darling Motherdear, please give darling Papa and sisters my very best love and kisses...I remain your very loving son Georgy."[72]

A twenty-three-year-old schoolmaster named James Sims was appointed to assist Dalton, and both tutors agreed that the boys should keep a diary of the voyage. Later, Dalton obtained permission to publish the journal but it is clear from both the style and content that Dalton himself heavily doctored the original entries, filling them with dull details about the history and geography of every place they visited. Nonetheless, from the daily accounts of their activities aboard the *Bacchante*, it is clear that, while they continued their studies and participated in various duties, there was also plenty of time for recreation. In Minorca, they enjoyed donkey rides; in Fiji they played cricket; polo in Argentina; and, in Japan, on their father's instructions, they were taken to a Master Tattooist named Hori Chiyo[n], and had their arms tattooed with blue and red dragons. Between boat races, games on the deck, and visits to ancient monuments, Eddy occasionally performed an official duty such as opening a new building or giving away a bride. George was called on to perform the sadder service of attending the funeral and interment of the unfortunate Mr Sims, who died suddenly of a heart complaint while visiting Barbados

An even more tragic event followed when a young seaman named William Foster fell from the top mast onto the

---

[n] Hori Chiyo had tattooed their father when he visited Jerusalem in 1862.

ship's deck and died almost instantly. The princes attended their first burial at sea, which left a deep impression on both boys, although Eddy's poetic description of the occasion was unmistakably doctored by his tutor:

"The sea to which the little cluster of his chums and messmates committed his body, was that evening of the darkest purple blue and over the whole height of heaven were spread at that moment bright and deep coloured clouds, some angry and lowering, others of a delicate emerald and olive green, and others again saffron and golden."[73]

Far and away, the boys' favourite recreation was hunting the wildlife in virtually every country they visited. In Australia, as Dalton recorded proudly, 'Eddy shot two kangaroo, a right and left shot, George shot three,'; but he was disappointed that, in Vigo Bay, despite Eddy killing two birds with a new gun, and finding plenty of rabbits and partridges, 'we shot next to nothing.'

After three years and forty thousand miles, the *Bacchante* finally returned to England in early August 1882. The Prince and Princess of Wales and their daughters sailed out on the Royal Yacht *Osborne,* to greet the young princes – 'so grown and looking so well' – and, after a joyful reunion, they were taken to Osborne House to dine with the Queen. The following day, they were examined by Archbishop Tait in preparation for their confirmation – a ceremony which marked not only their commitment to the Church of England but also their passage from childhood into adulthood – and, that afternoon, they were confirmed in Whippingham Church.

Having seen so much of the world, it was remarkable that neither of the princes had mastered a foreign language, and their grandmother was particularly distressed by their lack of fluency in French and German. At her insistence, therefore, after a brief spell relaxing at home, they travelled to the shores of Lake Geneva in the vain hope of improving their linguistic skills.

Although the Prince and Princess of Wales had done their utmost to keep the boys together, the time inevitably came for them to be separated. Three months after their stay by Lake Geneva, George, promoted to sub-lieutenant, set sail aboard the *Canada* bound for North America. Bertie and Eddy sadly accompanied him to the docks, with the Duke of Cambridge who noted:

"I was very sorry for him as it was his first real start in life, his brother remaining at home."[74]

But George survived the separation and, over the next seven years, serving on the *Dreadnaught* and his Uncle Affie's flagship *Alexandra,* he would continue to earn promotions, reaching the rank of captain at the age of twenty-eight in 1893.

Eddy, meanwhile, despite his lack of academic prowess, spent the summer of 1884 confined in Sandringham with a number of tutors led by the erratic and possibly bipolar scholar and poet, J.K. Stephen[o], whose duty was to prepare him for Cambridge University. After only a short time in Eddy's company, Stephen concluded that the prince would gain little benefit from attending lectures at the university, since, 'He hardly knows the meaning of the words *to read.*'

Refusing to give up hope, his parents and the Queen decided that a brief spell at the University of Heidelberg, would not only prepare him for student life but also enable him to improve his rudimentary German under the guidance of the distinguished Professor Ihue. Eddy returned to England in early autumn, and, in October, disregarding Stephen's assessment, Bertie delivered him – and Dalton – to Trinity College. There, the prince endeared himself to his

---

[o] J.K. Stephen is alleged to have developed a strange obsession with Eddy. When he heard that Eddy had died, he starved himself to death at the age of only thirty-two.

tutors and the other students but, as Stephen had predicted, he had so little interest in his studies that it was fortunate that Dalton had had the foresight to stipulate that he would be exempted from all examinations.

After two years at Cambridge, Eddy was awarded an honorary Doctorate of Law and embarked on a period of military training with his father's regiment, the 10th Hussars, stationed at Aldershot under the command of the Queen's cousin, George, Duke of Cambridge. Commissioned as a Major, Eddy received the standard fee of fifteen shillings a day – as compared to one shilling a day for the men in the ranks.

That the officer class was made up of wealthy young men and aristocrats was not due to any lack of skill on the part of the lower orders, but rather that the expense of maintaining an officer's lifestyle precluded virtually anyone without a separate private income. Out of Eddy's fifteen shillings day, he had to purchase his own uniform, boots, horses, bridles, saddles and other riding equipment, as well as incurring mess bills – two shillings a day for breakfast; two shillings and sixpence for lunch; a pound (twenty shillings) for dinner; plus additional costs for wine and beer. He and his fellow officers were expected, too, to pay for servants, contribute to the upkeep of the regimental band, and pay for the entertainment of their senior officers. Unsurprisingly, the majority of officers were the Public School educated sons of the rich, and, while some had entered the armed forces out of patriotism or a sense of duty, many did so solely to enjoy the lifestyle and the kudos of the uniform, or simply because they had no idea how else to spend their time.

Eddy clearly belonged to the latter category, for he was no more a career soldier than he had been a career sailor. His senior officers reported that he had little enthusiasm for the mundane aspects of a military life, and he dawdled so much that, like his mother, he was constantly late for engagements. He did, however, enjoy military trappings and shared Cousin Willy's passion for uniforms.

Eddy's sartorial interest was not confined to battle and ceremonial dress. He was equally taken by the fashion for starched collars and long cuffs, which served to conceal his very long neck and long arms. His father, who was equally fastidious about clothes, was so amused by Eddy's style that he nicknamed him 'collar and cuffs' and urged his young cousins to address him by that epithet.

In spite of the jibes, Bertie was devoted to his son; and, in the eyes of the Princess of Wales and his sisters, Eddy could do no wrong. The rest of the family might consider him vacant and even, as one cousin suggested, 'quite stupid', but his sisters and his mother – to whom he was devoted – saw only his gentleness and kindness. Even the intellectual Vicky, who was so often critical of her own sons, described him as charming and kind, and for a while she considered him as a prospective husband for one of her daughters.

On his twenty-first birthday, January 8th 1885, Queen Victoria announced that henceforth he should be known by his correct name, Albert Victor, but the family had become so used to 'Eddy' that they found it impossible to comply with the command. The celebrations for the occasion lasted the entire day beginning in the morning when he received his numerous presents.

> "…Then," according to George of Cambridge, "he received addresses and deputations…to all of which he made very suitable replies and did it very well, with simple manner, without appearing to be nervous. All the retainers…then passed by in procession and gave him hearty cheers, and then Sanger's Circus passed by, previous to a performance in the Circus which we attended after luncheon, and which was given by the Prince to the labourers on the Estate and children of the several schools hereabouts. The

Circus was a very good performance and not too long. Dinner at 8.15 in uniform, at which I gave Eddy's health, who replied very nicely, though in but very few words. The day finished with a great Ball, 600 invitations, the Gentlemen in uniform..."[75]

Now that Eddy had officially reached adulthood, the question of what to do with a young man who showed no specific aptitudes and who was clearly wasting his time in the army, began to trouble his parents and the Queen. In the winter of 1887, the Prince of Wales contacted his commanding officer, the Duke of Cambridge, to ask his advice about whether or not Eddy should continue to serve with the regiment. In his reply, the Duke had no qualms about speaking bluntly, as he explained that the regimental headquarters was about to move to London and:

"...I do not think that this would be a desirable station at present for so young and inexperienced a man, who would be surrounded by temptations of every description, which it requires great firmness of character to resist."[76]

What was more, said the Duke, Eddy had been with the regiment long enough to have mastered the basics of a cavalry officer's duties and to continue along the same route would merely be wasting his time. He suggested that Eddy could be assigned to a different regiment and posted to Gibraltar where there was so much work to be done that he would be too busy to sink into dissipation.

"Great interests are involved in Eddy's future career, and certain sacrifices must be made to attain the objects in view to teach him and accustom him to habits of discipline and the knowledge of the business which he can better attain in the manner proposed than in any other way that presents itself to my mind."[77]

Eventually it was decided that, while maintaining his connection to his regiment, he should embark on another

125

series of tours to the furthest parts of the Empire. In April 1889, preparations began for a seven-month trip to India via Egypt, but, by the time he set out on the voyage that autumn, a scandal gave rise to the suspicion that his apparently sudden departure was simply a means of avoiding the press or even prosecution.

That summer, three months after preparations had begun for Eddy's Indian tour, the police were called to investigate a theft at the London Telegraph Offices. A young messenger boy was arrested and found to have in his possession a sum of money which far exceeded his wages. Under interrogation, the boy explained that he had earned the money by working in a male brothel on Cleveland Street, which was subsequently raided. As other rent boys were questioned, they revealed that their clients included several prominent men, including the son of an equerry to the Prince of Wales. Rumours rapidly spread that Eddy, too, had been a Cleveland Street client, sometimes arriving dressed as a woman and calling himself 'Victoria'. Whether or not the stories had any foundation in truth, Eddy's departure for India three months later, fuelled the speculation and, although the British press remained silent on the subject, American newspapers openly reported his involvement.

Fortunately for Eddy, the scandal had virtually blown over by the time that he returned to England in May 1890. Within three weeks of his homecoming, the Queen gave him the title Duke of Clarence and Avondale, and, while he was still officially stationed with the Hussars in York and in Dublin, he was given a series of royal duties while he and his family embarked on a desperate quest to find him a suitable wife.

Chapter 10 – Mere Love of Potsdam

The Hohenzollerns (Prussians)

Vicky (Victoria) – Eldest child of Queen Victoria; wife of
Fritz, Crown Prince of Prussia
Fritz (Frederick William) – Vicky's husband; Crown Prince
of Prussia
Willy (William/Wilhelm) – Fritz & Vicky's eldest son
Henry – Fritz & Vicky's second son
Moretta – Fritz & Vicky's second daughter

The heir to the British throne might not have been
interested in military affairs, but the same could not be said
for his counterpart in Prussia. Three years after the Austro-
Prussian War, the memory of his father's triumphant return
to Berlin continued to fire Willy's imagination, and since it
was the custom for Prussian princes to be assigned to a
regiment while they were still children, as his tenth birthday
approached, he anticipated his first commission with
boundless excitement.

On 27th January 1869, he proudly donned a miniature
uniform of the First Infantry Regiment of the Guards, and
stood in line with his fellow officers to receive his command
and the prestigious Order of the Black Eagle from his
grandfather. So deep was the impact that the ceremony made
upon him that even decades later, he recalled with pride:

"With a deep bow the Emperor told me that I was
still too young to gauge fully the importance of the
fact that I was now a Prussian officer. But the time of
understanding would come, and then I should
discharge my duty as my father had done. The
solemnity of the moment made a deep impression
upon me; it was like receiving my knighthood."[78]

To his delight, he was appointed a military tutor –
First Lieutenant O'Danne, and later the 'delightful' and

'congenial' Major-General von Cottberg – to work alongside his academic tutor, the uninspiring Hintzpeter.

Willy could not have been happier than when he was strutting around in his uniform, imagining himself to be the new Siegfried or some other hero of Germanic lore; and when, a few months later, he stood to attention as the King inspected the troops, he truly believed that he was already a noble and courageous soldier.

"...and the boy's heart beat faster as the King's eye met his," he wrote later. "Then the battalions formed up for the march-past and I marched by in the rear. It was a never-to-be-forgotten day. For what could be finer for a Prince of the Blood, a grandson of the King and an officer of the First Infantry Regiment of the Guards than to stand on duty before his great and awe-inspiring liege!"[79]

Sadly, as happened so often, Willy's self-concept was at odds others' perceptions of him. As he proudly marched in what he believed to be the first steps of a glorious military career, his mother wrote dismissively that, 'Poor Willy in his uniform looks like some unfortunate, little monkey dressed up.'[80]

For all his desire to appear heroic, Willy's greatest asset was his intellect, for, despite his mother's disappointment in his progress, he had an excellent memory and excelled in those subjects which interested him. He mastered languages easily; was a keen historian and archaeologist; he was well-read; cultivated in the arts; and had a broad general knowledge. Lady Emily Russell, who dined with him when he was fourteen years old, told Queen Victoria that:

"Everyone who has the gratification of speaking to Prince William is struck by his natural charming and amiable qualities, his great intelligence and his admirable education."[81]

It was a sentiment shared at the time by his uncle, Bertie, Prince of Wales, who told his mother that 'it would impossible to find two nicer boys than Willy and Henry.'

Vicky, the perfectionist, was not so convinced. By the time that Willy was eleven years old, she was so concerned about the malign influence that the court was having on her sons, that she agreed with their tutor, Hintzpeter, that they would benefit from the company of their peers in a gymnasium (public school) in Kassel. Initially, Fritz and his father's court had their doubts about the plan, fearing that if the future Kaiser proved to be less gifted than his fellow pupils, the mystique of All-Powerful Sovereign, would be shattered. Eventually, though, Fritz agreed that the benefits outweighed the risks, and both he and Vicky hoped that the distance from Berlin would remove the unhelpful influence of Otto von Bismarck, who had recently been appointed Chancellor.

Willy, however, had his own reservations which, despite his bravado, revealed the depths of his shyness:

"...now I was to leave the parental home in whose protection I had grown up, was to be given into the hands of new teachers, and now, all at once, was to learn with strange boys in a public school, was to compete with them, and – to come out lower in the list!"[82]

He was consoled by the knowledge that he would be accompanied by Henry and his civil and military tutors, Hintzpeter and von Cottenberg, and he gradually came round to the idea and accepted his parents' decision.

In the weeks leading up to the boys' departure for Kassel, Willy's behaviour improved dramatically. He made a deep impression on his mother during his confirmation ceremony, and, as the day of parting approached, Vicky dreaded the separation.

"Today is a sort of break up," she told the Queen in August 1874. "In two days the boys leave us for school where they will stay for three years – only returning for the holidays – then Willy will go into the army and Henry to the naval school. I feel giving them up like this very much."[83]

With surprising ease the boys settled into the new environment where, although they were careful to avoid particular friendships, they were popular with their classmates and devoted to several of their masters. The two years spent at Kassel were married only by disagreements between Hintzpeter and von Cottenberg, and the excessively long hours of study, which often lasted from five or six in the morning until seven in the evening.

Graduating from the gymnasium, Willy moved on to Bonn University, ostensibly to study political science though much of his time was spent with fellow members of the Borussia Corps – a military fraternity of students, who were renowned for drinking and duelling. His student days were pleasant enough, but, for Willy, nothing could live up to the years that followed when, at his grandfather's suggestion, he embarked on a course of military training in Potsdam.

'I really found my family, my friends, my interests – everything of which I had up to that time had to do without,'[84] he wrote later. Again, though, his mother and grandmother dismissed his obsession with the military as nothing more than a whim which he would outgrow.

"[Willy's] want of interest or taste – and mere love of Potsdam is quite provoking –," wrote Queen Victoria, but I think young people have such an esprit de contradiction that it very likely will get better if no notice is taken of that."[85]

In fact, at Potsdam the future Supreme War Lord gained no greater grasp of modern warfare, than he had had as a ten-year-old child. It was not the actuality of battles that appealed to his wild imagination, but rather a romantic dream of chivalric glory. In this, he differed little from 'mad' King Ludwig of Bavaria – the 'Swan King', who sought to recreate a legendary world by building fairy-tale castles – or many contemporary writers, artists and architects, who, in the midst of rapid industrialisation, sought to recapture an idyllic Golden Age of heroes and fabled Knights-of-yore. This was an era when mock-castles sprang up all over England; when readers avidly followed the adventures of Walter Scott's *Ivanhoe,* and Tennyson's *Lady of Shallot*; and the pre-Raphaelite brotherhood produced works of art depicting Arthurian legends.

Willy was far more interested in pageantry and show than he was in tactics. Over the years, he would amass more than four hundred uniforms, which he treasured in much the same way as Cousin George of Wales treasured stamps[p]; and, it made little difference to which regiment the uniform belonged for he was as happy to be seen dressed as a British Admiral as he was to be seen in the helmet of his Death's Head Hussars. Like his cousin, Ella of Hesse, who was renowned for disappearing partway through a ball and reappearing later in a new dress complete with matching jewellery, Willy frequently excused himself from the company he was with, to return in a different uniform. Observers who saw him strutting about as a Prussian Hussar or a British Field Marshal, had no idea of the struggles faced by his attendants as they hurried to dress him.

"We would not care if [he] changed his uniform ten, instead of three or four times per day," a valet wrote, "it's the fear of injuring his lame hand that makes us nervous and gradually wears away our usefulness. And, besides, we must always be prepared to forestall the collapse of the all-highest master when he balances himself on his left leg, as is his wont sometimes, when he is in a hurry to put on a different pair of trousers."[86]

Even after his accession, he was so desperate to add to his collection of uniforms that, like a schoolboy trading

---

p See Chapter 22

sports cards with his classmates, he offered foreign princes the honorary commandership of various German regiments, in the hope that they would return the favour and he could acquire a new uniform to add to his rather meaningless collection.

Queen Victoria viewed this obsession with mild amusement. While entertaining her family or foreign guests to dinner, she made a point of insisting that civilian dress should be worn. When, however, after Willy's accession, a German general appeared in uniform with the explanation that the Kaiser had commanded him to do so, the Queen turned to him, smiling and said,

"I wonder if His Majesty's envoy thinks we are *impressed* by uniforms?"[87]

Second only to his passion for the army, was Willy's love for the navy – an interest which he shared with his brother, Henry, who made a career at sea. Their childhood holidays at Osborne were surpassed only by a visit to the new Prussian harbour at Wilhelmshaven in 1869, when ten-year-old Willy 'gazed speechless' at the great ironclad, *Konig Wilhelm* – a colossal battleship armed with rows of twenty-one centimetre guns. The experience left such a deep impression on the boy that, from that moment, he dreamed of creating a great Prussian navy to rival that of Great Britain.

Henry, though less ambitious, had been so drawn to a nautical life that even before he attended school in Kassel, plans were afoot for his future as a naval cadet. He already had a rudimentary knowledge of sailing, for, while he was still a small child, the officers of his grandmother's Royal Yacht had taught him to understand signal codes, how to hoist a flag, and how to use a compass. On his tenth birthday, August 14th 1872, he was officially created 'Unterleutnant zur See' – a second lieutenant in his grandfather's navy.

Five years later, he entered the Imperial Naval Cadet Training School, where he would share the duties of his fellow cadets and gain much practical experience. Queen Victoria followed his progress with interest and, observing that his first ship was named *Sedan* after the decisive Prussian victory in the Franco-Prussian War, she suggested that, to avoid offending the French, an alternative name should be found. Vicky passed her suggestion to the Admiralty and the vessel was re-named *Prinz Adalbert.*

Henry's cheerful nature and affability earned him many friends but his mother, distressed by his adherence to Bismarck's policies, continued to find fault with him.

'Much as dear Henry is loved I do not feel very proud of him,' she told the Queen, who, despite having written an almost identical line about her own sailor son, Affie, several decades earlier, responded by suggesting that Vicky should show greater leniency to her children.

To complete his naval training, Henry embarked on a two-year round-the-world voyage aboard the *Olga,* which gave him his first unnerving experience of almost being shipwrecked in a storm. Queen Victoria was shocked to hear of what had happened but, when he stayed with her at Osborne soon after his return, she had nothing but praise and admiration for him.

"I must write you a line to say how delighted we were to see Henry again; my particular child looking well though thin, and no wonder; they had such an awful (really dangerous) passage back...He is as dear, simple and affectionate as ever, very fond of his profession but delighted to be home. Count von Seckendorff...gives the very best report of dear Henry, how well he does his duty and how good he is."[88]

Having successfully completed his cadetship, Henry graduated to the Imperial Naval Academy where, once again his commitment and ability impressed his superiors. Over the next two decades he continued to earn his promotions, captaining different kinds of vessels, and eventually being appointed Admiral of the Fleet.

"Prince Henry is a sailor-man through and through, an admiral first and a Prince afterwards," wrote one observer in 1913. "He has had little time, and less inclination for the luxurious pastimes of his royal estate. The fashions and frivolities of Court life have never appealed to him. His hobby is the sea, and he is happiest when cultivating it."[89]

The Italian naval commander, Marquis Lorenzo d'Adda, was greatly impressed by the way in which Henry addressed his subordinates with gentleness and such a profound knowledge of his profession that, rather than barking out commands, he needed only to speak quietly to 'inspire absolute confidence'.

"He has," said the Marquis, "charm, simplicity and the distinction of an English gentleman of high birth....I never noticed a single gesture of impatience or anger."[90]

His love of the sea soon distracted him from politics, and although he remained Willy's staunch friend and supporter, he increasingly withdrew from the political intrigues of Berlin, where, by then, his brother was making a strong impression as the Kaiser.

Chapter 11 – A Mere Passing Shadow

The Hohenzollerns

Vicky (Victoria) – Eldest child of Queen Victoria; wife of
Fritz, Crown Prince of Prussia; later Empress Frederick
Fritz (Frederick William) – Vicky's husband; Crown Prince
of Prussia; later Emperor Frederick III
Emperor William I – German Emperor; Fritz's father
Willy (William/Wilhelm) – Fritz & Vicky's eldest son
Henry – Fritz & Vicky's second son
Irene – Princess of Hesse; daughter of Queen Victoria's
second daughter, Alice; bride of Henry.
Moretta – Vicky's second daughter

For much of his adult life, Willy and Henry's father,
Crown Prince Fritz of Prussia, had been silenced. Since his
liberal views were not in keeping with the opinions of
Bismarck and his father's court, he was prevented from
speaking publicly on affairs of state, and he was often
dismissed as nothing more than a mouthpiece for his
dominant wife. As Willy grew into adulthood, he, who had
once admired his father, did nothing to correct this unjust
assessment, but rather encouraged it by telling the Tsar of
Russia that his father was completely under the thumb of his
mother, who was likewise under the sway of Queen Victoria.
Groomed by Bismarck, Willy viewed his parents'
opinions as weak and he saw himself as the true face of a
young and powerful Germany. So eager was he to ascend the
throne, that he had scrawled across his own photograph, 'I
bide my time'; and he envisaged his reign as being a
repetition of that of his ancestor, Frederick the Great. In spite
of this ambition and his sense of rivalry with his parents,
Willy still loved his father and he was as shocked as anyone
to discover that he was seriously ill and possibly even dying.

Troubled by hoarseness through the winter of 1886-1887, Fritz believed his sore throat was the result of a recent bout of measles combined with a severe cold which he caught while on holiday in Italy. Since the dust of Berlin exacerbated the condition, his hoarseness improved when he left the city, creating the impression that the root cause of his problem was stress. The improvement, though, was short-lived and, by the time of Queen Victoria's Golden Jubilee, he had begun to suspect that something was seriously amiss. Various doctors examined him and initially diagnosed a severe inflammation of the larynx before discovering a small growth on his vocal cord, which they attempted to cauterise.

In May 1887, at Vicky's request, a celebrated British throat specialist, Dr Morell Mackenzie, arrived in Berlin to assist in the Crown Prince's treatment. He, too, observed the small growth but, while the German doctors believed that the tumour was cancerous, Mackenzie stated it would be impossible to make such a diagnosis without a biopsy. The German doctors refused to perform the necessary surgery so Mackenzie himself carried out the procedure and arranged to meet Fritz again when he was in London for the jubilee celebrations.

Despite his attempts to play down his complaint, by the time that Fritz arrived in England, rumours had already spread that he was seriously ill. With great fortitude he dispelled the stories by making an impressive appearance in the procession of princes, for, although one observer noticed that 'a slight change had come over him', his manner and bearing gave no suggestion that he might be dying.

"Prince Frederick," recalled the editor of Lloyd's newspaper, "was in the white uniform of the Cuirassier Guard, with the Imperial Crest on his helmet. He sat with the firm easy seat of a cavalry soldier; an ideal prince among princes. Though my notes described him as looking 'pale and grey', there was no thought of impending doom."[91]

Despite appearances, Vicky and her mother were aware of how ill he felt, and, to avoid the smog of Central London, had agreed that he and Vicky would stay at Upper Norwood in the suburbs.

As arranged, Mackenzie examined him again and, after removing another growth, recommended a period of convalescence. Fritz, sharing his mother-in-law's belief in the benefits of sea air, chose to stay on the Isle of Wight before spending some time with the Queen at Balmoral, and continuing his recuperation in the mountains of the Austrian Tyrol. Doctors frequently came and went and noticed little improvement, and so, as the weather grew colder, Fritz, Vicky and their younger daughters, moved to the warmer climes of San Remo.

His prolonged absence from Berlin, meanwhile, provoked a good deal of conjecture, and when the Emperor's health began to fail, hostile articles appeared in the press questioning why the Crown Prince was not carrying out his duties for him. As time went on, increasingly outlandish stories began to appear in the papers. Some said that Fritz was suffering from cancer but his wife insisted on keeping it secret as she only wanted English doctors to attend him. Others claimed that he had been prescribed mercury and, since this was the usual treatment for venereal disease, it was evidence that Fritz had contracted syphilis while attending the opening of the Suez Canal almost twenty years earlier. Most salacious of all were the tales that Vicky had taken a young lover whom she wished to marry, and so she and her English doctors were conspiring to kill her husband.

Willy and Henry were horrified by the stories but, rather than defending their mother, they urged her to leave Fritz's treatment solely in the hands of German doctors. When the brothers arrived in San Remo in November 1887, Henry told his mother plainly that her English medics were killing his father.

"[Henry] becomes so rude and impertinent that I really cannot stand it," Vicky complained to Queen Victoria. "... [He] is quite dreadful in this respect! He is so prejudiced and fancies he knows better than his Mama and all the doctors here, and that we do not speak the truth."[92]

Willy, meanwhile, claiming to act on behalf of his grandfather, the Emperor, demanded a conference with of Fritz' surgeons and physicians, and behaved in such a high-handed manner that Vicky adamantly refused to permit him to see his father. Seething with anger, Willy returned to Berlin where, to Vicky's annoyance, one of the German doctors was presenting public lectures on the Crown Prince's condition. Soon, to Vicky's consternation, she learned that a number of powerful ministers were intriguing with Willy to ensure that he, rather than his father, would act as Regent for the Emperor if his condition continued to deteriorate; and already Willy was dealing with his grandfather's correspondence and taking over many of his duties.

Despite Vicky's anger, Willy's actions were not entirely motivated by self-interest. His grandfather was too ill to deal with much pressing business and, since Fritz was far away, who else but the next-in-line should take on his responsibilities? Nonetheless, in his mother's eyes, her 'unfeeling' son was, without any reference to his father, behaving as though he were already Emperor, issuing orders to all and sundry, including his younger brother, Henry, whom he used as a messenger to take unpleasant news to their parents.

"Henry arrives," Vicky told the Queen, "pulls a paper, or rather a letter from Willy out of his pocket, in which letter it says that he has been appointed Stellvertreter des Kaisers [Vice-Emperor], and gives it to Fritz, who was much upset, very angry, and much excited..."[93]

Stressed and feeling attacked from all sides, Vicky clung to the vain hope that Fritz would recover. Repeatedly she reassured herself and her mother that his health was improving and only Willy's intrigues with Bismarck prevented the newspapers from reporting that he would soon be well.

If Vicky were deceiving herself, Fritz was far more pragmatic. When Mackenzie next examined him, he asked directly if the growths were cancerous and, if so, was there any possibility of a cure. Mackenzie regretfully replied that they were cancerous and that, beyond making him more comfortable, nothing could be done.

"The Crown Prince received the communication with perfect calmness. After a moment's silence, with a smile of peculiar sweetness, which so well express the mingled gentleness and strength of his character, he grasped my hand and said, 'I have lately been fearing something of the sort. I thank you, Sir Morell, for being so frank with me.' In all my long experience, I have never seen a man bear himself under similar circumstances with such unaffected heroism."[94]

By February 1888, the tumours were so large that a tracheotomy had to be performed to enable Fritz to breathe. The surgery was carried out under chloroform by a German doctor, while Vicky, Henry and his sisters waited in an adjoining room. This time, Henry was far more supportive of his mother, who described him as being 'sensitive' and 'so nice'.

The operation was successful but before Fritz had had time to recuperate, news arrived that the Emperor's condition had deteriorated and the Crown Prince must return at once to Berlin. Despite Mackenzie's warning that he was not fit to travel, Fritz decided that his duty was more important than his health and ordered the necessary arrangements to be made as quickly as possible. On the morning of his departure, however, a telegram arrived informing him that his father had already died.

For thirty years Vicky and Fritz had dreamed of being in a position to create a more liberal Germany but the opportunity had come too late. For the new Emperor Frederick III, the journey to Berlin was torturous and, by the time he arrived in the city in the midst of a snowstorm, he was so exhausted that it took every ounce of determination for him to greet the ministers and ambassadors who had assembled in the Charlottenburg Palace. Less than a week later, he had not yet regained sufficient strength to attend his father's funeral:

> "His Majesty was more depressed than I had ever seen him," Mackenzie wrote. "His countenance expressed the deepest sorrow; he was restless and agitated, and twice he pointed to a window looking toward Berlin, saying, 'I *ought* to be there!'" [95]

While Henry and his sisters offered what support they could to their father, Willy let it be known to anyone who cared to listen, that a man who could not speak could not be Emperor, and his father should, therefore, abdicate in his favour.

> "I think people in general consider us a mere passing shadow," Vicky wrote mournfully to her mother, "soon to be replaced in the shape of [Willy]." [96]

Appalled by Willy's unfilial behaviour, Queen Victoria was even more incensed by his continued opposition to a match between his sister, Moretta, and Prince Alexander (Sandro) Battenberg, an elder brother of Beatrice's husband, Liko. Backed by Bismarck, Emperor Wilhelm I had adamantly refused to permit them to marry, and when Vicky had pleaded Sandro's cause, the Emperor had warned that if their relationship continued, both Moretta and her mother would be banished from the court. Willy had volubly backed his grandfather's decision, denigrating the Battenbergs at every opportunity, and provoking an intensely annoyed

Queen Victoria into reminding him that his own wife was a 'poor little insignificant princess'[q]

Now, though, with her father's accession, Moretta had every reason to believe that finally her hopes would be fulfilled for, although Fritz had initially opposed the match, he had come round to the idea that daughter's happiness was of greater importance than any dynastic considerations. Willy, on the other hand, remained intransigent and, when he heard that his father had invited Sandro to Berlin, he succeeded in persuading him to withdraw the invitation on the grounds that he was not well enough to receive him.

"How Bismarck and still more William can play such a double game is impossible for us honest, straightforward English to understand," Queen Victoria huffed. "Thank God we *are* English!"[97]

Infuriated by her grandson's behaviour, and deeply saddened by Fritz' illness, the Queen announced her intention of visiting Vicky and Fritz to offer them her support. Knowing of Bismarck's antagonism towards her, her ministers advised her against the trip but she dismissed their concerns, insisting that she had a right and a duty to be with her daughter and son-in-law in their hour of need.

Her mother's arrival in Berlin on April 24th 1888 gave Vicky a much-needed opportunity to vent the feelings which she had suppressed for so long. She wept much of the time as she poured out her heart to the Queen, who made a public demonstration of her support by driving out with her through the streets of the city. To Vicky's surprise, she was greeted with cheers and applause, which seemed so at odds with what 'Willy and his clique' had told her of her unpopularity.

Queen Victoria attempted to raise Vicky's spirits by remaining cheerful and inviting Fritz to visit her in England when he was better, but it was all a façade, for she knew as well as anyone that, in reality, Fritz was dying. Within a

---

[q] See Chapter 15

couple of weeks of his accession, the tissue around the site of the cannula, which had been inserted into his windpipe, had begun to crumble and, as new tubes were regularly inserted, abscesses formed causing him even greater difficulty in breathing. He nonetheless was determined to be present at his son, Henry's wedding on 24th May 1888[r].

The evening before the ceremony, he had hoped to be able to welcome his new daughter-in-law to Berlin, but he lacked the strength to remain awake and was forced to retire. The following morning, his family assumed that he would be too ill to attend the service and therefore they began to civil ceremony without him. To his chagrin, he arrived too late to see the register signed, but he was able to join them for the religious service, doing his utmost to appear well and cheerful, although witnesses could not help but notice the whistling through his tracheotomy tube and the pallor of his gaunt features.

'He was never so well after Prince Henry's wedding,' Mackenzie wrote; and shortly afterwards he asked to be moved to his favourite home in Potsdam – the New Palace, in which he and Vicky had spent most of their married life, and which he now renamed Friedrichskron.

Throughout the first two weeks of June, his health deteriorated rapidly and, although he continued to sign documents and keep abreast of affairs of state, he was soon confined to bed and, unable to swallow, being fed by a tube. Vicky and his younger daughters barely left his side until finally he breathed his last on the morning of 15th June 1888, having reigned for only three months. One of his final acts was to write a note to Willy:

> "I wish to have set in evidence as my unbiased personal opinion that I entirely acquiesce in the betrothal of your second sister with Prince Alexander of Battenberg. I charge you as a filial duty with the accomplishment of this my desire, which your sister

---

[r] See Chapter 18

Victoria [Moretta] for so many years has cherished in her heart. I count upon your fulfilling your duty as a son by a precise attention to my wishes, and as a brother by not withdrawing your co-operation from your sister."[98]

It was a vain hope, for Willy had no intention of honouring the request and, even as his father lay on his deathbed, he had ordered a cordon of soldiers to surround the Friedrichskron to prevent anyone from leaving. His first act, therefore, as Emperor was to place his mother under house arrest and, as she and her daughters wept over Fritz' body, desks were rifled and rooms were searched and the broken-hearted widow was not even permitted to go into the garden to cut a rose to place in the hand of her dead husband.

Much has been made of Willy's apparent cruelty at that time but his actions were not entirely without justification. He was well aware that, since her marriage, his mother had kept a diary, containing numerous secrets of the Prussian Court, including the part her husband had played in the unification of Germany, as well as detailed notes about confidential and potentially damaging information about Germany's military capabilities. As his father's health was rapidly deteriorating, Willy had been informed – probably by Bismarck – that the moment he died, his mother intended to send her diaries back to England with Morell Mackenzie. In order to protect state secrets, it was vital to prevent the diaries from being taken out of the country, which was why Willy immediately sent in the soldiers. Within a couple of hours after a fruitless search, the soldiers were withdrawn and Vicky was left to mourn in peace.

In fact, unbeknown to Willy, his mother had already given the diaries to Queen Victoria when she visited Berlin the previous April. More circumspect than her daughter was in this instance, the Queen realised the potential danger of possessing the documents and therefore she kept them sealed in locked boxes until Willy's accession, at which point she

143

returned them to him with the seals unbroken. It was her first, but would not be her last, show of respect for the position of the new German Emperor, Kaiser Wilhelm II.

Chapter 12 – The Art of Self-Deception

The Hohenzollerns

Vicky (Victoria) – Eldest child of Queen Victoria; Empress Frederick

Fritz (Frederick William) – Vicky's husband; Emperor Frederick III

Willy (William/Wilhelm) – Kaiser Wilhelm II; Fritz & Vicky's eldest son

Henry – Fritz & Vicky's second son

Charlotte – Princess of Saxe-Meiningen; Vicky's eldest daughter

Moretta – Vicky's second daughter

Sophie – Vicky's third daughter

Mossy – Vicky's youngest daughter

Others

Sandro (Alexander) – Prince of Battenberg; suitor of Moretta

Bernhard – Prince of Saxe-Meiningen; Charlotte's husband

Tino – Crown Prince of Greece; Sophie's husband

From the moment of his accession, twenty-nine-year-old Kaiser Wilhelm II sought to demonstrate his authority in his typically flamboyant fashion. Although he eschewed a lavish coronation in order to avoid unnecessary expense, within ten days of his father's death he had organised a grand opening of the Reichstag and a triumphant entry into Berlin to receive the homage of the various German rulers. In his first official speech on that occasion, he pointedly omitted any mention of his predecessor, promising instead to follow in his grandfather's footsteps. All traces of Emperor Frederick III's brief reign were clearly being erased as Willy prepared to present himself to the world as the powerful face of a young and dynamic Germany.

In their anguish, Vicky and her younger daughters retreated to their country estate at Bornstedt, while Willy, in his haste to establish himself, wrote to his mother, demanding that all his father's uniforms should be delivered to him; and informing her that, contrary to Fritz's expressed wishes, a post mortem would be performed at the request of the German doctors, who hoped to prove that Mackenzie was responsible for his death.

Worse was to follow. The Friedrichskron, which had been a family home for most of Vicky's married life, was to revert to its former name – the New Palace – and the Dowager Empress and her daughters must vacate it as soon as possible since Willy wished to live there. This decision, though painful for Vicky, was not quite as cruel as it first appears, for the Friedrichskron was the most prestigious place in Berlin, and therefore the most appropriate residence for an Emperor. In asking Vicky to leave, Willy offered her the choice of several other palaces in the city, but, ousted from the home she had loved, she chose to present herself as a 'homeless' victim of her son's heartlessness.

Queen Victoria, aghast at such apparently heartless behaviour, pointedly remained aloof when Willy's envoy arrived in Windsor bearing greetings from the new Kaiser. When news of their meeting reached Willy, he let it be known that he was hurt by his grandmother's coldness and from now on he wished to be treated as an Emperor and not merely as a grandson. The Queen, however, was not to be bullied by his grandiose statements. She laughed at his insistence on signing himself as Emperor Wilhelm, even when sending her private messages, and she asked her secretary to inform him that:

> "The Queen intended [the meeting with Willy's envoy] to be cold. She last saw him as her son-in-law's A.D.C. He came to her and never uttered one word of sorrow for his master's death, and rejoiced in the accession of his new master."[99]

Despite her refusal to bow to his grandiosity, Queen Victoria recognised the need to respect Willy's position as Emperor. When Vicky and her daughters arrived in England in November, she, who had been one of Sandro Battenberg's staunchest supporters, gently told Moretta that she must abandon all hope of marrying her erstwhile suitor, since she could not contravene the dictates of the Emperor[s].

Willy was equally harsh in the treatment of another sister, Sophie, who, shortly after his accession, married Crown Prince Constantine (Tino) of Greece. Soon afterwards, she decided to adopt her husband's Greek Orthodox faith and, although her mother was a little shocked by the news, she accepted the decision and agreed with Queen Victoria that religion was a matter for individual conscience. Willy, however, was appalled and, convinced that his mother had encouraged Sophie to convert, declared that he absolutely forbade her to abandon her German Protestantism.

As the Crown Princess of the Hellenes, Sophie paid little attention to her brother's diktat, and she laughed when Willy's wife, Dona, squawked that, if she disobeyed the Kaiser, she faced eternal damnation. Matters took a more unpleasant turn, however, when Dona gave birth to a premature baby, and Willy informed several relations that if his son should die, the blame would be entirely Sophie's.

"I think," Vicky warned Sophie, "you had better say a little word to Grandmama when you write, as it is sure to reach her ears in a very different form and she should hear the truth. I am sure she will listen to all you say."[100]

'Grandmama' did indeed listen to all that Sophie said and, when Willy wrote to her seeking support, she did not even bother to answer his letter. He had no more success with Sophie's father-in-law, King George of the Hellenes,

---

[s] In fact, Sandro soon lost hope of marrying Moretta and, nine months after Willy's accession, he married an actress from the Darmstadt theatre.

who calmly replied that he could not interfere in what was a private matter, before sending copies of all his correspondence with Willy to Vicky. Fuming with rage, Willy declared that, since Sophie had disobeyed him, she was no longer permitted to set foot in Germany and, if she dared to enter his country, she would be instantly arrested.

Though slightly perturbed that the ban would prevent Sophie from visiting her mother, Queen Victoria remained convinced that the situation, which she put down to Willy's narrow-mindedness and Dona's interference, would soon blow over. In the meantime, she sought the advice of the Prince of Wales, who recommended that whenever Sophie wished to visit her mother, she should be accompanied by her husband since not even Willy would dare to arrest the Crown Prince of Greece. The ban was never enforced but officially remained in place for four years until it was quietly lifted.

Notwithstanding his apparent lack of concern about the welfare of his family, in the early months of his reign Willy made a point of attempting to ameliorate a difficult situation for his eldest sister, Charlotte. At the age of seventeen, Charlotte had married her father's cousin, Prince Bernhard of Saxe-Meiningen, which prompted numerous allegations about both Charlotte and her mother. Some claimed that Vicky was so anxious to be rid of her wayward daughter that she had forced her into the match; while others suggested that Charlotte was so desperate to escape from her mother's overbearing control that she would have married any available prince at the first opportunity. Whether or not the latter suggestion were true, marriage did not bring an end to Vicky's influence over her daughter. By royal standards, Bernhard was not a wealthy man and he and Charlotte were forced to depend on Vicky for financial support, which gave her mother a measure of control over Charlotte's lifestyle.

Shortly after his accession, Willy rectified the situation by arranging a private allowance for Bernhard and

Charlotte, but while his actions seemed generous at the time, they might well have been simply another way to irk his mother. After all, Charlotte, described by a cousin as 'one of the most fickle and changeable women', did little to endear herself to her brother, for, unlike her younger sisters, Charlotte was not afraid to stand up to him, and no matter how forcefully he attempted to demonstrate his authority, she refused to treat him as anything but a rather troublesome elder brother. She mocked his wife relentlessly, and regularly attempted to humiliate Willy by making jokes at his expense. On reading an article about the World Champion boxer, John Sullivan, for example, she was heard to remark,

"I hope that Sullivan had not the bad taste to wear as many rings as my brother."

Initially, Willy responded in kind to Charlotte's jibes. While attending a ball at which one of the guests was dressed as a flower, with two huge lilies protruding from her hair, Willy said loudly enough for others to hear:

"Good Lord, I hope Bernhard won't see her. He might take it for an allusion to the pretty calf-coloured antlers his wife is growing on her forehead."[101]

Dona laughed loudly at the joke, for it was a rare occasion when she could get the better of Charlotte.

There were times, though, when Charlotte's mischief-making went far beyond harmless banter. To impress foreign princes, she was happy to impart confidential information from the Prussian Court, and her intriguing became so legendary that Willy would eventually confine her to her home before suggesting that she should leave Germany altogether. Unsurprisingly, in view of her intrigues, she became the chief suspect when, in the spring and summer of 1894, a series of scandalous letters were sent to various members of the court including the Kaiser and Kaiserin. Cleverly amalgamating truth and fiction, the letters described actual incidents from the lives of the recipients but distorted events with semi-pornographic descriptions. Whether the purpose was blackmail or simply to shock, the fact that the letters demonstrated an intimate knowledge of the court, led Willy and several of his ministers to suspect that Charlotte was the culprit. It was not until Charlotte herself received a series of letters accusing her of promiscuity and claiming that she was pregnant at the time of her marriage, that Willy realised she was not responsible for the obscenities.

Eventually, a former friend of Charlotte and Bernhard was arrested and, although he was eventually released without charge, it came to light that much of the content of the letters was based on Charlotte's diary which had been stolen some months earlier. It was widely believed that the diary had been taken by the suspect's wife, but, whoever had stolen it, it eventually landed in Willy's hands and he found it to contain many insulting descriptions of him and the entire Imperial Family. Salacious stories of his younger sister, Moretta's, numerous lovers were interspersed with descriptions of his own 'intolerable swagger' and his wife's puritanical prudishness. Instead of returning the diary to its owner, Willy kept it and ordered Charlotte to spend some time out of the country.

Harsh as she often was, Charlotte was perfectly capable of withstanding Willy's banter and responding in the same vein, but her younger sister, Moretta, had such a low opinion of herself that his words were often deeply wounding. Following the Sandro Battenberg debacle, Moretta had become anorexic and convinced that she was far too ugly to ever find a husband. Since all she had ever wanted was a husband and a family of her own, Willy cruelly joke that she was willing to marry 'anyone who was manly'. His words, though wounding, were not entirely without foundation, for already the court was rife with rumours that, in her desperation, she had indulged in 'several flirtations of a rather sensational character with …several gay diplomats and noblemen, which were a source of amusement to the court.'

Nonetheless, when Moretta finally married the 'rather scruffy' Prince Adolf of Schaumburg-Lippe, Willy was particularly kind to the couple, who spent much of the season in Berlin, and his teasing of his sister was far gentler.

"Her brother, the Emperor," wrote one witness, "who is not given to take fancies to anyone is devoted to Prince Adolf & says sometimes, 'Isn't he handsome – is he not charming?' to which she answers "Don't be so silly Willie"—but she said it with pleasure & pride."[102]

So fond was he of Adolf that he considered creating him Viceroy of Alsace-Lorraine, or even Regent of Brunswick, had the position become available.

Willy was equally contrary in his relations with his youngest sister, Mossy. When Mossy married the brother of the Landgrave of Hesse-Kassel, Willy remarked that a mere landgrave was unworthy of a sister of the Kaiser, and yet, when he attended their wedding, he behaved with extraordinary gentility.

Of all his siblings, he had always been closest to Henry, and, although, following his accession, he was prone to ordering him around, their relationship never floundered. Issuing commands without explanation, Willy thought nothing of sending Henry thither and yon on official visits, and insisted that he should request permission before leaving his home in Kiel to visit Berlin. When, in 1897, Henry was sent to China in the hope of securing the lease of the naval port of Kiao Chau, his wife, Irene, remained at home with their young children until Willy, for no apparent reason, ordered her to go and meet her husband in Hong Kong.

Happily, Henry's good humour enabled him to laugh at some of Willy's more pronounced characteristics and the sycophancy of his friends. Referring to a popular satirical magazine, Henry asked:

"Why is my brother like the *Fliegende Blatter* in a

foreign country?...Because he is always sure of raising a laugh whether he offers something witty or inane. So it is with the *Fliegende Blatter*. It has a reputation for being funny, and, where German is not understood, is applauded indiscriminately."[103]

Amusingly, too, considering his love of ships and pride in his navy, Willy was often seasick – a condition possibly exacerbated by a painful and persistent ear complaint, which also affected his balance. While out on one of Henry's yachts, the Kaiser was forced to withdraw to a cabin to vomit, at which point Henry leaned in through the door and laughed,

"Well, Willy, how do you feel now, and what has become of your imperial dignity?"[104]

The cordiality of the relationship between the brothers was all the more remarkable in view of the fact that Willy had always felt that Henry was his father's favourite son – an opinion which appeared to be justified by two incidents which took place during his brief reign as Emperor Frederick III. On one occasion, the American Ambassador, who had recently spent some time with Willy, praised him effusively, to which his father replied,

"Yes Wilhelm's a fine lad, but you should see my boy, Heinrich!"[105]

Again, on the day of Henry and Irene's wedding, his father, although too ill to speak, handed him a paper which, pointedly comparing him to Willy, read:

"You at least have never given me a moment's sorrow, and will make as good a husband as you have been a loving son."[106]

In spite of the obvious favouritism, Willy bore Henry no ill-will but appreciated his good nature and was happy to listen to his advice concerning improvements to the navy.

He was not, though, content merely to dominate his mother and siblings. As the Kaiser, he saw himself as the head of all his German relations and was quick to impose bizarre punishments on those who infringed his erratic rules. When his pregnant sister-in-law fell through the ice while skating, Willy blamed her husband for permitting her to undertake such a dangerous activity in her condition, and banished them both to their house for several days, with the order that all the lights must be extinguished by eight in the evening!

While busily alienating many members of his family, Willy was simultaneously attempting to win friends across the continent. Determined to impose himself on the world stage, he embarked on a series of tours, starting with visits to the various courts within his German Empire. He graciously greeted and fawned over the King of Württemberg and the Grand Duke of Baden, while making long speeches to their people about his divine right to rule, and portraying himself as a great peacemaker who would create strong relationships with his fellow sovereigns to maintain the stability of a Europe in which Germany would play a prominent role.

In 1889, he outstayed his welcome during a ten day visit to St Petersburg where he told Tsar Alexander III of his hope of creating stronger relations between their nations, before journeying on to repeat the same message in Sweden, Denmark and France. In his euphoria, he was taken aback when the French replied that if he truly wished to restore good relations between the two nations, he should return the provinces of Alsace-Lorraine, which had been seized by Germany during the Franco-Prussian War. In September that year, he upstaged his uncle, the Prince of Wales, by announcing his intention of visiting the Austro-Hungarian Emperor Franz Josef, at a time when the Prince had planned to visit, compelling Uncle Bertie, to travel to Roumania instead. In Vienna, he complimented the aged Franz Josef, describing him as a great victor when, in fact, he had lost virtually every war his country had ever fought; and, on arriving in England, he flattered his grandmother by describing her as 'a very superior lady on account of her wisdom and counsel.'

The arch-showman was in his element during these tours, truly believing that he was the bearer of good tidings, and delighting in the acclamation of the crowds. At approximately five-feet-seven-inches tall, he nonetheless had a noble bearing, creating the impression that he was much bigger than was the case. With his dramatic and carefully-waxed moustache, a bellowing voice and a powerful right arm, he was perfectly capable of concealing his disability and presenting an image of self-confidence and personal power. Beneath the bluster, however, as he naively sought to gloss over decades of international rivalry, diplomacy and hostility, his deepest desire was to win the love and admiration of everyone he met.

"He lived continually in a world of fiction," wrote Princess Louise of Belgium. "In short he was an actor....and his skill is greatest in the art of self-deception." [107]

Bismarck watched his protégé with increasing consternation. Willy's mother had once described him as the Chancellor's creature but now he seemed to be very much his own man. In his eagerness to make friends of all nations, he appeared to be oblivious of the intrigues and machinations in which the Chancellor had indulged to create the unified Germany, and Bismarck felt obliged to warn him that it was impossible to make everyone happy.

For the first time, perhaps, Bismarck began to understand Willy's parents' reservations about introducing their son to foreign affairs. Only two years before his accession, Willy had persuaded his grandfather to involve him in affairs of state and to grant him access to the dealings of the Foreign Office. His father was appalled on hearing that his request had been granted, and he wrote at once protesting that Willy was not yet ready for such responsibility:

"...Considering [his] unripeness and inexperience...together with his leaning towards vanity and presumption and his own overweening estimation of himself, I must frankly express my opinion that it is *dangerous* as yet to introduce him to foreign affairs."[108]

Bismarck had dismissed Fritz's warning, believing that the malleable little boy, whom he had repeatedly flattered, would forever remain a puppet whom he could control. The Chancellor, though, had underestimated Willy's intelligence and powers of observation. He was far too astute to be unaware of the way in which Bismarck had treated his parents, and, despite his difficult relationship with his mother, he resented the wily statesman's interference in his family affairs. Moreover, Willy had firm ideas about how he intended to rule Germany, and, unlike his grandfather, he was not prepared to yield at every turn to Bismarck's manipulations. Even at the start of his reign, he had doubts about some of Bismarck's underhand methods and within two years he was looking for a way to remove him from office.

Matters came to a head in the winter of 1889-1890 when the Reichstag was involved in a heated debate about the rising threat of socialism – a cause which Bismarck detested. Willy, who was deeply interested in social affairs and was eager to support the welfare and rights of workers, eventually discovered that Bismarck was again playing a double-game, attempting to provoke the socialists into an uprising so that he would have an excuse to send in the army to crush them. Willy was appalled that Bismarck would have had him begin his reign by turning his troops on his own people, and, when he discovered that the Chancellor had given orders that no document should be given to the Kaiser without his approval, he needed no further prompting: Bismarck had to go.

155

That winter, as the elderly Chancellor was suffering from rheumatism, Willy advised him to take a break at his country estate. Realising that power was gradually slipping through his fingers, the Chancellor desperately continued his secret political manoeuvrings but Willy, aware of what he was doing, summoned him to give and explanation. In a final vain attempt at manipulation, Bismarck foolishly attempted to demonstrate Willy's need for guidance by producing a letter which the Russian Tsar had written following his visit to St. Petersburg. He had not, he said, mentioned the letter before since the contents would be wounding for the Kaiser, and, even now, he could not bring himself to read it aloud. Willy snatched the letter from him, to discover that the Tsar had described him as 'a badly brought up boy', clearly showing that his visit to Russia had not been as successful as he had believed. Bismarck was sure that Willy would be so distressed by this insult that he would have even greater need of the Chancellor's support. His plan, however, backfired. According to Bismarck's account, Willy simply 'rose and offered me his hand...more coldly than usual.' Two days later, under intense pressure from the Kaiser, Bismarck had no option but to tender his resignation[t].

Nowhere did Willy practise the 'art of self-deception' more fully than in his dealings with the army. Still fired by the dreams of heroism and glory which inspired him as a boy, he viewed his troops with the same affection with which a child might look upon a favourite box of toy soldiers. There were no actual enemies whom he wished to attack, but rather he revelled in thoughts of victories and, in his fantasy, he was ever the great hero, whose feats and courage commanded a loyal following. The great showman's

---

[t] Ironically, as he fell from favour, Bismarck sought Vicky's help, asking her to use her influence over her son to persuade him to accept advice in both domestic and foreign affairs. Vicky could only reply honestly that, thanks to Bismarck, she had no influence over her son.

bombastic outbursts about Prussian military superiority often drew on ancient legends as he sought to inspire his troops with his own romantic dream, but despite his rousing words, he never saw active service or commanded a battalion; and, despite his swagger, experienced Generals were aghast at his lack of real knowledge. On one occasions, when he had led a series of manoeuvres, an elderly officer remarked with disgust that his:

> '...idea of military operations consisted mainly in arranging dramatic cavalry charges, more in keeping with the conceptions of an elaborate military display...than with the root principles of modern warfare. Sheer military nonsense!'[109]

He did, however, care deeply for the ordinary soldiers and had little time for the practice of granting promotions only to those whose families could afford to pay for their commissions. He studied the lives of his troops and took strong measures to curb the brutality with which junior soldiers were often treated:

> "In my army," he said, "every soldier should be justly, lawfully and worthily treated, so as to arouse and promote in him delight in, and devotion to, his calling, love and confidence in his superiors"[110]

He interested himself, too, in creating military manuals and, of course, in 'raking up hitherto unknown appendage to uniforms, with all ostentation.' Again, it was, above all, the pageantry which so appealed to his imagination.

Chapter 13 – A Real Loss to the Army

The Christians

Lenchen – (Helena/Princess Christian) Queen Victoria's second daughter
Christle – (Christian Victor) Lenchen's elder son

Other family members

Charlie – (Charles Edward) Duke of Albany; only son of Queen Victoria's fourth son, Leopold, Duke of Albany
Young Arthur – Prince of Connaught; only son of Queen Victoria's third son, Arthur, Duke of Connaught
Drino – (Alexander) Eldest son of Queen Victoria's youngest daughter, Beatrice
Vicky – Crown Princess of Prussia; Queen Victoria's eldest daughter
Fritz – Crown Prince of Prussia; Vicky's husband
Willy – Eldest son of Vicky and Fritz

While Eddy of Wales whiled away his time with the 10th Hussars, and the new Kaiser Wilhelm played at military manoeuvres, some of their cousins took military service far more seriously. From the moment he was born, Charlie, the little Duke of Albany, had been adopted as the Commander of his late father's regiment, the Seaforth Highlanders, and, at the age of six, dressed in a miniature uniform, he proudly marched out to review the troops. Having been carefully instructed on how to issue orders, he called out several commands 'as gravely as if the fate of a battle depended upon his words' and was delighted to see how quickly he was obeyed.

Lenchen's son, Christle, meanwhile, had embarked on a far more daring military career which reads like the story of a hero in the popular boys' novels of the era. After leaving Wellington College, he progressed to Magdalen College, Oxford, where he obtained a Master of Arts degree and, again, displayed his skills on the cricket pitch. As the Captain of the First XI, he demonstrated great prowess as a wicketkeeper; and, in August 1887, he participated in a celebrated match between I Zingari – the old Harrovians – and the Gentlemen of England. Despite being out for a duck in the second innings, he earned his place in the record books as the only member of the Royal Family to have played First Class cricket.

Had he not been a prince, Christle could certainly have made a career as a sportsman, but cricket was merely a pastime for him while military service was a duty to which he applied himself with great diligence. His devotion to his troops and his commitment to his duties earned him the respect not only of his commanding officers but also of his cousin, Willy of Prussia; and he was so dedicated to the British army that, when he was offered the position of heir to the Duke of Schleswig-Holstein, he declined, leaving the position to his younger brother.

Having trained at the Royal Military College at Sandhurst, he was commissioned as a lieutenant in the 60th King's Royal Rifle Corps in August 1888. Within two years he had been promoted to captain and, after a period of service at Aldershot, he was posted to India at the age of twenty-four.

Britain's involvement in the subcontinent had begun many centuries earlier with the arrival of the East India Company in the reign of Queen Elizabeth I. As the trading company expanded, it gained greater control over large areas of the country, employing its own armies of sepoys (local soldiers), and gradually taking over the administration of several regions. By the middle of the nineteenth century, however, the sepoys had many grievances against their employers, and the final straw came in 1857 when they were equipped with the new Enfield rifles, the cartridges for which

159

had to be bitten open. When the predominantly Muslim sepoys discovered that the cartridges had been greased with beef or pork fat, a mutiny erupted, which escalated into a widespread revolt of the civilian population.

Horrific reports about the violence of the uprising soon reached England, where Queen Victoria was aghast to hear that British women were being raped before being murdered with their children.

"We are in sad anxiety about India, which engrosses all our attention," she wrote to her uncle. "...The horrors committed on the poor ladies and children are unknown in these ages, and make one's blood run cold."[111]

Her government sent troops to protect the British settlers and for several months fierce fighting took place across the country.

"Our poor troops have again behaved wonderfully," the Queen wrote some months later, blissfully ignorant of the cruel revenge inflicted by her armies on the innocent civilians of the towns that offered resistance.

Queen Victoria had stressed to the Governor, Lord Canning, that the troops were to act with moderation but his attempts to carry out her wishes were met with derision. The press mocked him as 'Clemency Canning'; and in many areas his orders were simply ignored. At Delhi and Cawnpore, whole families were bayonetted or shot, women being forced to watch while their husbands were slaughtered.

When Canning was eventually able to give the Queen a full account of the atrocities her armies had committed, she was horrified.

"Lord Canning will easily believe," she wrote, "how entirely the Queen shares his feelings of sorrow and indignation at the unchristian spirit shown alas!"[112]

While she believed that those who had committed murder and rape should be dealt with severely, she concluded that,

"...to the nation at large – to the peaceful inhabitants, to the many kind and friendly neighbours who have assisted us and been faithful and true, there should be the greatest kindness."[113]

Eventually, by the end of the year, the rebellion had been put down, and talks ensued between the Indian princes and tribal chiefs, and representatives of the British government. It was agreed that the authority of the East Indian Company should be transferred to the Crown, which led to the establishment of an India Office in London, and the appointment of a Viceroy to oversee the administration of the country. Almost twenty years later, in 1876, Queen Victoria, to her great delight, was named Empress of India.

The Queen viewed India, the 'jewel in the crown', with great affection. Although she never visited the subcontinent, she learned Hindustani, began eating curries, and surrounded herself with Indian servants, most notably the infamous Munshi, Abdul Karim, whose arrogance and ubiquity deeply irked other members of her family. So great was Queen Victoria's devotion to her 'Indian teacher' that she wilfully failed to see the number of mistresses he installed in the cottage she provided for him; and she wept copiously when her son, Affie, refused to allow him to join the Royal Family at his daughter's wedding.[u]

It was a matter of great importance to the Queen that the traditions and religious practices of her Indian servants should be observed and respected; and she was equally insistent that her troops should not interfere with the customs of beliefs of native populations. On hearing one of her generals rejoice that the British presence in India was undermining local religions and spreading Christianity, she wrote indignantly that:

"...the deep attachment which Her Majesty feels to her own religion, and the comfort and happiness which she derives from its consolations, will preclude

---

[u] See Chapter 18

her from any attempt to interfere with the native religions, and that her servants will be directed to act scrupulously in accordance with her directions."[114]

Thoroughly entranced by all things Indian, the Queen was pleased when Christle received his posting, but her delight was tinged with anxiety about the dangers he would face, participating in the Hazara – or Black Mountain – Expedition. The purpose of the expedition was to protect the British Indians by enforcing an agreement with the Hassanzai and Akazai tribes of Pathans. The fighting was fierce and, throughout March and April 1891, as Christle served on the front line, the Queen could only sympathise with his anxious mother, Lenchen, and take comfort from the regular reports she received of her grandson's courage and popularity with his men. When, however, he came home on leave, Christle modestly dismissed her compliments, playing down his own role to praise instead the courage of his wounded Indian comrades whose stoical serenity in the face of great pain never ceased to astound him.

After a brief holiday in England for the wedding of his sister, Marie Louise, in July 1891, Christle returned to India to participate in further expeditions along the North-West Frontier, regularly being mentioned in despatches, and earning promotions and honours for his courage and diligence. By the time of the Ashanti Expedition of 1896, he had become so accustomed to adapting for foreign climates that, although he contracted malaria, he quickly recovered and was able to resume his command, again being mentioned in dispatches and earning the Ashanti Star. Recurrences of the illness did not prevent him from continuing his military career or experiencing numerous adventures, as on the occasion when his gunboat was sunk and he had to swim some distance to the shore; or when, at Colenso, he narrowly escaped death when a bullet passed through his wallet.

In 1898, he served in the Sudan with Lord Kitchener, and participated in the Battles of Omdurman and Khartoum;

and, the following year, after almost a decade of active service in some of the most dangerous parts of the Empire, he was offered a more sedentary position at the Staff College at Sandhurst. He had hardly had time to settle into the post when the Second Boer War broke out and, as he immediately volunteered for active service, he was posted to South Africa as a Staff Officer with the Second Infantry Brigade.

He set sail on 6th October 1899, and arrived at the Cape almost three weeks later, keeping his mother and grandmother informed by telegram of his progress. For almost a year he was actively involved in some of the most ferocious battles, including Spion Kop, where the British suffered over a thousand casualties and, according to the war correspondent, Winston Churchill, corpses, mutilated by shells and shrapnel were lying everywhere. Between assignments he did, however, manage to find time to indulge in his favourite sport – cricket.

In early October 1900, his period of service was drawing to an end and his commanding officer, Field Marshal Roberts, was about to recommend him for further gallantry awards, 'which he so well deserved. His sterling qualities as a soldier, his unfailing courtesy and attention to his duties had endeared him to all with whom he came in contact.' Already, plans had been made for him to return home when he was struck by a recurrence of malaria. Within a week, enteric fever developed but after a few days he appeared to be recovering and wrote home to tell his family that the worst was over. Hardly had his letter been sent when he suffered a relapse and sank into a coma.

Three days later, on 29th October 1900, having come safely through so many battles and adventures, Christle died of enteric fever at the age of thirty-three.

"His early death," wrote Roberts, "is a real loss to the army."

On 1st November, he was buried in Pretoria with full military honours. His coffin was carried by no fewer than six generals, including Robert Baden-Powell, the future founder of the Boy Scouts – a movement of which Christle would undoubtedly have approved.

The news was devastating for his siblings and his parents.

"Lenchen's grief makes my heart bleed," wrote Vicky. "He was her *idol* and gave her such joy, and proved such a good, steady boy."[115]

It was left to his sister, Thora, to break the news to the Queen, whose first thoughts, despite her own grief, were for his fellow officers. She had already agreed to open the Marble Arch for a parade of the returning soldiers, and not wishing to dampen their rejoicing, she asked that the news of Christle's death be kept secret until the procession was over.

Ironically, in the light of later events[v], on hearing of his death, Christle's young cousin, Maurice Battenberg, went late one evening in his dressing gown to Thora's room at Balmoral and told her softly, 'It may comfort you to know that I have decided to join the 60th when I am old enough.'[116]

A bronze statue of the prince was commissioned, which still stands outside the North Gate of Windsor Castle.

Interestingly, in her autobiography, his sister, Marie Louise recalled an encounter with Christle (whom she called Kicky) several years after his death. Following the annulment of her marriage[w], Marie Louise had just moved into a house in Kensington when she suddenly saw her brother enter the room.

"'Oh Kicky…how nice to see you again.' He replied: 'I just came to see that you were all right and happy.' He sat down in the chair next to the fire, and I then noticed he had his favourite dachshund on his knee. We talked a little, then he got up and told me I was

---

[v] See Chapter 24

[w] Marie Louise had married Prince Aribert of Anhalt, who appeared to have married her solely to conceal his homosexuality. See *Queen Victoria's Granddaughters 1860-1918* by Christina Croft

not to follow him downstairs, that he was very happy and all was well with him. After he had gone and shut the door, I realised that he was in khaki but did not have his medal ribbons on. I then remembered that during the South African War, an order had been issued that officers were not to wear their ribbons so that the enemy would not be able to distinguish them from their men. Only then did I suddenly realise that this dearly beloved brother had died eighteen months previously and lay in his last resting place in South Africa.

"My sister came to see me that same afternoon and I told her of what had taken place. She was sitting in the same chair as he had done and when she got up she remarked, 'I know he has been here – I can feel it.'"[117]

Christle was not the only one of Queen Victoria's grandsons to forge a career in the armed services. On leaving Eton, his cousin, Young Arthur of Connaught, followed Christle to Sandhurst, where, at the age of eighteen, he received his commission as a lieutenant in the 7th Hussars before being posted to South Africa towards the end of the Second Boer War.

The following year, Drino Battenberg, began his naval cadetship aboard the *Britannia,* on which his Wales cousins had trained. Drino's naval career was short lived but, in 1910, he joined the exclusive Castaways Club for retired naval officers who wished to keep in contact with their fellow seamen. Nine years after joining the Royal Navy, he was commissioned as a lieutenant in the Grenadier Guards where he showed a marked penchant for uniforms, medals and other young officers in his regiment. His pompousness continued to irk his cousins and companions, who now added effeminacy to the list of his less desirable characteristics.

While these cousins served in their grandmother's forces, others were commissioned in the Kaiser's armies. Like his brother, Christle, Abbie of Schleswig-Holstein graduated from Sandhurst and gained a British commission but, having been made heir to the Duke of Schleswig-Holstein, and being due to inherit 'vast estates in Silesia', he left England for Germany, rising to the rank of captain in the Prussian Dragoons. For several years he was stationed in Hesse-Darmstadt, while, ironically, his cousin, Ernie of Hesse-Darmstadt was serving with the Prussian Dragoons in Potsdam.

Ernie, a free spirit with a passion for art, would never have chosen a military career but, after completing his degree at the University of Leipzig, he was compelled to enrol in one of the Kaiser's regiments. Life for officers in Prussia was dominated by a series of numerous regulations. They were never allowed to be seen out of uniform even when entertaining friends in their own homes; there were streets in Berlin where they were not permitted to smoke; and if, while out riding, they happened to pass a member of the extended Royal Family, they were expected to dismount at once to stand to attention.

For Ernie, Potsdam was a dull inconvenience but for his cousin, Young Affie, the only son of Alfred, Duke of Edinburgh, it would ultimately prove a disaster.

Chapter 14 – Too Giddy to Resist Temptations

The Edinburghs/Coburgs

Affie (Alfred) – Duke of Edinburgh & Coburg; Queen Victoria's second son
Marie – Duchess of Edinburgh & Coburg; Affie's Russian wife
Young Affie (Alfred) – Only son of Affie & Marie
Missy (Marie) – Eldest daughter of Affie & Marie

The Albanys

Helen – Duchess of Albany; wife of Queen Victoria's late son, Leopold
Alice – Daughter of the Duchess of Albany
Charlie (Charles Edward) – Duke of Albany; only son of Helen and Leopold
Dick – (Victoria Adelaide) – Princess of Schleswig-Holstein; Charlie's wife

As a second-in-line to the Duke of Coburg, Young Affie of Edinburgh had been sent to complete his education and military training in the duchy, but, following Cousin Willy's accession, he was summoned to Berlin and enrolled in the prestigious military academy at Potsdam. Willy, who greatly enjoyed playing the father-figure to his younger cousins, promised to supervise his progress and, even when Young Affie's father succeeded to the Dukedom and moved to Coburg in 1893, he continued to take overall charge of his training. He invested him with the Prussian Order of the Red Eagle, ostensibly awarded to recognise valour or long service to the country; and in 1895, when Young Affie was twenty, he permitted the publication of an announcement of his engagement to a daughter of the King of Württemberg.

In fact, the engagement came to nothing, and Willy, for all his good intentions was far too engrossed in affairs of state to pay close attention to his cousin's rapid decline, for already Young Affie was living:

"...a terrible fast life...put into the 1st Prussian Corps, the fastest of all Regiments with a thoroughly bad man to look after him. He simply had no chance whatsoever..."[118]

As in Britain, Prussian officers required a private income to support their extravagant lifestyle, and so, at Potsdam, the somewhat unstable and easily-led young man had come into contact with many wealthy officers who squandered fortunes in the pursuit of pleasure. He threw himself into a dissipated lifestyle, frequenting brothels and gaming tables, accruing debts and becoming increasingly reliant on alcohol.

"Potsdam!" his Aunt Vicky wrote in disgust, "– that was not the place for him. He was too inexperienced and heedless and giddy to resist temptations, bad examples etc."[119]

By the time that Willy realised the extent of his dissipation, the twenty-four-year-old prince had contracted syphilis, which, at that time, was incurable and frequently led to insanity and an agonising death from what was euphemistically described as 'General Paralysis of the Insane.'

When his condition became pronounced, Young Affie was dismissed from the army and, on Willy's orders, returned to his parents in Coburg. His alcoholic father and proud mother had no idea how to deal with their difficult son, whose health was already irreparably damaged.

In January 1899, his parents – now Duke and Duchess of Coburg – were preparing to celebrate twenty-five years of their unhappy marriage and, as guests would be arriving from across the Continent, his mother was anxious to keep Young Affie out of the way. The exact details of what happened next are shrouded in hearsay and rumour but, in the midst of the Silver Anniversary preparations, and argument erupted between mother and son, during which, according to some unverified sources, Young Affie confessed to having secretly married or intending to marry a girl deemed by his family to be an unsuitable bride.

It is often reported that, in the heat of the argument, Young Affie seized a gun and shot himself, but there is little evidence to support that claim. What is certain is that by now his doctors had told his mother the full details of the nature of his illness and he was suffering from 'paralysis of the larynx, caused by the state of the brain.'

In view of his mental state and the shame of his illness, the Duchess decided he must leave Coburg before the guests arrived for the anniversary celebrations. Disregarding the doctors' warnings that he was too ill to travel, she arranged for him to be taken at once to a castle in Thuringia, and, three days later, without her husband's agreement, had him transferred to a sanatorium in Merano. Accompanying him was a British Naval doctor, Arthur Reginald Bankart, who had proved his worth some years earlier by performing surgery on Young Affie's father. Bankart kept the family informed of his patient's progress, and on 5th February 1899 sent a telegram to the Duke, warning him that his son's condition was rapidly deteriorating.

The following day the telegrams were even more ominous, and the Duke, angered that his son had been sent away without his consent, prepared to leave at once for Merano. Before he departed, however, a further telegram informed him that Young Affie had died.

On hearing the news, Young Affie's cousin, Ernie of Hesse, went straight away to Merano where he met his uncle, the Duke of Coburg, who broke down completely on seeing his dead son. Blaming his wife for having sent Young Affie away, it is alleged that, from that moment, the Duke never spoke to her again.

The young man's death *was* a tragedy, and one which might have been foreseen. The only son of an alcoholic father and intolerant mother, he had been simultaneous spoiled and severely criticised. While at home, he was frequently upbraided by his mother, who failed to understand his sensitive nature; and, according to his sister:

"...people were too impatient with him, and mama, hoping to find perfection, was often disappointed in her son. Mama had a supreme horror of the shady side of life and in every way tried to ignore it...She was never able to talk with Alfred; she thought that severity and religious principles must keep him straight; he found no mercy when he sinned, so he lost confidence in those who might have helped him."[120]

While still young, he had often been separated from his family and placed under the supervision of overbearing tutors. Once released from their control, he found himself ill-equipped to cope with the freedom of Potsdam and, with no reliable mentor to guide him, it is unsurprising that he floundered and sank deeper and deeper into his dissipation. The horrific physical and mental effects of syphilis were undoubtedly exacerbated for him by the shame he felt when his mother insisted on concealing his illness, and by the general attitude towards venereal diseases at the time.

"It is true," wrote his Aunt Vicky, "that he was always giddy & wild, as many young men are, & that he contracted an illness of which I know next to nothing, as I have never asked or heard anything about it, one dislikes thinking about it and still more speaking or writing about it."[121]

With clearer guidance, Young Affie might have become an excellent Duke of Coburg, for, as his sister wrote, he had the charm and ability to speak easily with people of all classes and all ages, and 'there were the makings of a real prince in him.'

His body was brought back to the family castle in Gotha, from where, on 10th February 1899, his funeral procession began. Overwhelmed with grief and guilt, his mother, who was normally so restrained, 'sank to her knees, crossing herself many times and then burst into tears.'

Apart from his parents' grief, Young Affie's death had wider implications for Coburg and for his extended family. Salic Law precluded his sisters from succeeding their father to the Dukedom, and the next in line was the Duke's younger brother, Arthur, Duke of Connaught. Arthur briefly toyed with the idea of accepting the position but his commitment to the British army, and the prospect of showing obeisance to his nephew, the Kaiser, persuaded him to renounce the position. He was equally eager to prevent his son, Young Arthur, from slipping into the same kind of lifestyle as his deceased cousin, Young Affie, and actively discouraged him from accepting the role.

Young Arthur had no desire to leave England and, according to some reports, he met the next-in-line – his fifteen-year-old cousin, Charlie of Albany – on a corridor at Eton, where he threatened to give him a thrashing unless he agreed to be their uncle's successor.

Meanwhile, Charlie's mother, the widowed Duchess of Albany, faced a difficult dilemma. Charlie was happy at Eton but, if he were to become his uncle's heir, he would have to move to Coburg and undertake appropriate military training. Since he did not even speak German and had no interest in the duchy, the Duchess of Albany realised that the upheaval could be traumatic for him. On the other hand, she felt it could be a mistake to deny him the opportunity of becoming a reigning duke and collecting the £300,000 income.

For several months discussions continued, hindered, in Queen Victoria's opinion, by Willy's interference, but eventually it was decided that Charlie would accept the

171

position with the proviso that, should he died childless, the duchy would pass to Young Arthur. Should the current Duke die before Charlie reached his majority, his son-in-law, Prince Ernst of Hohenlohe-Langenburg, would act as regent until he came of age.

By June 1899, everything had been settled and, two months later, on the 5th August – the day after his confirmation in St. George's Chapel – Charlie set out with his mother and sister to visit Affie, Duke of Coburg, at his hunting lodge of Rheinhardsbrunn in Gotha. Affie, already a very sick man, explained that he not only wished to make Charlie his successor, but also intended to adopt him and take him to live with his own family. The Duchess of Albany was astounded. Apart from not wishing to be parted from her son, she could see that his alcoholic uncle was hardly suited to raise an impressionable boy, especially in the light of what had happened to Young Affie. Unsurprisingly, she declined his offer.

The Duke, however, had not expected such an outcome and had consequently made no alternative arrangements to accommodate Charlie and his family. Moreover, he was annoyed that his plans had been foiled and refused to provide the Duchess of Albany with a home in the duchy. Fortunately, the Duchess' brother-in-law, the King of Württemberg, was far more helpful and gave the family a suite in his palace in Stuttgart where Charlie began his training for his future position under the direction of a German tutor.

Adjusting to a new way of life did not come easily. Charlie had difficulty learning German and, confined with a tutor, he missed the company of his former school friends. In an effort to ease his situation, his mother began looking for an appropriate school in the region in the hope that, by mixing with his peers, he would soon feel more at home in this foreign country. Vicky, who, according to Charlie's sister, Alice, was 'constantly meddling', suggested a modern establishment in Frankfurt, while the Duke of Coburg wished him to attend 'a horrid scruffy place' near Rheinhardsbrunn. Neither of these suggestions satisfied Charlie or his mother and they were grateful when Cousin Willy came to their assistance, arranging for Charlie to enrol in the Leitchertfielde Military Cadet Academy in Potsdam, and providing his mother and sister with a house – Villa Ingenheim – nearby.

Although the villa was smaller and far less luxurious than the suite in Stuttgart, the Albanys soon settled in and became regular guests of the Kaiser and Kaiserin[x] at the New Palace in Berlin, where Willy was a congenial host and Charlie spent many happy hours playing with his children. Having learned his lesson from the demise of Young Affie, Willy was quick to do everything possible to support his cousin, Charlie. When, for example, the Duchess of Albany approached him about why he had not answered her request that a particular lieutenant at the college should be appointed as Charlie's mentor, Willy was furious that his aide-de-camp had not bothered to deliver the Duchess' message, and arranged for the appointment to be made without delay.

Notwithstanding the pleasant days spent with the Kaiser's children, and the efforts made to prepare Charlie for his new role, he still missed his former life in England, and found himself an outsider in the military academy where his fellow cadets regularly bullied him as a foreigner. Moreover, he was not popular among some of his own cousins, and Queen Victoria rebuked her grandson, Ernie of Hesse, for saying that he did 'not like Charlie, who is a remarkably nice boy.'

Charlie hardly had time to adjust to the transition to life in another country when his position was significantly altered by the death of the Duke of Coburg, who finally succumbed to throat cancer on 30th July 1900.

---

[x] See Chapter 15

"I cannot understand it at all yet," wrote the Duke's sister, Vicky. "He had a sore throat it seems, and in June it was discovered that it was cancer of the root of the tongue."[122]

In fact, it could hardly have been such a shock, for Affie's health had been rapidly declining for several years due mainly to his intemperance and his refusal to adhere to his doctors' advice to abstain from alcohol and to take more exercise. The death of his son had been the final straw, and, broken completely, he had survived him by only eighteen months.

Four days after his uncle's death, sixteen-year-old Charlie arrived in Coburg as the new Duke. Along with his £300,000 annual income, he had inherited huge swathes of profitable farmland, thirteen castles, hotels, hunting lodges and even a power station. For the next five years, Prince Ernst would act as his regent but, now that he had come into his inheritance, Charlie began to settle more comfortably into life in Germany.

In England, however, questions were asked in parliament about whether, in view of his accession to a German duchy, he should remain on the Britain's civil list. In Germany, too, there were discussions about whether or not he should renounce his British titles and declare himself wholly German.

"It is his affair," argued one professor, "to decide how far his duty to England extends, and how far he will fulfil it. It is within my knowledge that he is firmly resolved to regulate it in such a way that it shall not clash with his duty to Germany."[123]

Having completed his training at the military academy, Charlie followed in the Kaiser's footsteps by undertaking a course of legal studies at the University of Bonn, where, according to his sister, he was happier than he had ever been since leaving England. Participating in the activities of the students' regiment, the Borussa Corps, he continued his military training, and over the next decade he would rise to the rank of General in both the Prussian Guard and the Saxon Hussars.

Willy continued to keep a fatherly eye on his young cousin and even went so far as to find him a suitable bride. Princess Victoria Adelaide of Schleswig-Holstein, known familiarly as Dick, was Willy's niece by marriage – the daughter of Dona's brother, the Duke of Schleswig-Holstein-Sonderburg-Glücksburg. The wedding took place in the romantic Glücksburg Castle on 11th October 1905, and so began what was to be a very happy marriage, which would produce five children, one of whom would go on to become the mother of the present King of Sweden.

Blue-eyed and handsome, Charlie became a popular Duke of Coburg, devoting much of his time to sorting out the duchy's finances and becoming a great patron of the arts, as his grandfather, Prince Albert, would have wished. He donated large sums of money to the Coburg Theatre and turned one of his castles into a museum, continuing the tradition established by his predecessors to maintain the duchy as a place where:

> "Nature and art joined hands. There were no showy processions, no studied etiquette; only a charming and distinguished simplicity."[124]

He was equally keen to prosper the duchy's industry, and, in October 1913, established a large chemical factory to make use of the by-products of potash salts.

Part III – 'A Rare Guest at Princely Unions'

Husbands & Fathers

Chapter 15 – His Slightest Whims Are Obeyed

The Hohenzollerns (Prussians)

Vicky (Victoria) – Eldest child of Queen Victoria; wife of Fritz, Crown Prince of Prussia
Fritz (Frederick William) – Vicky's husband; Crown Prince of Prussia
Emperor William I – German Emperor; Fritz's father
Empress Augusta – German Empress; Fritz's mother
Willy (William/Wilhelm) – Fritz & Vicky's eldest son
Dona (Augusta Victoria) – Princess of Schleswig-Holstein; Willy's wife
Charlotte – Fritz & Vicky's eldest daughter
The Crown Prince – Wilhelm, eldest son of Willy & Dona
Sissy (Victoria Louise) – Willy's daughter

The Hessians

Victoria – Eldest daughter of Queen Victoria's second daughter, Alice
Ella (Elizabeth) – Second daughter of Queen Victoria's second daughter, Alice

It is said that only two women were ever able to reduce the excitable Kaiser Wilhelm to silence. The first was his grandmother, Queen Victoria, whom he respected and sometimes feared; the second was his cousin, Ella of Hesse.

During his student days at Bonn University, Willy had regularly visited his Hessian relations in Darmstadt, and, in later years he would describe these visits as some of the happiest days of his life. Playing tennis and boating in the grounds of the New Palace, he taught his cousin, Victoria, how to smoke, but his eyes were transfixed by the blossoming beauty of her younger sister, Ella, whom he would later describe as 'the most beautiful woman I ever saw.'

Willy was so infatuated by Cousin Ella that, speechless in her presence, he was reduced to expressing himself in poetry. He did, however, find the words to confess his feelings to his mother, who was delighted to hear that he had fallen in love with a girl of similar age. During his adolescence he had developed a strange obsession with Vicky, writing her romantic letters and describing his dreams of her beautiful hands. She had chosen to ignore his rather embarrassing outpourings but when he told her of his love for Cousin Ella, her immediate reaction was relief.

At first, Queen Victoria was cautious. Ella's mother, the recently deceased Alice, had, said the Queen, never 'wished to catch' Willy for any of her daughters, and, since he was rather immature, it would be better for him to wait a while before considering marriage. The more she ruminated over the potential match, however, the more pleased she became at the thought of a marriage between two of her grandchildren. Gentle and sensible, Ella had the ideal temperament to calm her volatile cousin and her beauty and intelligence would make her an excellent German Empress. Willy's paternal grandmother, Empress Augusta, was equally enthusiastic, viewing Ella as beautiful and malleable, and, most importantly, more German than English.

The only person who seemed to oppose the match was Ella herself, who confided in her sister that she thought Cousin Willy was 'quite horrid'. Willy, though, had mistaken her kindness and polite attention for affection, and was devastated when she declined his proposal. Her rejection played into his deep-rooted sense of inadequacy; and, some months later, he confessed to an admirer that he was amazed that she found him attractive for, just as he had mistakenly believed that his mother could not love him because of his malformed arm, he had come to the erroneous conclusion that all women found him repulsive.

Queen Victoria, though deeply disappointed, accepted Ella's decision, but Willy's paternal grandmother was far less phlegmatic. Months later she publicly snubbed Ella and her sisters and made several rather cruel remarks about their late mother. Bismarck, on the other hand, breathed a sigh of relief, for he had already set his sights on a different bride for the prince – one by whose marriage a long-standing feud could be ended.

For over fifteen years a land dispute between the Prussian court and the Dukes of Schleswig-Holstein had undermined the sense of German unity that Bismarck had worked so hard to create. In the Chancellor's eyes, there could be no better way to heal the rift than by a royal marriage, particularly if a daughter of the Duke should one day become German Empress.

The Duke, known familiarly as Fritz Holstein, was not only the brother of Queen Victoria's son-in-law, Christian, but also a good friend of Willy's parents. The families had often spent time together, and Willy had regularly come into contact with the Duke's elder daughters, Augusta Victoria (Dona) and Caroline Mathilde (Calma). Still smarting from Ella's rejection, Willy was eager to marry as quickly as possible and it was not long before he seemed to be showing such an interest in Calma that his parents believed he was about to propose.

Unpredictable as ever, Willy had different ideas, for in the autumn of 1879, Dona paid him so much attention that he decided that she, not her sister, would be his bride. Dona was overjoyed; Willy's parents and Bismarck were content; and, although Queen Victoria had never met Dona, she had sufficient regard for her father to support the match. Not everyone, however, was so supportive. Willy's grandfather, Emperor Wilhelm I felt that the daughter of a somewhat impoverished and rather insignificant duke was unworthy of a future Emperor; and the Duke himself was convinced that

Bismarck had engineered the match simply to subsume Schleswig-Holstein into his Prussian Empire.

Objections apart, Willy was not to be dissuaded. In a romantic gesture, he secretly proposed to Dona on St Valentine's Day 1880 – little over a fortnight after his twenty-first birthday – and within a month the secret was out and Queen Victoria had invited his future bride to England so that she might 'look her over'. A few days later, the German Emperor yielded and gave his consent to the marriage.

In England, Dona stayed with her cousins, the Christians, at Cumberland Lodge, from where she travelled to Windsor to be presented to the Queen. Queen Victoria confessed that she did not find her pretty but she was 'ladylike and gentle' and would surely make Willy happy. Her fiancé, meanwhile, soon followed her to England, where his grandmother gave the couple her blessing; and Willy – 'a nice young fellow' in the opinion of Prince George of Cambridge – behaved so courteously that everyone agreed that romance was very good for him.

As wedding preparations were soon underway, Vicky did her utmost to welcome 'thoroughly amiable' Dona into the family, but, as the day of the ceremony approached, she became increasingly maudlin at the prospect of losing her son:

> "It is the last time we have Willy, unmarried, in the same house in his old room with us," she wrote on New Year's Day 1881. "He thinks me absurdly sentimental to observe this and says it is all the same to him in what place or house or room he lives."[125]

In spite of his obvious excitement at his forthcoming nuptials, and his apparent love for his bride, nothing could compete with his love for the army. On the morning of his wedding, 27th February 1881, he was seen on the parade ground, drilling a company of Grenadiers, until just under an hour before the service. Even more surprising for observers, was the fact that the following day he set out at dawn to Potsdam to present a medal to a young subaltern.

What Dona made of his sudden disappearance is not recorded, but it is unlikely that she raised any objections since she epitomised Willy's ideal of a docile wife. Submissive to the point of fawning, in many ways Dona was the very antithesis of Willy's mother. She had little interest in politics and expressed few opinions of her own, but flattered her husband's ego by agreeing with everything he said. Her brother, whom Queen Victoria once referred to as 'the odious Gunther', observed that the couple 'never fight, because he sees to it that his slightest whims are obeyed, nay, more, anticipated.'[126]

Immediately after their marriage Willy and Dona moved into the Marble Palace, where Willy's rule was law and Dona happily acquiesced to his demands. When, for example, he let it be known that he did not wish to see her bedecked in jewels, she took to wearing only her wedding ring. In public, though, he insisted on making a striking impression and was most put out when 'Gustel', as he affectionately called his wife, attended a theatre performance in one of her habitual German-made dresses, and looked exceeding dowdy beside the sparkling Queen of Italy. From then on, Willy chose her dresses for every occasion but his sartorial expertise was clearly limited to military uniforms, for observers often commented on Dona's 'sumptuous' but 'tasteless' gowns, and smiled behind her back at her outlandish hats.

Life with such an excitable and erratic man was not always easy, and while no one doubted that Dona loved Willy deeply, his impulsive and often imperious behaviour sometimes reduced her to tears. At a moment's notice, he might decide that the entire household should move from one palace to another; and he often embarked on lengthy tours, leaving her at the mercy of a court which still viewed her as inferior, due to her relatively humble origins. Nor was Willy entirely faithful in the early years of their marriage. Although his infidelities were fewer and far more discreet than those of many of his contemporaries, he was reputed to have had at least two affairs within a decade of his wedding.

In 1884, he made the acquaintance of a divorcée, Countess Elizabeth von Wedel, who, according to an eye-witness, simultaneously shared her favours with several other powerful men. In 1887, she was living with her most recent lover, the Persian Ambassador, at the Embassy in Berlin when the infatuated Willy sent her a number of passionate letters. At the same time, she received a series of 'filthy' and anonymous missives, which she presented to the Ambassador in the hope that he might discover their author. When he contacted the Head of Police, von Richthofen, he was told that:

"This lady is the notorious wife of Count von Wedel. For some time she has been in intimate relations with Prince William von Hohenzollern."[127]

Furious that the police should have pried into her private life, the Countess arranged a meeting with von Richthofen who informed her that she was not the only one to enjoy a relationship with Willy, for he was already seeing Countess Hohenau, and, since 'favourites soon fall' it was time for Countess Wedel to 'vanish'. As she pressed him further, he explained that the police followed every woman in whom the prince showed any interest and they knew every detail of all his comings and goings.

Soon afterwards, Willy sent the Countess a ring to assure her of his eternal love, but, within a few months, his passion had cooled and she was paid a small sum of money for the return of his billets-doux. Although from then onwards their relationship was purely platonic, they remained in contact until the Countess left Germany for America in 1893

Whether or not Dona knew of the affair, in public as well as in private she remained so obviously devoted to

Willy that Queen Victoria's acerbic lady-in-waiting viewed her as 'insipid and boring'. Willy's sisters found her equally dull and prudish, and the eldest, Charlotte, took every opportunity to ridicule her. On one occasion, during a military parade, Charlotte arrived drunk, and mounted a horse in a cruel impression of Dona; and during a family performance to celebrate her parents' silver wedding anniversary, Charlotte made a point of upstaging her nervous sister-in-law.

In the face of Charlotte's humiliations, Vicky remained Dona's strongest champion until, little by little, she began to realise that her seemingly biddable daughter-in-law, was exacerbating her already difficult relationship with Willy.

Within five years of his marriage, Willy had distanced himself more than ever from his parents, and months might pass before he deigned to pay them a visit. In the early summer of 1886, he was suffering from a serious ear inflammation – the effects of which would continue to plague him throughout his life. When his anxious mother had been to see him, she told Queen Victoria that she found him:

"...in the garden and I thought him looking all right. He did not condescend to remember that he had not seen me for two months, or...that his sisters had the measles. He never asked after them or you, or any of my relations in England, so that I felt hurt and disappointed as I had been tormenting myself so much about him. He is a curious creature."[128]

Following Willy's accession, relations between Vicky and Dona became increasingly tense. Often the new Empress snubbed or made cutting remarks to her mother-in-law, and when, following Fritz's death, she wrote to her for support, Dona did not even bother to reply. Despite knowing how fond Vicky was of small children, Dona allowed her only limited access to her grandsons for fear that she might infect them with her liberal ideas; and when, after bearing six sons, she gave birth to a daughter, she was quick to point out that, although she was called Victoria, she was *not* named in honour of her grandmother. It was, however, her influence over Willy that most concerned his mother, for Dona flattered him constantly and neither he nor she, who 'thinks she knows better than everyone because she is the Empress', were prepared to listen to advice.

Despite Vicky's increasing disappointment and irritation, Dona's sons adored her, but the tension between Willy and his parents was reflected in his relationship with his sons. Despite her alleged prudishness, Dona announced quite openly that during her seven pregnancies she and Willy continued to share a bed right up to the day of her confinement, and there is no doubt at all that he was immensely proud to be the father of new fewer than six Prussian princes. As Emperor, though, he desperately wanted the respect and admiration of his people, and, within his own home he expected the same from his sons. While, to her boys, Dona was 'ever sympathetic, comprehending...so clear-sighted and wide-visioned in her simple modesty'[129], Willy often appeared distant, aloof and unyielding. His duties left him limited time to spend with his family and, while his children were young, he made a point of rising early, breakfasting with his wife, and seeing the boys for about half an hour before attending to the business of the day. He was seldom available to join in their games, and became almost a frightening stranger who lacked the ability to laugh with them or to unbend in their presence.

"...It seems to me," wrote his eldest son, Crown Prince Wilhelm, "as though he were unable so to divest himself of the dignity and superiority of the mature adult man as to enable him to properly engage with us little fellows."[130]

Even Dona allegedly told a friend that she doubted that Willy would be interested in any of his children until they were old enough to undertake military service.

Nevertheless, Willy was keen to keep abreast of their progress and, as was the custom of the time, thought nothing of ordering a beating if they misbehaved. Understandably, then, the boys were afraid of their father and, on the rare occasions when he softened a little in an effort to win their confidence, his behaviour was so unusual that they were merely 'abashed in his presence'.

Fortunately, their mother was always there to support them, and the nursery was the one domain in which she dared to correct her husband. On one occasion he marched unexpectedly into the schoolroom and, when his children could not answer his questions, he shouted so loudly that they cried.

Hearing the commotion, Dona hurried to the room in time to hear him bellow, "I will be obeyed! I am master!"

To which she firmly replied that he was indeed master in the country but not in the schoolroom, which was her responsibility.

As the boys grew older and their education was placed in the hands of tutors, they saw even less of the Kaiser, so that, by the time they eventually entered the military, their relationship was so strained that they viewed him as less of a father and more as a Commander-in-Chief to whom they could only relate as a senior officer.

Basically, Willy found it difficult to understand his sons, and his erratic nature made it equally difficult for them to understand him. On being told, for example, that the Crown Prince's tutor had had to reprimand the boy for swearing, Willy jokingly responded:

"The devil! He must be broken of that; but where did the little Schcisskerl (the very same phrase complained of) hear that expression?"[131]

When, however, the Crown Prince complained that he was shocked by the coarseness of his fellow-students at Bonn University, Willy scoffed at his sensitivity. On discovering that his eldest son had accrued a number of debts, Willy not only refused to settle them but rather accused him of being 'not enough of a soldier; not enough of a Hohenzollern.'

Despite his aloofness and apparent hard-heartedness, however, Willy cared for the boys far more deeply than he was prepared to admit. He was particularly keen to ensure that their Christmases were memorable and happy occasions, asking them for lists in advance so that he could select the choicest presents. He always provided each child with his own Christmas tree, and gave him sufficient money to purchase gifts for his siblings. During his foreign visits, he missed them deeply, confessing to a friend that, although the visit was a great success, it did not compensate for the absence of his family, and,

"I shall have soreness in the heart until I see my wife and youngsters again."[132]

As in so many areas of his life, Willy was constantly torn between his genuine feelings of love and affection, and his desperation to appear superior and invulnerable. Laughing too loudly, talking too bombastically, appearing domineering and aloof, the entire charade was an attempt to conceal his true, somewhat timid nature, and it was not until his sons were older that they began to understand how deeply he had cared for them. Many years later, the Crown Prince wrote that:

> "In the depths of his nature my father is a thoroughly kind-hearted man striving to make people happy and create joyousness around him. But this trait is often concealed by his desire not to appear tender, but royal and exalted above the small emotions of sentiment."[133]

When, in 1887, his fourth son, Joachim, was born, Willy's determination to appear above sentimentality was evidenced in his response to his mother, who suggested that it would have been pleasant to have had a girl. Willy replied sharply that he had no use for daughters since girls were useless creatures and he only wanted sons, but this reaction was either designed either to shock or to conceal his own disappointment, for when, five years later, his only daughter, Victoria Louise ('Sissy'), was born, he could not have been more excited.

Sissy, a bright and precocious little girl who in many ways resembled Willy's mother, was without doubt her father's favourite child. In her company he was far more relaxed than he had ever been with his sons, and of all his children she was, according to her brother, 'the only one of us who succeeded...in gaining a snug place in his heart.' She alone was able to tease him in a manner that would, from anyone else, have elicited an angry response; and father and daughter often rode together along the Unter den Linden, solely to give her the pleasure of receiving the salutations of the crowd. With her, too, Willy felt no need to accentuate his authority or to attempt to impress.

"My daughter," he said, "is proud to be known as the daughter of the Kaiser, but it never enters her head that he is actually an Emperor."[134]

No matter how difficult Willy's relationships with his sons might have been, they were, however, virtually perfect compared to those of his cousin, George, and his children.

Chapter 16 – I Have Buried My Angel Today

The Waleses

Eddy (Albert Victor) – Duke of Clarence & Avondale; eldest son of the Prince and Princess of Wales
George – Eddy's younger brother; second son of the Prince and Princess of Wales
Bertie (Albert Edward) – Prince of Wales; Queen Victoria's eldest son
Alexandra – Princess of Wales; Bertie's wife
Toria (Victoria) – Second daughter of the Prince & Princess of Wales

Others

Alix – Princess of Hesse; daughter of Queen Victoria's deceased daughter, Alice
Vicky – German Empress Frederick; Queen Victoria's eldest daughter
Willy – Kaiser Wilhelm II; son of Vicky
Lenchen – Queen Victoria's third daughter
Christian – Lenchen's husband
Beatrice – Queen Victoria's youngest daughter
Mary of Cambridge – Duchess of Teck; Queen Victoria's cousin
May (Mary) – of Teck; only daughter of the Duchess of Teck

At the time of Willy's wedding, a journalist for an English newspaper commented that there was far more interest in the nuptials of an heir to the German throne than there was in the marriage prospects of his English counterpart, Prince Albert Victor (Eddy). The journalist explained this phenomenon by stressing that, since Germany was an autocracy, the succession was of greater significance than was the case in Britain with its constitutional monarchy. In fact, though, the lack of interest in Eddy's romantic aspirations was part of a wider indifference to him, since people knew so little about him. As Willy was beginning to make his mark on the world stage, the more reticent Duke of Clarence performed only occasional public duties and, to the majority of the British people, he was little more than a name on a family tree or an image on a photograph.

To his family, however, Eddy's prospects were of paramount importance, and, as random rumours about his private life reached the Queen's ears, she was desperate to find him a wife to prevent him from following his father's wayward example. As always, her first thought was to seek a bride among her granddaughters, and none seemed more appropriate than Alice's youngest daughter, eighteen-year-old Princess Alix of Hesse.

Since her mother's death when she was only six-years-old, Alix had spent a good deal of time at her grandmother's court and consequently not only shared many of the Queen's values but also many of her traits.

"She shared her grandmother's love of law and order, her faithful adherence to family duty, her dislike of modernity, and she also possessed the 'homeliness' of the Coburgs..."[135]

Unsurprisingly, Queen Victoria saw Alix as an ideal candidate for 'the highest position there is' and she made a point of arranging meetings between the cousins. To her delight, Eddy soon appeared to be smitten with the beautiful Alix, but she, alas, had already given her heart to the Russian Tsarevich. Under intense pressure from her family, Alix wavered for several months before finally rejecting Eddy's proposal in the spring of 1890.

"It is a real sorrow to us," wrote the Queen, "and they have tried to persuade her, but she says that if she is forced she will do it, but that she would be unhappy and he, too."[136]

Disappointed but not despairing, the Queen was certain that she would soon find him an equally suitable bride and, as Eddy returned to his regiment in York, her thoughts turned to a second granddaughter – Willy's youngest sister, Princess Margaret (Mossy) of Prussia.

Eddy's mother, the Princess of Wales, was not happy; and when his brother, George told her, 'I think, Motherdear…that both Grandmamma & dear Papa wish him to marry a German,' she was horrified. Despising Germany in general and Prussia in particular, the prospect of a Prussian daughter-in-law was anathema to her, and it came as a relief to discover that, despite Eddy's professed disappoint over Alix of Hesse's rejection, he had already fallen in love with someone else.

Three years earlier, at the home of his married sister, Louise, Eddy had first met Hélène of Orleans, the beautiful daughter of a claimant to the defunct French throne. Seven years younger than Eddy, Hélène had been born in England following the overthrow of the French monarchy, but she had spent much of her childhood and youth in France and consequently displayed all the grace and charm of a Parisian beauty. Intelligent and beautiful, Hélène was clearly as attracted to Eddy as he was to her, and both sets of parents were eager to encourage the romance.

Politically and constitutionally, the affair was doomed from the start. Hélène was a Roman Catholic, and Catholics were barred from marrying the heir to the throne; and, what was more, her father repeatedly called for a restoration of the French monarchy, so marriage to Eddy could damage Britain's relations with Republican France. The Princess of Wales dismissed these objections and continued to encourage the couple to write to one another and to meet in secret. Gifts and letters were regularly exchanged as Hélène and Eddy swore eternal love until, at last, prompted by his mother, Eddy proposed and was immediately accepted.

Now it was necessary to gain the Queen's support, and so the couple travelled to Eddy's sister's Scottish home, Mar Lodge, at a time when his grandmother was staying at Balmoral. Initially, Queen Victoria urged him to re-consider Mossy of Prussia instead, but, after meeting the couple together, her heart was swayed by the romance and by Hélène's assurance her that she was willing to convert to Anglicanism, and Eddy declaration that he was willing to renounce his place in the succession in order to marry her. The Queen promised to do what she could to help them, and she wrote at once to the Prime Minister, Lord Salisbury, asking if it were possible to facilitate the marriage.

Salisbury was far from optimistic. Hélène's conversion was essential, he said, but even then there could be insurmountable difficulties concerning relations with France. Moreover, Hélène's father adamantly opposed her plans to convert and, when she eventually gained an audience with Pope, the Pontiff told her firmly that it was beyond his power to grant her request. Realising that the situation was hopeless, Hélène urged Eddy to go away and forget her, but he responded by telling her that separation was too much to bear, and assuring her that she would ever remain the one true love of his life.

The great romance was not, however, quite as tragic as it first appears, for, even as Eddy was pouring his heart out to Hélène, he was simultaneously pursuing another woman. In February 1891, while Vicky was half-heartedly parading Mossy around Sandringham in the hope of attracting Eddy's attention, he was busily writing to Sybil, the beautiful daughter of the Earl of Rosslyn. He would never have believed it was possible, he said, to be in love with two women at the same time, but that was exactly the situation in which he found himself with Sybil and Hélène. With the latter's departure, his love for the former intensified but, within a couple of months, he heard that she was about to be engaged. Eddy wrote to her, wishing her well and telling her not to be surprised if she heard that he, too, was soon to be married, since his family, and particularly his grandmother, were becoming increasingly anxious to see him 'settled'.

That autumn, Eddy was stationed with his regiment in Dublin, where his brother, George, who had just returned from a voyage as the Commander of the *Melampus,* paid him a visit. On returning soon afterwards to Sandringham, George began to display the symptoms of typhoid, and within a few days his condition was critical. The Princess of Wales, who was visiting her sister in Russia, anxiously hurried home, but, by the time she reached England the worst of the crisis was over. Only as he began to recover was the seriousness of his condition made public, but the news of his near-fatal illness, convinced the press as well as his family, that Eddy must marry as soon as possible in order to secure the succession.

By late autumn, having kept her eyes open for a suitable candidate, Queen Victoria believed she had found him a perfect bride. Victoria Mary (May) of Teck, was the twenty-four-year-old daughter of the Queen's frequently impoverished and permanently obese cousin, Mary of Cambridge, and her equally impecunious husband, Francis, Duke of Teck. In the past, Queen Victoria had often despaired of Cousin Mary who was prone to shocking royal guests by her appalling dress sense and uninhibited conversation. Nonetheless, her joviality and winning smile had won the hearts of the public and it was widely reported that during processions, Mary's carriage was always greeted with the loudest cheers. It was also rumoured that Mary had long harboured the hope that one day her only daughter, May, would wear a crown.

May was the very antithesis of her mother. Sensible, serious, shy and slim, she had been a 'merry and healthy' child but, in Queen Victoria's opinion, 'not as handsome as she ought to be'. As she grew older, her shyness increased, creating the impression of aloofness. Vicky considered her 'cold and stiff' and probably not very clever; while Eddy's sisters thought her dull and too studious to be able to hold an interesting conversation. May shared, though, her mother's great reverence for the monarchy, and that fact, combined with her sensibleness, appealed to the Queen, who saw her as a potentially stabilising influence on her fickle grandson. As the Queen's admiration of her qualities increased, so, too, did her admiration of May's appearance. By autumn 1891, she was regularly describing her as pretty and she told Vicky that she was:

"A particularly nice girl, so quiet and yet cheerful and so very carefully brought up and so sensible."[137]

Due to her parents' financial restraints, May had spent much of her childhood travelling on the Continent to avoid the expense of living in London, but during their regular sojourns in England, May and her brothers had often played with the Wales children, and in 1885 the family took up permanent residence in White Lodge in Windsor Park.

In November 1891, as George recovered from his illness, the Queen invited May to Balmoral to assess her as a potential candidate for the 'highest position there is'. Throughout the ten day visit, May could not have impressed the Queen more, and when she recommended her to the Prince of Wales, he replied that he was personally fond of May and would waste no time in 'suggesting' to Eddy that she would make him an ideal wife. With the same impulsiveness with which he had once offered to renounce the throne for Hélène, he willingly accepted his father's suggestion, and promised to propose at the first opportunity.

Within a matter of days, arrangements were made for the couple to stay at Luton Hoo, the home of the Danish Ambassador. There, on December 3rd, Eddy asked May to marry him, and, despite being slightly taken aback by the speed of events, she accepted him without hesitation. Four days later their engagement was officially announced.

"We are much excited and delighted at the happy event of May Teck's engagement to dear Eddy," Vicky wrote to her daughter. "Aunt Mary Teck will be in the seventh heaven, for years and years it has been her ardent wish, and she has thought of nothing else. What a marriage, and what a position for her daughter!"[138]

The sentiment was reiterated by several equally cynical courtiers who believed that the Tecks had been desperately trying to engineer the match; but Cousin Willy was far more sincere in his felicitations. He liked May, he said, and he was delighted in Eddy's happiness. Although Eddy's somewhat possessive sisters were not overjoyed by their brother's choice of bride, his parents welcomed her into the family and did their utmost to help her to feel at home.

Queen Victoria, whose respect for May deepened by the day, wanted the wedding to take place as soon as possible – perhaps to prevent fickle Eddy from changing his mind – and the date was set for February 27th 1892. Throughout the December days, the couple often appeared together in public, attending the opera or the theatre and receiving great applause from the crowds.

After a festive Christmas, the year 1891 ended on rather a sad note when Lenchen's husband, Prince Christian, was accidentally shot in the face[y]; and, on New Year's Eve, Prince Victor of Hohenlohe-Langenburg, the son of Queen Victoria's half-sister, died of throat cancer. On a damp and windy day, January 4th, Eddy and his father attended the funeral at Sunningdale, and, on returning to Sandringham, Eddy developed a slight cold while his hypochondriacal sister, Toria, repaired to her bed with influenza.

Two days later, while out shooting in the grounds of Sandringham, Eddy felt so unwell that May persuaded him to return to the house. George took his temperature and, finding it was high, asked the doctor to visit. The following day,

[y] See Chapter 22

194

January 8th, was Eddy's birthday and he managed to get up to open his presents and attend the entertainment that had been prepared for him but, by that evening, the doctors had diagnosed influenza. Initially, there was little cause for alarm. Influenza was rife at Osborne as well as at Sandringham and several members of the Queen's suite had been affected but had quickly recovered. Eddy was not so fortunate. Pneumonia developed and he became increasingly delirious.

"Heard to-night...that dear Eddy had been attacked at Sandringham by Influenza in a very serious form, which distresses me much,"[139] wrote his fiancée's uncle, George of Cambridge; while his Aunt Vicky pessimistically told her daughter:

"...They are still very anxious about Eddy and the news is not so good from Sandringham this morning. It worries and torments me very much. Poor Eddy, I do trust he will pull through all right. It is so dreadful to be constantly cast from one anxiety into another, dreading and fearing what may come, trembling for those one loves. Such is Life, such is its uncertainty, and we are weak and helpless creatures."[140]

As his mother sat mopping his brow, and his future bride sat awkwardly with her parents in an adjoining room, Eddy rambled incoherently, occasionally calling out, 'Hélène! Hélène!' By the evening of the 13th January his condition had deteriorated and, in the early hours of the following morning, his family gathered in his tiny bedroom as the chaplain began reading the prayers for the dying. According to his mother, shortly before the end, he suddenly raised his head from his pillow and asked:

"Who's that calling? Who's that calling me?"

"It is Jesus calling you," she replied[141].

At nine-thirty in the morning on 14th January, the twenty-eight-year-old Duke of Clarence and Avondale died.

The distraught Prince of Wales stood holding his face in his hands and sobbing violently, while his wife, numb with grief, 'looked as if she were turned to marble'. Eddy's sisters sought to come to terms with their loss by describing him as little less than a saint or a knight of old; and from Prussia, Aunt Vicky wrote that she could think of nothing else and had a headache from crying and feeling so bewildered at the death of the 'gentle, good and affectionate' boy.

"It is a fearful catastrophe, so sudden, so unexpected and in the very prime of life and in apparent health when I last saw him this day week," wrote the Duke of Cambridge. "It is really overwhelming one can hardly realise the painfully sad event which has so suddenly come upon us and the results which may arise out of it."[142]

As news travelled across the Empire, Eddy's parents received overwhelming support from every part of the globe. In England there was an outpouring of sympathy the like of which had not been witnessed since the death of Prince Albert, twenty years earlier. In London, nine thousand cabmen were reported to have draped their whips in black crepe; and in every British city as well as in Canada, Australia, South Africa and India, shops were shuttered and flags at half-mast hung over every public building. Even the Zulu Chief sent a message of heartfelt condolence to the grieving parents.

The Princess of Wales, who adored her son, never recovered from the loss, and, even years later, at George's coronation she was heard to whisper, "It should have been Eddy." The Prince of Wales was no less heartbroken, writing to the Archbishop of Canterbury:

"...We can hardly realise the terrible loss we have sustained...You know what a happy family party we have always been, so the wrenching away of our first-born son under such peculiarly sad circumstances is a sorrow the shadow of which can never leave us during the rest of our lives."[143]

The Princess of Wales would have liked her son to be buried quietly at Sandringham but, due to his position, it was deemed necessary for him to be interred at Windsor. Queen Victoria, who had recently tripped and hurt her ankle, planned to make the journey from Osborne but her daughters, Lenchen and Beatrice, persuaded her to heed her doctor's warning that the journey in the height of winter would be too traumatic. Amusingly, when her doctor, James Reid, suggested that the service would be too depressing for her, she replied crossly that she was never depressed at a funeral![144] It was a marked contrast to her response to the marriage of one of her granddaughters when she sighed, 'I *hate* weddings!'

On 20th January, Eddy's coffin, draped in a union flag, was taken on a gun carriage from Sandringham to Windsor under an escort of his regiment, the 10th Hussars. A simple military funeral followed in the dimly-lit chapel which was awash with flowers sent from across the Empire. All eyes were fixed on the recently-recovered George, who bore up well although many an old soldier was seen to have tears in his eyes. After the service, before the body was taken to the vault in the Albert Memorial Chapel, his bereaved fiancée left a wreath of orange blossom on his coffin. Eddy's uncle, Liko Battenberg, had the unenviable job of directing all the carriages, which was made more difficult since the mourners were leaving the chapel by different doors. That evening, Alexandra, who insisted that Eddy's rooms should remain exactly as he left them, wrote to her mother:

"I have buried my angel today and with him my happiness."[145]

Now she would focus all her attention on her second son, George.

Chapter 17 – What a Difference for Poor Georgie

The Waleses

Bertie (Albert Edward) Queen Victoria's eldest son; Prince of Wales
Alexandra – Bertie's Danish wife; Princess of Wales
Eddy (Albert Victor) – Duke of Clarence & Avondale; Bertie's eldest son
George – Duke of York; Bertie's second son
Louise – Duchess of Fife; Bertie's eldest daughter

Others

Vicky – Empress Frederick, Queen Victoria's eldest daughter
Willy – Kaiser Wilhelm II; Vicky's eldest son
Affie – Duke of Edinburgh; Queen Victoria's second son
Missy (Marie) – Affie's eldest daughter
Lenchen (Helena) – Queen Victoria's third daughter
Thora (Helena Victoria) – Lenchen's daughter
Mary – Duchess of Teck; Queen Victoria's cousin
May – Princess of Teck; Duchess of York; Mary's daughter; George's wife
David – Eldest son of George & May
Albert (Bertie) – Second son of George & May
John – Youngest son of George & May

"What a difference for poor Georgie now suddenly hurled into quite a different position," wrote Vicky shortly after Eddy's death. It was a position which George had neither expected nor wanted. Unlike Cousin Willy, who had hardly been able to restrain his eagerness to ascend the throne, George had envisaged a very different future and had no ambition to succeed his father as King.

Enjoying his career, he felt secure in the masculine discipline of a naval life and would far rather have remained at sea than to stand second-in-line to the throne of a mighty empire. At the time of his brother's death, he had never made a speech, had attended very few official engagements, and had been away on so many voyages that the public knew even less of him than they had known of Eddy.

The first few months of 1892 were particularly trying for the twenty-six-year-old prince, who was still recovering from typhoid as he sought to come to terms with the adjustment in his status and the loss of a brother from whom he had once been inseparable.

"I am sure," he wrote to his grandmother, "no two brothers could have loved each other more than we did. Alas! it is only now that I have found out how deeply I did love him; & I remember with pain nearly every hard word & little quarrel I ever had with him & I long to ask his forgiveness, but, alas, it is too late now!"[146]

To aid his emotional and physical recovery, George joined his parents on a tour of the Continent, including a visit to Vicky's home in Homburg where she observed that, although he looked much thinner, he was cheerful and 'a great darling.' His Prussian cousins were equally effusive in their praise of his 'sweetness' and sense of humour.

To mark the significant alteration in his position, Queen Victoria created him Duke of York – a title which pleased him immensely, despite his grandmother's reminder that anyone could become a duke, whereas princes are born princes. She quietly asked him, too, whether, in view of his becoming his father's heir, he would consider changing his name to Albert. Uncertain how to respond, George asked the advice of the Queen's private secretary, Henry Ponsonby, who replied that 'he would gladly lay down his life for the Queen, but if she asked him to change his name to Thomas, he would certainly refuse.'[147] Neither the Queen nor George raised the subject again.

At his own request, it was agreed that for a little while longer he could continue his career in the Royal Navy, but his active service would gradually decrease as he was expected to participate more fully in public duties. The most pressing consideration, however, at least in the eyes of his grandmother, was finding him a suitable wife to secure the succession.

Even before Eddy's death, Queen Victoria had been urging George to think about marriage. Perhaps she had heard the rumours about a mistress in St. John's Wood, whom he shared with his elder brother; or the suggestion that he was having an affair with an Admiral's daughter in Malta. Whatever her reasons, she had several times written to him, urging him not to be led astray by decadent companions, and, in February 1891, she had suggested that both he and Eddy should find wives. George, somewhat ingenuously, responded by reminding her of the dangers of marrying too young, citing the case of Crown Prince Rudolf, the heir to the Austrian Empire, who had been all but forced to marry a Belgian princess, and who subsequently committed suicide in seedy circumstances. Eddy, George said, was twenty-seven, which was a reasonable age for settling down, but he himself was not yet ready and:

> "The one thing I never could do is to marry a person that didn't care for me. I should be miserable for the rest of my life."[148]

In his late teenage years, George had formed an attachment to the daughter of one of his mother's ladies-in-waiting, Julie Stonor, but, though his feelings were reciprocated, both knew that, in view of her relatively lowly station, nothing could come of their romance. Now, Eddy's death had made him significantly more eligible to European princesses, and one of his aunts was determined that her daughter should be first on the list of candidates for the position of future Queen Consort.

Queen Victoria's third daughter, Lenchen, had been most put out when she heard of the engagement of Eddy and May of Teck, as she had harboured the belief that her own daughter, Thora, would make him an ideal wife. Now that George was second-in-line to the throne, Lenchen urged Thora to make herself noticed. Thora dutifully obeyed, seeking him out whenever possible, hovering in his presence and offering him her photograph – a sure sign, at that time, of romantic intentions. Her awkward efforts backfired when the Princess of Wales who had never liked Thora's mother, and who could not forgive her father's family's role in the seizure of Schleswig-Holstein, cruelly mocked her, calling her by a nickname adopted by her brothers on account of her long nose:

> "So the Xtians have been following you about with their lovely Snipe!" she wrote to George. "Well it will be a pleasure to expect that beauty as your bride – when may we expect the news? You see she is quite prepared to take you by storm already offering you her contrafeit (sic) in a frame."[149]

Scornful as she was of Thora's attempts to win her son's heart, the Princess of Wales was still more perturbed to discover that George had already fallen in love with a far more flamboyant cousin – Marie (Missy) the eldest daughter of his Uncle Affie, Duke of Edinburgh.

In the late 1880s, as Commander of the Mediterranean fleet, Affie, was stationed on Malta, and while serving in the navy, George often stayed with him and his family at the San Antonio Palace. There, Affie had introduced his nephew to the joys of philately – an interest which was to become one of his greatest passions[z] – and during that time, to the mild amusement of his family, George first grew a beard in an attempt to make himself

---

[z] See Chapter 22

appear older than he was. His brother, Eddy, was unimpressed, advising him to shave it off before he returned home, but his young Edinburgh cousins liked it, and Missy in particular enjoyed the attention of a mature-looking cousin, ten years her senior, who nonetheless treated her as an equal.

The Edinburgh girls were used to entertaining young naval officers, several of whom were frequent guests at their home. They all became, in Missy's words, 'great chums', and George was just one among many. Although Missy enjoyed his company on picnics, rides and outings, she never saw him as anything other than a cousin and a friend.

"Cousin George was a beloved chum," she wrote later, "...but I proudly remember that...I was [his] decided favourite; there was no doubt about that whatever. What fun we had with George; what delightful, harmless fun!"[150]

Unfortunately, what Missy saw as innocent amusement, George mistook for romance and soon declared to his parents that he wished to marry her. His father approved of the match; after all, Affie was his favourite brother, and Missy had sufficient sparkle, beauty and intelligence to make an ideal bride. Affie was equally in favour; and Queen Victoria, who saw no difficulties in marriages between first cousins, was happy at the prospect of a union of two of her grandchildren.

Their mothers, however, were far less enthusiastic. The Germanophobic Princess of Wales, believed that, since Affie was due to inherit the Duchy of Coburg, the Edinburgh girls had been raised as Germans and even spoke English with a German accent. Besides, she said, Missy was far too young – 'a mere baby barely out of petticoats' – and she had never been particularly fond of Missy's mother, the Russian-born Duchess of Edinburgh. Her feelings were reciprocated by the Duchess of Edinburgh, whose overbearing mother-in-law and unhappy marriage had created such a jaundiced view of England that she had no intention of allowing any of her daughters to marry an English prince.

It was Missy herself, however, who made the final decision, and, when George eventually summoned the courage to propose, she gently refused him. Affronted and angry, the Prince of Wales berated Missy's father for the outcome, while the Princess of Wales, for all her opposition to the match, was insulted to think that the 'mere baby' would dare to reject her son. Within a couple of months, news reached Sandringham that Missy was engaged to the heir to the throne of Roumania, and, though she and George would always be friends, it was clear that he would have to look elsewhere for a bride.

In the meantime, having lost one son, the Princess of Wales lavished all her affection on George. By 1892, he was twenty-seven years old and commanding some of the most powerful vessels in the British Fleet, yet in her letters she still addressed him as 'little Georgie' and his replies to 'Motherdear' usually ended with great big kisses. Reluctant as she was to think of it, she knew that George had a duty to marry, and, although it would be hard to share his affection with any other woman, she raised no objections to Queen Victoria's suggestion that the perfect solution was for him to marry his late brother's fiancée, May of Teck.

Eddy's death had left May in an awkward situation, for she had almost risen to one of the foremost positions in the Royal Family but now she was left uncertain about her future. Following the funeral, she had withdrawn to live quietly with her mother at White Lodge, and, as George occasionally visited her there, it did not take long for their friends and the press to start speculating about the nature of their relationship. Soon, people were calling openly for them to marry, and, while May complained that the constant interference was more than she could bear, her mother – and probably May herself – saw that a crown was still within her grasp.

May and George genuinely enjoyed one another's company but both were reticent when it came to expressing their feelings. George had, after all, received a painful and humiliating rejection from Cousin Missy; and May had been only a month away from her wedding when Eddy died. So shy were they about their romance that it would take a good deal of prompting for any hope of marriage to develop. Eventually, it fell to George's sister, Louise, to spur him into action. Having invited the couple to her home, Sheen Lodge, she all but pushed them into the garden together, making the obvious point to George that now was the moment to propose. He finally managed to do so, and, as just as May had responded without hesitation to Eddy's proposal, she now immediately accepted his younger brother's.

The Queen, who was at Balmoral, was delighted when George arrived two days later to tell her what had happened, and, when the engagement was officially announced on 3rd May 1893, the general consensus of opinion was that this was a fitting resolution to the tragedy of the Duke of Clarence's death. The *Times,* while drawing attention to the peculiarity of May's situation, reported that:

> "The Duke of York enjoys not only the popularity attaching to the Navy, but also a personal goodwill, founded on his own frank and manly bearing on the few occasions when he has come before the public."[151]

Only George's mother felt a pang of regret at the thought of losing her 'darling Georgie boy.' A few days before the engagement was announced, she had written to him of her sadness that 'we shall never be able to be together and travel in the same way'[152] but reminding him that the bond between mother and child was indestructible.

After an engagement of only two months, the wedding took place in the Chapel Royal at St. James' Palace on a beautiful summer's day, 6th July 1893. Royal guests arrived from across the Continent, including George's grandparents, the King and Queen of Denmark, and his cousin and friend, the Tsarevich Nicholas, heir to the Russian Empire. Among other cousins in the congregation were four of Queen Victoria's grandsons: Henry of Prussia, representing the Kaiser; Young Arthur Connaught; Drino Battenberg; and Abbie of Schleswig-Holstein.

Immense crowds gathered to cheer the procession to and from St. James' Palace, and later the well-wishers migrated towards Buckingham Palace, where George and May stood on the balcony, amazed by the cheering and goodwill of the masses below. The honeymoon was spent in York Cottage, a wedding gift from George's father, which was to become their home. The house on the Sandringham estate had originally been built to accommodate the Prince of Wales' suite and guests, and, by royal standards, it was small and unimpressive with narrow corridors and cluttered rooms. To George, who loved the confines of ships, it was an ideal home.

There, the couple lived like a country squire and his wife; George enjoying the rural pursuits of shooting and sports, May involving herself in charitable works and providing her husband with heirs. To outsiders the marriage appeared to be perfectly happy, for May submissively yielded to her husband in everything, recognising him as her future king. They found, wrote an equerry, 'extraordinary delight in each other' and, although they displayed none of the obvious passion of several of George's relations, the reticent couple developed a deep fondness for one another. It was difficult, though, for May to adjust to life with a husband who had few intellectual interests, for she had been better educated and was generally viewed as his intellectual superior. She loved art and enjoyed touring galleries and museums – interests which George, poring over his stamps or shooting birds, could not share.

"Sometimes," wrote her early biographer, John Gore, "the Duchess's intellectual life...may have been starved and her energies atrophied in those early years...For many women, then and now, the daily call to follow the shooters, to watch the killing, however faultless, to take always a cheerful appreciative part in man-made, man-valued amusements, must have been answered at the sacrifice of many cherished, constructive and liberal ambitions."[153]

Nor was May made to feel totally welcome by her new family. While the Queen and Prince of Wales treated her with respect and kindness, George's sisters thought her boring since she could not participate in their idle chit-chat and did not appreciate of some of their childish ways. Occasionally, they quietly laughed at her, scornful of her lowly origins: 'Poor May, poor May with her Württemberg hands!' they were heard to say.

Although York Cottage had been gifted to the couple at their wedding, May was not permitted to make any alterations without the express permission of George's parents, and May's own artistic tastes often different sharply from those of her in-laws who preferred to keep everything just as it had always been.

Naturally reticent, May's shyness increased due to her feeling of a lack of support from George's family, but, knowing the strong bond between him and his mother, there was little she could do to change it. Even her attempts to initiate new charitable schemes around Sandringham were hampered by her mother-in-law who saw all such activities as her own prerogative.

When in London, the Yorks occupied a suite of rooms in St. James' Palace from where they carried out their official duties, opening hospitals, laying the foundation stones of building, and dutifully attending state functions. For the most part, though, their lives continued in the routine of shooting parties, reluctantly following the social season, and, to the annoyance of their staff, living quietly in the increasingly cramped York Cottage.

Eleven months after the wedding, a son was born at May's mother's home, White Lodge in Windsor – an event which, almost inevitably, provoked a letter from the Queen asking that the child should be named Albert after his late great-grandfather. George was compelled to explain that he and May had already decided that their first son should be named Edward, after Eddy, the Duke of Clarence. The Queen accepted the explanation but sensibly pointed out:

"...only I think you write as if Edward was the real name of dear Eddy, while it was Albert Victor."

In the event, the little boy was christened Edward Albert Christian George David – and, by the family, he would always be addressed as David.

The following year, a second son was born, and this time the Queen was gratified to hear that he was to be called Albert. Her only regret was that his birthday occurred on 'the terrible 14th' – the 14th December 1895, the thirty-fourth anniversary of the death of his great-grandfather.

Over the next decade, four more children – Mary, Henry, George and John– were born in the small white bedroom of York Cottage; and Cousin Willy's often strained relationship with his offspring was magnified many times over in the relationship between Cousin George and his five sons.

Often away on his extensive tours, his absence was more of a blessing than a sorrow to his children, one of whom was so terrified of him that he would faint in his presence. George and May might have been content in each other's company with no overt expressions of affection but they were equally undemonstrative towards their children. May had few obvious maternal instincts and, as in so many aspects of her life, she viewed producing heirs as a royal duty rather than a pleasure. George, who had grown used to barking orders in the Royal Navy, treated his sons like recalcitrant midshipmen, and is alleged to have said that, since he was afraid of his father, he was 'going to be damned sure that my children are afraid of me.'

In that, he was extremely successful. In the cramped rooms of York Cottage on the Sandringham estate, the children were relegated to the care of nannies, one of whom, according to a possibly spurious tale which David liked to tell, would pinch her little charges and twist their arms before taking them to meet their parents for a brief spell each evening. George bellowed questions at the boys, and if they did not answer immediately, they were given such a severe dressing down that they literally trembled. David frequently disappointed his father by his lack of self-discipline; while his younger brother, left-handed Albert (Bertie), was forced to write with his right hand, and placed in splints to cure his supposed knock-knees. George's hot temper was legendary and, even allowing for exaggeration in his alleged mistreatment of his sons, the effects of his behaviour were obvious as the boys grew older. David became attracted to older married women who would mother him; while Bertie – the future King George VI – developed a pronounced stammer which made giving a speech a terrifying ordeal. The fourth son, George, would later enjoy a series of bisexual affairs, and sadly became addicted to morphine and cocaine.

Only one son seemed immune to his father's strict discipline – the youngest boy, John, whose carefree outspokenness amused visitors but was originally viewed by his parents as naughtiness. By the age of four, however, John had become prone to epileptic fits and it was clear that he suffered from what would probably now be diagnosed at autism. His behaviour was both an embarrassment and a concern for parents who believed in the importance of presenting a dignified image of royalty to the world. When, John was eleven years old, they decided to provide him with a separate household, Wood Farm on the Sandringham estate, under the supervision of a caring nanny, Charlotte Bill. His parents occasionally visited him there but he was seldom seen in public and, for the most part, quite forgotten by the outside world.

Like Willy, George was gentler in his dealings with his only daughter, Mary, with whom he often went riding along Rotten Row; but it is difficult to comprehend how an indulged, cheerful and mischievous little boy could become so tyrannical a father to his sons. Perhaps years of naval discipline had hardened him; or perhaps the fact that he had been forced to abandon his chosen career in order to prepare for his role as king, had created a deep-seated bitterness within him. Whatever his reasons, his lack of obvious affection for his sons contrasted sharply with the devotion with which several of his cousins treated their own children.

Chapter 18 – Too Young & Inexperienced

Hohenzollern (Prussians)

Vicky – Queen Victoria's eldest child; Empress Frederick
Willy (Wilhelm/William) – Vicky's eldest son; Kaiser Wilhelm II
Dona – Willy's wife
Henry – Vicky's second son
Irene – Henry's wife and cousin; daughter of Queen Victoria's second daughter, Alice

Hessians

Louis – Grand Duke of Hesse; husband of Queen Victoria's late daughter, Alice
Ernie – Grand Duke of Hesse; son of Louis and Alice
Victoria – Ernie's sister
Ella – Ernie's sister
Irene – Ernie's sister; wife of Henry of Prussia
Alix – Ernie's sister
Elizabeth – Ernie's daughter
Ducky (Victoria Melita) – Ernie's cousin and wife; Grand Duchess of Hesse

Others
Affie (Alfred) – Duke of Edinburgh & Coburg; Queen Victoria's second son; Ducky's father
Ducky (Victoria Melita) – Princess of Edinburgh/Grand Duchess of Hesse; daughter of Queen Victoria's son, Affie; wife of Ernie of Hesse

Like their mother, the daughters of Queen Victoria's second daughter, Alice, were strong-willed young women whose legendary beauty and intelligence made them some of the most sought-after princesses in Europe. As was shown, both Ella and Alix had rejected their grandmother's choice of marriage partners –Willy of Prussia; and Eddy of Wales – and both would go on to horrify the Queen by marrying *Russians!* The marriage of their sister, Irene, however, would certainly have pleased Queen Victoria, were it not for the fact that she did not know about the romance until the engagement was announced.

Willy might have been unlucky in his pursuit of a Hessian princess, but his younger brother, Henry, was more successful. Like Willy, Henry had often visited his cousins in Darmstadt, and as all eyes were fixed on Willy's attraction to Ella, Henry was quietly developing a strong attachment to her younger sister, Irene. Well-travelled and good-humoured, he made a dramatic impression on the twenty-year-old princess during a visit to Hesse in 1886, and the following January, when he returned to propose, Irene gladly accepted him.

Somewhat overshadowed by her elder sisters, Irene was graceful, quiet and gentle, and so deeply in love with her twenty-four-year-old cousin that his parents were delighted by the outcome. Queen Victoria, though offended that she had not known in advance of what was happening, soon recovered from her indignation and was happy to give the couple her blessing; but Henry's paternal grandmother, the sour Empress Augusta peevishly objected to the match, for, since Ella's rejection of Willy, she had taken a strong dislike to all of the Hessian princesses.

The engagement was formally announced on 22nd March 1887, in the midst of celebrations for the ninetieth birthday of Henry's grandfather, Emperor Wilhelm I. The streets of Berlin were festooned with garlands and flags, buildings were adorned with decorations, and, to the sound of orchestral performances of music from German composers, a flamboyant procession made its way to the Emperor's palace where the family and foreign dignitaries presented him with their gifts. Willy's young sons were among those who stepped forwards with flowers, and their great-grandfather received them with immense joy at the realisation that three generations of his heirs were present.

Henry's father, Fritz, made the official announcement of the engagement – an event which the reticent Irene anticipated with trepidation – but, by then, he was already in the early stages of throat cancer and his voice was so hoarse that he could barely be heard.

The wedding took place in May the following year, and the couple moved into the 'peaceful and harmonious' Königliches Schloss in Kiel, from where Henry continued his naval duties. Irene's concern for the poor soon endeared her to the local people, and it was noticed that she was a calming influence on her husband's occasional short temper.

"[He] was a tall and handsome man, but inclined to be – let us say – temperamental," wrote one observer. "At times he was overbearing and very satirical, and at others friendly and charming."[154]

When the couple were together, Henry's friendliness and charm easily outshone the overbearing aspect of his character, and they made such an impression on their family and suite that they were nicknamed the 'Very Amiables'. After his marriage, one of Queen Victoria's ladies-in-waiting, thought him so friendly and courteous that he was 'the nicest male royalty going'; and observers regularly commented upon the couple's mutual devotion.

"She is a magnificent equestrienne," wrote one contemporary, "and a very clever shot, being infinitely more successful in this respect than her husband, who is so devoted to her that he bears this superiority with the greatest equanimity."[155]

This devotion, however, did not prevent Henry from being involved in a minor scandal, when, during a tour of the United States[aa], he specifically asked to be taken to the somewhat notorious Everleigh Club in Chicago. Founded by

[aa] See Chapter 20

two sister in February 1900, the club was an expensive, high class brothel where the agile 'Everleigh butterflies' catered to the requirements of wealthy clients. On hearing that the prince had expressed a desire to visit the place, the Everleigh sisters prepared exclusive entertainment for their German guests, including a performance of the mythical slaying and dismembering of Zeus' son; and, as champagne flowed freely, Henry was reputedly spotted with several pretty prostitutes sitting one after another on his knee. Whether or not Irene heard of the escapade, she and Henry remained mutually supportive and openly affectionate to one another in a stable and happy marriage.

Unlike Willy's wife, Irene was fond of Henry's mother, and was happy to welcome her into her home. When, in 1894, Henry bought a new country house, Hemmelmarck – 'a fine large property with barns and cow houses, some woods and good sheet of water' – Vicky was one of the first visitors; and she was usually on hand to help Irene through her confinements.

A year after the wedding, as the birth of Irene's first child approached, Vicky hurried to Kiel and was shocked to see that Irene made no attempt to conceal her pregnancy. She was more disappointed to note that there were very few books in the house and it was incomprehensible to her that neither her son nor her daughter-in-law had any interest in visiting museums or galleries. At least, though, they were welcoming and were happy to have her in their home.

On 20th March 1889, a son was born and named Waldemar after Henry's younger brother who had died of diphtheria a decade earlier. To Irene's great sorrow, it was not long before the little boy was diagnosed with the hereditary disease, haemophilia, which had contributed to the death of her little brother, Frittie, almost twenty years before. Despite knowing the dangers that Waldemar would face, Henry and Irene encouraged him to live as normal a life as possible, and Henry was delighted when, at the age of ten, his son was officially commissioned in the German Navy.

Due, perhaps, to Waldemar's haemophilia, or quite simply because Henry was so often away from home, it was seven years before a second son was born. He, too, was named after one of his late uncles – Henry's little brother, Sigismund, who had died of meningitis in 1866. At the time of the birth of a third child, Henry was away in China on what his mother viewed as a puerile mission, and Vicky, assisting Irene during her pregnancy, noticed that the house was 'so silent and sad' in his absence. To Henry's chagrin, his mother was unable to stay with Irene through her confinement but he was overjoyed when, in January 1900, he received news that he had another son. On his way home from China he visited his mother, who found him in excellent spirits and 'very anxious to get home to his wife and children and see the new baby.'[156]

His joy was complete when he set eyes on the blonde-haired, blue-eyed little boy, whose cheerfulness endeared him to everyone, and who would be named Henry after his father. Sadly, it was not long before little Henry, too, was diagnosed with haemophilia, and his parents could only hope that he would survive the childhood bumps and bruises which could so easily prove fatal. In February 1904, however, in an almost identical replay of what had happened to her mother and brother, Frittie, Irene was watching Henry playing when she momentarily left the room. In the few minutes of her absence, the four-year-old climbed onto a chair from which he tumbled and fell onto his head. For any other child the injuries would have been barely noticeable but, when the doctors examined him, they discovered that he was suffering from a brain haemorrhage and, within a few hours, he was dead.

Naturally, his parents were devastated by their loss but, unlike King Alfonso XIII of Spain who blamed his wife for introducing haemophilia to the dynasty, Henry did not hold Irene responsible for the condition; and the tragedy drew the couple even closer together.

No one sympathised more with Irene's loss than her brother, Ernie, for, only three months earlier, he, too, had experienced the death of a beloved child.

Two months after the death of the Duke of Clarence in 1892, fifty-four-year-old Grand Duke Louis of Hesse – the widowed husband of the Queen's second daughter, Alice – suffered a stroke while dining with his family, and died ten days later, having barely recovered consciousness.

"I am broken-hearted at the loss of my beloved son...who was so devoted to me and whom I loved so dearly," wrote the Queen. "It is too terrible to be struck down in the prime of life and of strength, leaving his poor children orphans."[157]

Queen Victoria had always loved Louis, and although, since Alice's death thirteen years earlier, she had doubted his ability to raise his children unaided, she had admired his efforts and had done all she could to assist in him in their upbringing. By March 1892, three of his daughters were married – the first, Victoria, to the dashing Prince Louis Battenberg; the second, Ella, to Grand Duke Serge of Russia; and the third, Irene, to Henry of Prussia. Only the youngest surviving children, twenty-three-year-old Ernie, and nineteen-year-old, Alix, were still at home – and it was these two of whom the Queen was thinking when she wrote of the poor orphans.

Until then, Ernie had been enjoying a rather leisurely existence, pursuing his interest in the arts and enjoying the company of like-minded friends, particularly young men, with whom, it was rumoured, he formed a number of romantic liaisons. Whether or not the Queen knew of Ernie's alleged bisexuality, she felt that he was ill-prepared for his new role as Grand Duke.

'Ernie is much too young and inexperienced for his position,' Vicky agreed; while Ernie's own elder sisters believed that he would require a good deal of assistance to adjust to his new responsibilities.

Fortunately, he and his younger sister, Alix, were particularly devoted to one another, and she was happy to act as hostess to his guests and to participate in the running of the Grand Duchy.

"The bond that had always united the young Grand Duke of Hesse and his sister became a complete and harmonious understanding," wrote Alix's future lady-in-waiting. "The Grand Duke looked after his sister chivalrously, and acted as father, mother and friend. The innate motherliness of the Princess's character made her happiest when she could most devote herself to others, and she now centred all her thoughts on her brother. She shared his pursuits, identified herself with his interests, and gave up her life and aspirations to him."[158]

With his interest in architecture and natural flair for the arts, one of Ernie's first acts as Grand Duke was to insist on a re-working of the plans for a new museum in Darmstadt, since he considered the original design too ugly and out of place. Soon, he went further, for, like his grandfather, Prince Albert, he saw the potential of combining art and technology to create worthwhile employment to prosper industry and beauty in the Grand Duchy.[bb]

Despite his relations' misgivings, Ernie's simplicity and naturalness quickly won the respect of the Hessians, for, unlike many of his German contemporaries, he did not believe in the divine right to rule, but viewed his role as primarily one of service. Nonetheless, he was sometimes viewed as lackadaisical in areas which did not interest him, and Queen Victoria's charge d'affaires in Darmstadt, George Buchanan, observed that he was:

[bb] See Chapter 22

"...apt to leave many things undone which [he] ought to have done, and to do many things which [he] had better, perhaps, left undone."[159]

Throughout Ernie's childhood, he had often been criticised for his laziness in the schoolroom and his lack of attention to subjects which bored him. On hearing Buchanan's impressions, therefore, Queen Victoria feared he might take the same attitude towards his duties. In the months following his accession, she offered him plenty of sound advice, stressing most vehemently the necessity of finding a wife to assist and support him. Although Alix was performing her duties admirably, the time would come for her to marry; and, besides, a Grand Duke needed a Grand Duchess to secure the succession of the dynasty.

Ernie responded cheerfully to most of his grandmother's suggestions, but remained unmoved by her exhortations about marriage. Somewhat puzzled, the Queen asked his sisters why he was in no hurry to find a wife, and she was dissatisfied by their response that he was not yet ready to make such a commitment. His Aunt Vicky was probably more accurate than she realised, when she asked, "Who can tell what his tastes may be?"

Dissatisfied by the delay, Queen Victoria decided to take matters into her own hands and, as usual, began looking for a bride among her own granddaughters. Cousin Maud of Wales was her first suggestion but she had no desire to live in Darmstadt, and Ernie had no desire for Maud. Undiscouraged, the Queen turned her attention to another granddaughter, Victoria Melita (Ducky) of Edinburgh, with whom, at first sight, Ernie appeared to have a great deal in common.

Although Ernie was eight years older than Ducky, they shared the same birthday; they both loved art and music; they were young and fun-loving; and the Queen had often seen them laughing together, signifying a shared sense of humour. More importantly, Ducky was living with her

217

parents – then Duke and Duchess of Coburg – and therefore she was familiar with the mores of a typical German duchy. It did not matter that the 'rather passionate' young woman had already fallen in love with a Russian cousin, Kyril Vladimirovich, for Kyril's Orthodox religion forbade marriage between first cousins and so nothing could come of her dreams. All in all, Queen Victoria decided, Ernie and Ducky were ideally suited.

At every possible opportunity she brought the couple together, and the more she observed them, the more convinced she became of their compatibility. She could not understand, then, why Ernie kept prevaricating and making excuses for not having proposed, and she was rather put out when he told her he feared that their consanguinity could have a detrimental effect on their children. Ernie had, after all, seen his younger brother die of haemophilia, and, though the illness was little understood, it was becoming apparent that it was a hereditary condition which, Ernie suggested, could spring from the inter-marriage of so many close relations. Vicky agreed with Ernie and reminded her mother that Prince Albert had often spoken of the need to bring new blood into the family, but when the Queen sought the opinion of her doctor, William Jenner, he assured her that if two healthy cousins married, their union would simply 'strengthen the stock' and their children would be even healthier.

At length, finding all his excuses had been parried, Ernie yielded to the Queen's harrying and, while visiting Coburg in January 1894, he proposed and Ducky accepted him.

On receiving the news by telegram from Ducky's father, the Queen was overjoyed, but other members of the family were surprised by the unexpected announcement.

"Ernie and Ducky!" Vicky wrote to her daughter. "Perhaps you are not astonished? If she were only not his 1st cousin, what could be nicer? She is a charming girl, bright and clever, with plenty of spirit, which is rather what he wants, and then it is so nice to think that it will not be a stranger in dearest Alice's place."[160]

Surprised or not, all who met Ernie and Ducky in the months that followed, were struck by their obvious happiness, and, as invitations for a spring wedding in Coburg were sent to royal families across the continent, the general good cheer seemed to portend a very happy marriage.

In April 1894, the cobbled streets of Coburg thronged with so many royal relations that onlookers were amazed to see carriages stopping to allow empresses, grand duchesses and princesses emerge to embrace one another on the pavements. From Roumania, Russia, Prussia and Britain, they flocked to the Palais Coburg, and awaited the arrival of the star guest – the grandmother of both the bride and the groom, Queen Victoria. With so many grandchildren, the Queen could not attend every family celebration, but since Alice's death, she had made a point of supporting the Hessians and, just as she had travelled to Darmstadt for Ernie's confirmation ten years earlier, now she returned to Germany for his wedding.

Her pleasure in revisiting Coburg was, however, marred from the start by an argument with the bride's father. Having gone to meet his mother at the station, Affie was incensed to see, emerging from the Queen's carriage, her 'Indian secretary', Abdul Karim – the Munshi. His anger intensified when his mother insisted that the Munshi should sit with the family during the wedding service the following day, but only after a rather heated exchange of messages via their equerries, did Affie finally agree to permit him to join members of the suite in the gallery. The Queen made it clear that no servants should be seated near him as that would be too demeaning for a man of his station, but, as the wedding day dawned and Karim took his place in the gallery, he was disgusted to see that there were lowly grooms in the vicinity.

Without waiting to witness the greater part of the service, Karim walked out in disgust and wrote a long letter of complaint to the Queen, who, according to her doctor James Reid, 'was greatly distressed and cried a great deal.'[161]

Fortunately, the incident had little effect on the rest of the party, all of whom agreed that the bride and groom made a lovely couple and that the wedding was a peculiarly happy occasion.

"Happiness seemed to preside at the fete," wrote Princess Louise of Belgium. "Love had been invited – a rare guest at princely unions."[162]

For Queen Victoria, though, the Munshi's peevishness dwindled into insignificance when she was confronted with the far more shocking news that her favourite granddaughter, Ernie's younger sister, Alix, had finally accepted the proposal of the Russian Tsarevich, the future Nicholas II.

Nicholas and Alix had first met ten years earlier, when her sister, Ella, married Nicholas' uncle, Grand Duke Serge Alexandrovich. Although Alix was still a child at the time, she and Nicholas instantly fell in love, and, over the next decade their occasional meetings and frequent letters intensified their passion. Unfortunately, for the devoutly Lutheran Alix, the wife of the Tsarevich had to be of the Orthodox faith and, no matter how deeply she loved him, or how persistent his pleas, Alix simply *could not* abandon the religion of her childhood. For Queen Victoria, this hindrance was a blessing. The Romanov court, was, she felt, too decadent a place for her beloved granddaughter, and in a country rife with dissention, the position of a future Tsar and Tsarina was extremely perilous. Repeatedly, when Ella, who favoured the match, invited her sister to Russia, the Queen had bombarded Ernie with letters, telling him that he must insist that Alix would never be *allowed* to marry a Russian!

Ernie's first thought was always for his sister's happiness. He liked Nicholas and he had no objections to the idea of Alix converting to Orthodoxy, but, ironically, it was Cousin Willy –who, it was said, had to be 'the bride at every wedding and the corpse at every funeral' – who finally persuaded her to abandon her scruples to accept Nicholas' proposal[cc].

Meanwhile, despite the 'brilliant auspices under which the marriage took place'[163], Ernie and Ducky's honeymoon failed to live up to the bride's expectations. 'Completely shattered and disillusioned' by their wedding night, Ducky soon discovered her husband's penchant for young men; and, for all their shared artistic aspirations, she found life in Ernie's beloved Hesse dull and boring.

'To be entirely happy in marriage,' she said, 'the same things must be important to both' – and clearly they were not. For his part, Ernie was disappointed by Ducky's unwillingness to adopt his mother's charities, her lack of interest in Hessian affairs, and her refusal to take her duties as Grand Duchess seriously.

A year after the wedding, Ducky gave birth to a daughter, Elizabeth, upon whom Ernie doted with such possessiveness that, rather than drawing the couple closer together, their vying over the child's affection drove them further apart.

Two years after the wedding, in 1896, Ernie and Ducky attended the coronation of the new Tsar Nicholas II in Moscow, which inevitably brought them into contact with Ducky's cousin, Kyril, for whom she still harboured a passion. On returning to Darmstadt, she continued playing a role for the sake of appearances but her heart already belonged to Kyril, and her despair was exacerbated the following year when she allegedly returned home unexpectedly and found Ernie *in flagrante delicto* with one of his male servants.

Queen Victoria, who had specifically requested her charge d'affaires to keep her informed of the goings-on in

[cc] See *Queen Victoria's Granddaughters 1860-1918* by the same author

Hesse, was extremely disturbed to hear that, within two years of their wedding, the couple were living separate lives. At every possible opportunity, Ducky escaped from the Grand Duchy to stay with her relatives across the Continent, and, during her visits to England, she made no secret of her misery but let it be known that her promiscuous husband was fonder of his footmen than he was of his wife.

"The Grand Duchess is most amusing when describing her life in Darmstadt," wrote one of Queen Victoria's ladies-in-waiting, "and her loathing of Germans is quite extraordinary."[164]

The Queen did not find the situation in the least amusing, and when she heard of the extent of their unhappiness she sighed bitterly,

"I got up that marriage. I will never try to marry anyone again."[165]

Nonetheless, for the sake of their child, she refused to even contemplate permitting them to divorce, and the couple were reduced to living separately and bemoaning their fate. In Darmstadt, Ernie continued his duties as Grand Duke, while Ducky, moping in her mother's French villa, pined for her Russian lover.

The only bond that united the couple was their little daughter, Elizabeth; and, in 1899, they attempted a reconciliation in the hope that another child might help to restore their marriage. It was not to be. In spring the following year, Ducky suffered a miscarriage, and, realising that the relationship with Ernie was beyond repair, she left Darmstadt for Coburg. In the summer, she and her Russian cousin, Kyril, continued their supposedly clandestine affair at her mother's Château Fabron in Nice, leaving Ernie free to indulge in his liaisons, undisturbed by the presence of a dissatisfied wife.

It was only after the death of Queen Victoria[dd], that they were finally able to dissolve the sham of their marriage

---

[dd] See Chapter 19

on the grounds of 'invincible mutual apathy'. Despite Ernie's sisters' insistence that he had never wanted a divorce, their chief concern was to prevent any rumours of his alleged homosexuality. His youngest sister, Alix – by then Tsarina of Russia – urged her friends to dismiss any gossip by informing anyone who asked, that the couple had divorced quite simply because they 'did not get on.'

For Ernie, the most distressing aspect of the divorce was the fact that for much of the year he would be separated from his six-year-old daughter. Although the little girl made it clear that she would prefer to stay with her father, it was agreed that she would go to Coburg with Ducky, on the understanding that she could regularly return to Darmstadt. Her visits were sheer delight for Ernie, who loved to watch her playing in the little playhouse that he had created for her in the grounds of his hunting lodge, Wolfsgarten.

In the 'fascinating' gardens of Wolfsgarten with its 'stunted trees and rather sham-looking flowers and grass'[166] beautiful grey-blue-eyed Elizabeth trotted around on a white pony, displaying the equestrian skills she had inherited from her mother; and, there, in the summer of 1903, she entertained her young Russian cousins – Alix's daughters, the Grand Duchesses, Olga, Tatiana, Maria and Anastasia. The little Grand Duchesses looked up to their eight-year-old cousin, who, in turn, took charge of their games, initiating pranks and thoroughly enjoying their company.

"I never saw so sunny a nature;" wrote the Grand Duchesses' nanny, Miss Eagar. "I never saw the child out of temper, nor cross, and should any little dispute arise amongst my four charges, she would settle it with perfect amiability and justice."[167]

When the holiday in Wolfsgarten was over, Elizabeth and Ernie returned with the Russian Imperial Family to the Tsar's hunting lodge in Poland, where the happy games continued and the little girls enjoyed picnics in the autumn sunshine, cycling, and riding in a little carriage drawn by two tame deer.

One Saturday morning in early November, Elizabeth woke with a sore throat, which her English governess, Miss Wilson, believed to be nothing but a minor childhood ailment. Soon, however, Elizabeth felt worse and, after she had been put to bed, a doctor was called who reassured the governess and Ernie that the illness was simply a result of a change of diet and over-excitement.

By evening, she appeared much better, but when Miss Eagar approached the doctor and commented on the improvement, he told her bluntly that there *was* no improvement and the child was dying of heart failure. A shocked Miss Eagar immediately informed Ernie and his sister, the Tsarina, neither of whom could believe the new prognosis. Although Elizabeth's temperature had risen to 104 degrees Fahrenheit, when Ernie took her pulse it felt so strong and regular that he was certain that there was nothing to be alarmed about and he happily went out to the theatre with his sister and brother-in-law.

During their absence, the doctor became so anxious that he requested that a telegram be sent to the theatre, asking the Tsarina's permission to send for a heart specialist from Warsaw. Despite her conviction that he was overreacting, Alix ordered a private train to bring the specialist at once to the hunting lodge. On returning from the theatre, Ernie went straight to Elizabeth's room and was so reassured when she spoke to him brightly that he and the rest of the family retired to bed, leaving the little girl in the care of Miss Wilson and Miss Eagar.

In the middle of the night, the specialist arrived and detecting a 'paralysis of the heart' immediately injected her with camphor and caffeine. For a short while there appeared to be some improvement and the doctor continued to administer regular injections when, suddenly, Elizabeth sat up and called out,

"I'm dying! I'm dying! Send a telegram to Mama immediately!"

Ernie and Alix were sent for, and, as they finally realised the seriousness of her condition, a telegram was sent to Ducky in Coburg.

"We continued to fan the feeble spark of life," wrote Miss Eagar, "but moment by moment it declined. She began to talk to her cousins, and seemed to imagine she was playing with them. She asked for little Anastasie, and I brought the wee thing into the room. The dying eyes rested on her for a moment, and Anastasie said, 'Poor cousin Ella! Poor Princess Elizabeth!' I took the baby out of the room.

"Miss W. was kneeling beside the bed. The dying child turned and kissed her; another minute and her race was accomplished; the bright young life was ended."[168]

The death of his beloved daughter was devastating for Ernie, who had already experienced the tragic deaths of his younger brother, sister and mother. The speed with which Elizabeth's illness had developed made her passing all the more difficult to comprehend, for, only the day before she died, she had been running about happily and playing with her cousins. In order to make sense of what had happened, an autopsy was carried out and the doctors concluded that she contracted a particularly virulent form of typhoid, probably from drinking contaminated water from a stream.

The entire extended family was shocked by the tragedy, and one of the first messages of condolence came in a heartfelt letter from Cousin Willy. Tsar Nicholas ordered a silver coffin and the body was returned to Darmstadt where tearful crowds lined the streets for the funeral procession to the family mausoleum of Rosenhohe.

"It is impossible for me to pass over the sudden and tragic death of that sweet little sunshine," wrote the Kaiser to the Tsar. "...I feel for you all in this sad

225

affair...How joyous and merry she was...so full of life and fun and health...What a terrible heart-rending blow for poor Ernie...who adored that little enchantress!"[169]

To the end of his life, Ernie looked back on the loss of his 'sunshine' with intense sorrow, but it would not be long before he again enjoyed the pleasures of fatherhood. Two years after Elizabeth's death, he found happiness with a new wife, thirty-three-year-old Princess Eleanore (Onor) of Solms-Hohensolms-Lich.

"I am so glad that Ernie has again become engaged," wrote the Kaiser, and he happily accepted an invitation to the wedding in February 1905.

Quieter and less histrionic than Ducky, Onor was a conscientious Grand Duchess who carried out her duties effectively, and willingly adopted the charities founded by Ernie's mother. A year after the wedding, a son, George Donatus, was born, followed two years later by a second boy, Louis. Ernie was a devoted father, and, happy with his loving family, he continued to earn the respect of the people of his Grand Duchy.

Part IV – 'The Full Effect Will Not Be Realised For Some Years'

The Aftermath of the Death of Queen Victoria

Chapter 19 – The Emperor is Very Kind

In the early hours of 22nd June 1897, vast crowds swarmed through London, lining every street from the Buckingham Palace to St. Paul's Cathedral, and at three o'clock in the morning, with barely a space between them, Queen Victoria's loyal subjects were singing the National Anthem at the tops of their voices. Many had walked for miles and were prepared to wait outside all night, simply to catch a glimpse of the spectacle that had been prepared to celebrate Queen Victoria's sixty years on the throne. They were not to be disappointed, for the Diamond Jubilee was to be a colourful extravaganza of Empire, displaying the extent of the Queen's dominions and her position as the Grandmother of Europe.

Weaker than she had been at the Golden Jubilee a decade earlier, she was no longer able to walk the distance of the aisle of Westminster Abbey, so this time, an open air Thanksgiving Service was to be held outside St. Paul's Cathedral so that she could remain in her carriage.

A spectacular procession had been arranged, and the Queen stood at a window to watch as the dragoons, hussars and lancers left the palace and made their way along Constitution Hill. By the time she had descended the stairs to take her place in her carriage, the Life Guards had already arrived at St. Paul's. Behind them came the representatives of the Imperial Service Troops of India, followed by sixteen carriages occupied by the Queen's daughters and granddaughters, who had travelled from as far away as Russia to be present for so special an occasion. Canadian Highlanders, Maltese Militia, Jamaican Artillerymen, Australian Lancers, Dyak Policemen from Borneo, Cypriot Zaptiehs, the Natal Cavalry and the Mounted Police of the Cape of Good Hope were but a few of the numerous representatives of Victoria's mighty Empire who preceded an escort of princes, dressed in their striking uniforms and mounted, three-abreast, on some of the most magnificent horses Londoners had ever seen. Five of the Queen's grandsons took part in the escort: George, Duke of York; Grand Duke Ernie of Hesse; Henry of Prussia; and Christle and Abbie of Schleswig-Holstein.

Watching the proceedings from the roof of Buckingham Palace were Drino Battenberg, and his cousin, Charlie of Albany, who were so engrossed in the display that, when the time came for them to enter their own carriage, they gulped down their breakfasts quickly, and Charlie had to be taken into a St. John's Ambulance to 'be relieved of his hasty meal.'

Noticeable for his absence was the Queen's eldest grandson, Kaiser Wilhelm, whose support for the Turks in the Turko-Greek War had led to his being denied an invitation. To the annoyance of the pro-Greek British, he had not only expressed his hope of a Turkish victory but had also visited Constantinople to view a selection of captured Greek guns, which, according to his grandmother, made the public 'very angry at him'.

Willy was incensed at being excluded from the jubilee celebrations, and was even more furious when his brother, Henry, accepted an invitation to go in his place. In a fit of pique, he took out his anger on his own Reichstag, telling Henry that he could provide him with no better ship for his trip to England than the *Koenig Wilhelm*, because the 'unpatriotic scamps' in the Treasury had refused him greater funds.

The celebrations continued for a fortnight, with galas, balls, receptions and visits, and everywhere the outpouring of affection for the Queen left her feeling, as she told one of her granddaughters, 'very humble.'

The Diamond Jubilee was to be the last great spectacle of the Victorian age, and the years that followed were clouded with grief for the ageing Queen. By the time of Christle death, she had not only outlived three of her children and six of her grandsons but, by then, she knew, too, that her eldest daughter was dying.

Following Willy's accession, his mother had purchased a summer residence in Krönberg in the Taunus Mountains, where she resumed many of her greatest passions: art, gardening, riding, philanthropy and study. Filled with paintings, books and antique furniture, and surrounded by orchards and rose gardens, Schloss Friedrichshof, as she named the house, became a haven in which she could distract herself from the disagreeable goings-on in Berlin. There, among her guests, she entertained Christle's brother, Abbie, and his sister, Thora, who enjoyed games of tennis, while her grandsons played in the gardens.

In September 1899, Vicky was out riding at Krönberg with her youngest daughter, Mossy, when her horse was startled by a threshing machine and threw her to the ground. Although her dress had caught in the saddle and the horse trampled on her hand, she managed to walk back to the house, apparently unharmed. In the weeks that followed, however, she was troubled by persistent backache, which the doctors initially diagnosed as lumbago until eventually it was discovered that she had developed breast cancer which had spread to her spine.

Determined to continue living her life to the full, Vicky initially kept the diagnosis from her family, informing only her faithful chamberlain of the truth while, to everyone else, she maintained the pretence of having nothing more than lumbago. For several months she behaved as though nothing were wrong, even managing to take a holiday in Italy and continuing to entertain her grandchildren. Her mother, however, was unconvinced and discussed the case with her own doctors, who quickly deduced the real cause of Vicky's problems. The distraught Queen clung to the hope that the cancer was operable but, within a matter of weeks, it was obvious that it had spread too quickly to be cured.

By winter 1899, Vicky's pain was so intense that she was forced to stay in bed for long periods and, as she was obviously becoming thinner and paler, it was no longer possible to conceal the truth from her family. Her younger daughters were the first to be told, and eventually she broke the news to the wayward Charlotte, who, despite being sworn to secrecy, lost no time in telling everyone of her mother's condition. Vicky knew there was no alternative but to tell the Kaiser, who, genuinely concerned, went at once to visit her.

Although Willy's intentions were sincere, Vicky, recalling his behaviour during his father's last illness, was determined to disguise the seriousness of her condition. Consequently, not realising the extent of her pain, he ordered the doctors to prescribe less morphine which, he believed, was responsible for keeping her bedridden. Considering the difficulties of their relationship and their years of semi-estrangement, Willy was far more distressed by his mother's illness than she had expected. He visited her regularly and, as long as she steered the conversation away from politics, they were able to enjoy each other's company in a way that had not been possible since his childhood.

In July 1900, news of the death from cancer of her brother, the Duke of Coburg, came as a severe blow to Vicky at a time when her own sufferings were intense.

"Never have the spasms been so frightfully violent as these last days," she wrote shortly afterwards to her daughter. "If somebody had put me out of my misery I should have felt intensely thankful...When will it improve?"[170]

The improvement for which she hoped did not materialise; and, as her hand began to swell, she was forced to remove the wedding ring that had not left her finger in forty-two years. In the cold winter of 1900-1901, her anguish

231

was compounded when she realised that her mother was dying but she was too ill to be with her.

On a bleak December day in 1900, Queen Victoria made her usual crossing to the Isle of Wight to spend Christmas at Osborne. Accompanying her as always was her daughter, Beatrice, and her faithful companion of many years, Jane Churchill. The staff at Osborne, who had not seen the Queen for some time, were immediately struck by the change which had seemed to have come over her. The accumulated sorrows of recent years had taken their toll and the final straw came on Christmas morning when Jane Churchill was found dead in her bed.

The New Year began gloomily and, for the most part, Queen Victoria stayed in her own suite, not even going down to the Dining Room for meals. Within a couple of weeks, her mind was clouded as she rambled to her granddaughter, Thora of Schleswig-Holstein, and, by 17th January her strength had deteriorated so rapidly that members of her family began to gather. One person, though, was consistently excluded from communications about her condition: her eldest grandson, the Kaiser.

The Queen's doctor, Sir James Reid, was acutely aware of this omission as he had always enjoyed a good relationship with Willy, and had agreed to let him know if ever his grandmother were seriously ill. Now, suspecting that the Queen had suffered a stroke, Reid kept his promise and sent a telegram informing him that there was every possibility that she might die. Aware of the hostility he would face from his English aunts, Willy telegraphed 'Uncle Bertie', the Prince of Wales, graciously assuring him that he did not want to cause any trouble but wished only to see his grandmother one more time.

Bertie responded with equal grace, and tactfully agreed to meet his nephew at Buckingham Palace where he told him that the Queen was too ill to receive anyone.

Moreover, he said, if she realised that the Kaiser had come unannounced to see her, she might begin to believe that she was dying.

Bertie and Willy were still in London when, on 20th January, Reid sent a telegram urging them to come to Osborne as soon as possible. The following day, they travelled together to the island where so many other members of the family had gathered that Willy and his cousin, George, Duke of York, did not enter her bedroom but stood on the corridor outside, looking in through the open door. During the night, her breathing became more laboured and by nine-thirty in the morning, her doctors believed the end was imminent. Again, all the family gathered but, as her younger daughters whispered to her, telling her the names of all the relations who were present, they pointedly failed to mention the Kaiser, who was again waiting by the door.

Though wounded by the deliberate omission, Willy remained unobtrusive and, when the Queen rallied a little and the rest of the family dispersed, the kindly Reid sent a message asking if he would like to see her. Willy replied in the affirmative and, when the Prince of Wales' permission had been secured, the doctor took him into the bedroom and sent the maids away.

"'Your Majesty,'" Reid said, "'your grandson, the Emperor is here; he has come to see you as you are so ill,' and she smiled and understood. I went out afterwards and left him with her for five minutes alone. She said to me afterwards, 'The Emperor is very kind.'"[171]

That afternoon, the Queen asked for her little dog, Turi, to be brought to her bed, and soon afterwards she suffered a relapse. At about half-past four, the family again gathered in her bedroom but, this time, Willy was not only included but also given pride of place at her bedside. He remained supporting her head for almost two hours until her death at six-thirty in the evening, 22nd January 1901.

In the days that followed, as preparations were underway for the funeral, Willy's impeccable behaviour endeared him to the British public and to members of the household. Catching sight of a seamstress shivering as she stitched the pall, he immediately ordered a fire to be lit in her room; and over the subsequent days he left more than ten thousand marks in tips for the staff at Osborne and Windsor.

On 27th January, Willy soberly celebrated his forty-second birthday and ordered a fleet of German warships into the Solent to pay tribute to the late Queen. When the funeral preparations had been finalised, he and two of his cousins – Young Arthur of Connaught and Charlie, Duke of Coburg – helped to lift their grandmother's body into her coffin, while another cousin, George, Duke of York, was struck with German measles and no longer able to play any part in the ceremonies.

Five days later, a procession of royal mourners walked from Osborne House to the quay where the Queen's white coffin, draped in a crimson pall, was placed aboard the *Alberta,* and taken back to the mainland amid the sound of booming cannon and the tolling of distant bells.

The next day, Willy and his uncles, Bertie, now King Edward VII, and Arthur, Duke of Connaught, walked behind the coffin through the streets of London in a procession, described by one observer as 'too solemn to be sad'. The cortege was then taken by train from Paddington to Windsor where a gun-carriage was waiting to transport the coffin to St. George's Chapel for the funeral service. The horses pulling the carriage had been standing in the cold for so long that, when they were urged to move, they leaped, breaking loose from the traces, leaving the coffin behind and in danger of rolling back down the hill. Only the quick thinking of the Queen's grandson-in-law, Prince Louis Battenberg, prevented a disaster when he ordered the Royal Naval Guard of Honour to pull the gun-carriage instead. They sailors behaved so professionally that onlookers believed that this had been the intention all along; and, since then, a naval attachment has always played a major role in royal funerals.

According to the Queen's own wishes, the service was simple and included one of her favourite hymns: *I Know That My Redeemer Liveth,* after which her coffin lay in state in the Albert Memorial Chapel before being taken to the Royal Mausoleum at Frogmore, where, following a private service for her family, she was finally laid to rest beside her beloved Albert.

"The full effect of Her Majesty's death," prophesied a journalist for the Irish Times, "will not be realised for some years."

His prophecy was to prove accurate, for, with the death of the 'Grandmother of Europe', the bonds which had held her family together slowly began to fray and, in little more than a decade, brother would fight against brother, and the whole idyll of the European monarchies would be shattered.

Having acquitted himself well at the funeral, Willy returned to Germany to face a series of political disagreements which, combined, with the treatment he had received from his aunts in England, led him to the sad conclusion that he was not a popular monarch. The idea was brought home to him all the more violently when, while visiting Bremen in March, a deranged worker struck him with an iron bar so forcefully that even six months later the scar was clearly visible.

On a personal level, too, Willy faced the emotional trauma of watching his mother dying. The long standing tension in their relationship made the realisation of her imminent death all the more difficult to bear, but, in her final months, Willy did all he could to assure her of his affection.

"I wish I were dead, too!" she had cried when her daughter, Mossy, broke the news to her of the Queen's death.

Wracked with pain, sleepless and increasingly bedridden, she claimed that 'words cannot describe my agony of mind at this overwhelming sorrow,' but she tried to remain optimistic and told her daughter, the Crown Princess of Greece, that she hoped she would soon be well enough to visit.

In the weeks that followed, she was constantly attended by her daughters and daughter-in-law, Irene; and Willy's visits became more frequent as her condition began to deteriorate. It has often been reported that during his consultations with her doctors, Willy cruelly ordered a further reduction in the dosage of morphine, leaving her with insufficient analgesia to ease her pain. Vicky, however, made no mention of this, and her accounts of their relationship at this time, as well as her descriptions of the amounts of morphine she was prescribed, suggest that the story was invented solely to discredit him. At one point, she was being injected with 'morphia' every two hours throughout the night, and various other treatments were also attempted to ease her agony.

"The injections of morphia dull the pains a little for about a quarter of an hour, sometimes not at all, then they rage again with renewed intensity...The electricity does no good, nor poultices (hot), nor ice-bags, nor embrocations, nothing, nothing. It is fearful to endure. My courage is quite exhausted, and this morning I cried for an hour."

Her pain was so intense that even the footmen outside her room asked to be moved to another place as they were unable to endure the sound of her screams.

In late February, only a month after his accession, her brother, Bertie, visited her at Homburg, bringing with him his doctor, Sir Frederick Laking, and his equerry, Fritz Ponsonby. Greeted cordially by Willy at the station, the visitors were taken to the Friedrichshof, where, despite the objections of the German doctors to the intrusion of an English medic, Willy behaved with perfect tact and kindness. Despite their improved relationship, though, Vicky could not forget her son's behaviour following the death of his father and was determined to prevent similar scenes after her own demise. Summoning Ponsonby to visit her privately, she asked him to take her letters back to England with him.

"I know I can rely on your discretion," she said, "and I don't want a soul to know that they have been taken away, and certainly [Willy] must not have them, nor must he know that you have got them."[172]

Ponsonby did as she asked, leaving Vicky reassured that, after her death, her private correspondence and recollections of her life in Germany, would not be destroyed.

For five more months her agony continued until, by the beginning of August, it was clear that she was nearing the end. Having telegraphed the English cleric, Canon Teignmouth-Shore, asking him to come to Friedrichshof, Willy quietly remained by his mother's side for thirty-six unbroken hours. On 5th August, the Canon arrived and, kneeling by Vicky's bed, began the prayers for the sick.

"The dying Empress was at first slightly conscious," he recalled, "and I could see a gentle movement of her lips as we said the Lord's Prayer."[173]

At six o'clock in the evening, he returned to the room where Willy and his sisters were waiting. A charming incident occurred as a butterfly flew in and hovered above Vicky until, as 'the sweet, noble soul' breathed her last, it fluttered and escaped through the open window.

It has often been written that Willy denied his mother's final wish in refusing to allow her coffin to be draped in the British flag, but, in fact, he honoured all her requests: a simple funeral at Krönberg, during which her bier was covered with the Prussian ensign, accompanied by the music of one of her favourite composers, Felix Mendelssohn. Interestingly, too, considering that, throughout her lifetime, she had so often been denied access to Willy's children, his sons played a major part in the funeral service. In the middle of the ceremony, four of them rose from their seats, donned their military helmets and drew their swords to guard each corner of the coffin. Among the numerous wreaths, too, was a black-edged card, signed by each of Willy's seven children.

Apart from her own sons, two other grandsons of Queen Victoria were among the mourners – Ernie of Hesse, and Young Arthur of Connaught – and, when the simple service was complete, they accompanied Vicky's body to Potsdam to be laid to rest beside her beloved Fritz and their young sons, Waldemar and Sigi.

Willy might have attempted to erase from history his father's brief reign, but he did not allow his mother to be forgotten. Two years after her death, he unveiled a large statue of her in her coronation robes, opposite the statue of her husband outside the Brandenburg Gate in Berlin; and, many years later, in his memoirs he wrote:

> "Assuredly my mother was a woman of great gifts, full of ideas and initiative. If, however, she was never quite appreciated as she deserved...I am convinced that history will give her the full recognition that, like so much else, was dirtied in her lifetime."[174]

Chapter 20 – Courtly Platitudes

The Waleses

Bertie – Queen Victoria's eldest son; King Edward VII
Alexandra – Bertie's wife; Queen of Great Britain
George – Duke of York/Prince of Wales; Bertie's son
May – Duchess of York/Princess of Wales; George's wife
Maud – Bertie's youngest daughter

The Hohenzollerns

Willy – Kaiser Wilhelm II; eldest son of Queen Victoria's daughter, Vicky
Henry – Second son of Queen Victoria's daughter, Vicky
Irene – Henry's wife

The Battenbergs

Beatrice – Queen Victoria's youngest child; widow of Prince Henry (Liko) of Battenberg
Drino (Alexander) – Beatrice's eldest son
Leopold – Beatrice's second son
Maurice – Beatrice's youngest son
Ena – Beatrice's daughter

Others

Baby Bee (Beatrice) – Youngest daughter of Queen Victoria's son, Affie, the late Duke of Edinburgh & Coburg

Within a few days of Bertie's return from Friedrichshof in March 1901, his son and daughter-in-law, George and May, embarked on a grand tour of the British Dominions. Travelling aboard the *Ophir,* they crossed the globe, visiting places as far afield as Sumatra, Ceylon, Australia, New Zealand, Canada; and South Africa, where the Boer War was still raging. After performing numerous reviews and presenting many medals, George, now Prince of Wales, was promoted to the rank of General.

The couple returned home in time for the new King's coronation which was set to take place in June 1902. The eighteen month gap between Queen Victoria's death and Bertie being crowned as King Edward VII was due partly to the ongoing Boer War, which was finally concluded with the Treaty of Vereeniging in May that year. The delay gave Bertie time to make detailed preparations for the ceremony, which he hoped would be one of the greatest spectacles of Empire that the country had ever seen.

From the start of his reign, King Edward VII was determined to stamp his own personality on the monarchy. Although he maintained many traditions and insisted on receiving the respect due to his position, his was to be a very different reign from that of his mother. Attendants were allowed to smoke in his presence, and could come and go without seeking his permission. His dealings with advisors and ministers would be far more informal than had been the case in Queen Victoria's time; and, unlike his predecessor, who had so enjoyed seclusion, Bertie loved the limelight and revelled in seeing and being seen by his people.

Within his own homes, the changes were instantly apparent. Hardly had his mother been interred when the palaces were redecorated and all the Queen's mementos of John Brown and the Munshi were hastily removed from sight. More distressing for his sisters, was his decision to rid himself of his mother's beloved Osborne House. He first offered the place to his son, George, who could neither afford its upkeep nor had any desire to own such a stately mansion, before donating it to the nation with the proviso that his late mother's rooms should remain untouched and private.

By the middle of June 1902, the coronation preparations were complete and foreign guests began to arrive in London. Again, as during Queen Victoria's jubilees, the palaces were too full to accommodate all the visiting dignitaries; and Henry of Prussia stayed instead with Viscount Wimborne – a cousin by marriage to Winston Churchill.

Everything was going to plan when suddenly, twelve days before the event, Bertie fell ill, and his doctor, Sir Francis Laking, fearing that he was suffering from appendicitis, advised him to postpone the coronation. Convinced that he was suffering from little more than a chill, and refusing to disappoint the public, Bertie ordered the doctor from the room, telling him that nothing would induce him to change the arrangements. Anxiously, Laking contacted the renowned surgeon, Frederick Treves[ee] – the first English doctor to perform a successful appendectomy. No sooner had Treves examined the King than he told him he would die without immediate surgery, and Bertie was left with no option but to yield to his insistence on a postponement of the coronation.

As the royal guests returned to their homes, the Kaiser sent regular telegrams, asking to be kept informed of his uncle's progress, while George faced the real possibility that his father would die during the operation and he would find himself thrust unexpectedly into the role of monarch. For forty frightening minutes, Bertie's family waited in an adjoining room as Treves carried out the procedure with such skill that, by evening, his patient was sitting up in bed smoking a cigar. During his few weeks' recuperation aboard his yacht, it was left to George to perform many of the duties

---

[ee] Sir Frederick Treves had come to the attention of the then Prince and Princess of Wales when he worked at the London Hospital where he cared for Joseph Merrick, the 'Elephant Man', whom the Princess of Wales visited.

and make the public appearances which his father had planned, as well as assisting in rearranging the coronation.

A new date was set for the event – August 9th 1902 – but many of the foreign guests, whose diaries were prepared months in advance, were unable to return to London. The Kaiser's brother, Henry, was there, however and was most put out to find himself seated at the back of the Abbey during the ceremony.

In spite of the postponement, the colourful procession to Westminster Abbey was all that Bertie had dreamed it would be, but, once inside, it was clear that the stress of the occasion was taking its toll on the eighty-year-old Archbishop of Canterbury, Frederick Temple. He faltered so much that observers feared he was about to faint, and when a fellow bishop attempted to help him he angrily replied that, although his legs might be weak, there was nothing wrong with his head. After kneeling to pay homage to the King, he was unable to stand up again, but Bertie graciously leaned forwards to help him to his feet. George, Prince of Wales, followed the tradition of touching the crown and kissing his father's cheek, and the King responded by clasping him affectionately in his arms.

His father's accession had significantly altered George's position, since, as heir to the throne, he would be expected to perform more royal and ceremonial duties. For three years, therefore, he lived quietly in England, pursuing his two greatest passions – stamp collecting and shooting – and developing an interest in agriculture, including stocking rare breeds of Red Poll cattle and Berkshire pigs.

Ironically, despite his love of the sea and his enjoyment of the years he had spent in the Royal Navy, George disliked travelling abroad and had little interest in meeting 'more foreigners' so he was not initially overjoyed when, in 1905, his father decided it was time for another tour. His previous tour of the Dominions had not included a visit to India, and the King felt it was time to rectify this omission. That autumn, George and May set out on a six month tour of the subcontinent where, to George's delight, the itinerary included a good deal of hunting and shooting.

Following the success of the Indian tour, further trips were arranged and, over the next five years, George would return to Canada as well as journeying across Europe for holidays with his mother's Danish family; visits to his cousins, Tsar Nicholas of Russia and Kaiser Wilhelm of Germany; and attending various royal celebrations including the coronation of his youngest sister, Maud, as Queen Consort of Norway; and the marriage of his cousin, Ena of Battenberg, and King Alfonso XIII of Spain;

The death of her mother had left Queen Victoria's youngest daughter, Beatrice, in something of a vacuum. Since the age of four, her entire life had revolved around serving the Queen, and even after her marriage she had placed her mother's needs above those of her own children. Now with her brother's accession, she found herself out of place with no specific role to play in a modern court; and, to add to her woes, she had been ousted from her favourite home, Osborne House, and provided instead with the far smaller Osborne Cottage.

The death of their grandmother had an equally profound effect on Beatrice's children. Living in such close proximity to the Queen, they had assumed a special place in the family, and Drino in particular viewed himself as a person of great significance. With their uncle's accession, the proverbial pecking order changed dramatically and the former favourites found themselves in a rather inferior position.

After a suitable period of mourning, Beatrice realised that it was time to rebuild her life by creating experiences and adventures which would not have been possible during her mother's lifetime. In December 1903, she decided to escape from a dreary English winter to the warmer climes of Egypt and Sudan, taking with her, her daughter, Ena; her second son, the fourteen-year-old haemophiliac, Leopold; and her niece, 'Baby Bee' of Edinburgh and Coburg. Her eldest son, seventeen-year-old Drino, joined them soon after their arrival at the Cataract Hotel, Aswan, where Beatrice informed the manager, Herr Steiger that her children were to be treated no differently from any other guests. Herr Steiger agreed to her request but he could not resist making Christmas Day special for her children; and, as the family sat down to dinner, the lights were suddenly extinguished and white-clad, turbaned attendants entered by candlelight, carrying trays of gifts for the young princess and princes.

The four month stay was filled with adventures, from camel rides and Nile cruises to a visit to the Red Sea; journeys in the luxurious train of Khedive Abbas II; a guided tour of the Pyramids by the Inspector of Antiquities, Howard Carter; and participation in various archaeological digs during which Drino, Leopold, Ena and Baby Bee were lowered on ropes down a mine.

Returning home in late April, the family stayed in Baby Bee's mother's Château Fabron in Nice, which had become a haven for Baby Bee's sister, Ducky, recently released from her unhappy marriage to her cousin, Grand Duke Ernie of Hesse.

Three years later, Drino, Leopold and their younger brother, Maurice, set out for what was to become a far more frightening expedition to Madrid for the marriage of their sister, Ena, to the rakish Spanish King. That the wedding was to take place at all was something of a miracle since numerous objections had been raised from the moment that King Alfonso proposed. His mother felt that the mere 'Serene Highness', Ena, descended from the less than royal blood of the Battenbergs, was unworthy of her son; while in England there was such vociferous opposition to Ena's conversion to Catholicism, that Cousin George, Prince of

Wales, advised her mother to keep her out of sight in Osborne Cottage for a while.

Nonetheless, the challenges were eventually surmounted and the wedding was arranged for May 31st 1906. On May 24th, the Battenberg brothers set out with their mother and sister from Dover to Calais where they boarded a night train bound for Spain. Numerous other royal relations were also en route to the wedding, including Cousin George and his wife, May, representing the King; and Cousins Henry and Irene of Prussia, representing the Kaiser. At dawn the train crossed the Spanish border where the chain-smoking groom was waiting to greet his bride at the first Spanish station. The Battenbergs were taken to the El Pardo Palace in Madrid, where, despite the countless complaints from other royal guests about the heat and the dust, they were treated with great deference and kindness.

After a week of tours, celebrations and visits, the wedding day finally dawned. The brothers donned their distinctive uniforms – Drino in the ceremonial uniform of the Royal Navy; Leopold in the Stuart tartan of the Scotch Highlanders; and Maurice also in the Highlanders' uniform but, in his case, wearing a kilt – and preceded their sister into the magnificent Church of St. Hieronimo. As they walked down the aisle, bowing to all the dignitaries, their smartness and bearing made a striking impression on the congregation.

"No princes, young or old," wrote one observer, "showed more self-possession, more alertness, more manliness or more courtliness than these young boys."[175]

The lengthy and impressive ceremony passed without incident and, shortly before midday, the boom of a canon announced that the bride and groom were leaving the church. Ahead of them, in descending order of precedence, a procession of princes and ambassadors began the short journey to the palace. Leopold and Maurice travelled in the Semi-Gala Carriage, followed by Drino and his late father's sister, Princess Marie of Erbach-Shönberg, in a State Carriage. Several carriages later came Henry of Prussia in the Coach of the Ducal Crown; then George and May in the Gala Carriage, second only to the mothers of the bride and groom, before the newly-wed King and Queen.

The procession, surrounded by cheering crowds, moved slowly along the Calle Mayor when suddenly, for no apparent reason, Alfonso and Ena's coach stopped. In that moment, a bomb, hidden in a bouquet of flowers fell in front of the carriage, exploding on impact and blowing to pieces the King's equerry, several footmen and numerous bystanders.

> "Great chunks were literally gouged out of huge granite blocks in nearby buildings," a witness recalled, "and people on balconies where safety seemed absolute, met instant death."[176]

Having so narrowly escaped assassination, the young King leaped from the carriage to discover the extent of the devastation, before returning to his wife, who sat rigid in horror with her wedding dress splattered with blood. Alfonso helped her from the carriage and sent word at once to her mother and brothers that she was unharmed, before leading her to an alternative coach to continue more quickly to the palace.

Although none of the guests had been injured, the day's celebrations could not continue as planned, and, instead Ena and Alfonso spent the afternoon visiting the wounded and courageously appearing in public again in an open carriage. Eight days of festivities had been arranged and, after much deliberation, it was decided that events would continue as planned except that there would be no music or dancing.

As the assassin[ff] had yet to be apprehended, an atmosphere of fear pervaded the palaces, and George, Prince

---

[ff] When, eventually, Mateo Morral, the would-be assassin was arrested, he succeeded in killing a guard, who was taking him to prison, before

of Wales, irked his hosts by repeatedly cursing the police for their ineptitude. George irritated his hosts, too, by refusing to join the other guests at a bullfight, in order to make the point that the English considered such a 'sport' cruel. His stand might have won him greater respect had he not shot such a multitude of creatures during his many tours of the Empire.

At the turn of the century, George was not the only one of Queen Victoria's grandsons to cross the Atlantic, for, in late February 1902, the other 'sailor prince', Henry of Prussia, embarked on a tour of North America. The primary purpose of his trip was to witness the launch of the Kaiser's new yacht, *Meteor*gg., which Willy had ordered the previous year from the Townsend and Downey Shipbuilding Company on Shooter Island. A considerable number of German immigrants eagerly awaited his arrival and, by the time his ship, the *Kronprinz Wilhelm,* reached New York, large crowds had gathered, lining the route all the way from the harbour to the German Embassy. Later that morning, Henry journeyed to Washington for lunch at the White House with President Roosevelt, and despite the President's refusal to accede to the German Ambassador's request that a Hohenzollern Prince should take precedence and enter the dining room first, the meal passed off cordially. At midnight Henry and the Roosevelts returned by train to New York where, the following day, the President's daughter, Alice, officially launched the *Meteor.* Again, despite a lapse in protocol which led to the launch being made with French rather than German champagne, Henry's tact and affability endeared him to the Americans.

---

killing himself.

gg Despite its propitious launch, the *Meteor* did not quite live up to the Kaiser's expectations in international races; and just seven years later, it was sold to a renowned German chemist of Kiel University, Carl Dietrich Harries.

Over the next fortnight, he carried out a whirlwind tour of various states, including visits to Pennsylvania, Tennessee, Ohio, Kentucky, Indiana, Wisconsin, New Jersey, and Chicago, where the aforementioned visit to the Everleigh Club took place. After visiting the Niagara Falls, he crossed the border to spend a day in Canada at the express invitation of his uncle, King Edward VII; and one of the highlights of his tour was a visit to the United States Military Academy at West Point.

Henry performed so well and behaved with such tact that his brother, the Kaiser, was delighted by the improvement in relations between Berlin and Washington. By the time that he left the United States on 10th March 1902, he had made such an excellent impression on his American hosts that several English newspapers printed sombre letters, warning the Americans not to be taken in by 'courtly platitudes' of the Kaiser's representative, for, by then, relations between England and Germany were beginning to deteriorate rapidly.

Chapter 21 – Mad, Mad, Mad as March Hares

The English Royal Family

Bertie – King Edward VII
Alexandra – Consort of Edward VII
George – eldest son of Edward VII; King George V
May – George's wife
Toria (Victoria) – George's sister

Others

Willy – Kaiser Wilhelm II; son of Queen Victoria's daughter, Vicky
Henry – Willy's younger brother
Charlie – Duke of Coburg; only son of Queen Victoria's son, Leopold
Ernie – Grand Duke of Hesse; son of Queen Victoria's daughter, Alice
Young Arthur – Prince of Connaught; son of Queen Victoria's son, Arthur
Abbie (Albert) – Prince of Schleswig-Holstein; son of Queen Victoria's daughter, Lenchen
Drino (Alexander) – Prince of Battenberg; son of Queen Victoria's daughter, Beatrice

Kaiser Wilhelm had always loved and felt loved by his grandmother, and, regardless of his occasional ungracious comments about her interference, he had always known that she respected his position as Emperor. Indeed, on occasions she had even cited him to his Uncle Bertie as a good example of marital fidelity and commitment to his country – statements which, undoubtedly, grated on Bertie's nerves.

Uncle and nephew could not have been more dissimilar, and it was almost inevitable that Queen Victoria's death and Bertie's accession would lead to a deterioration of relations between Britain and Germany. To Bertie, Willy was an upstart who had 'not learned to control his rather unruly tongue'; his bombastic speeches and military displays were arrogant and incendiary; and, most important of all, Bertie could not forget the way that he had treated his parents.

For his part, Willy saw Bertie as the epitome of self-indulgence, who had not only shocked Berlin society by his numerous adulterous affairs, but had also accrued debts which were often settled by unscrupulous bankers, leaving him beholden to men whose personal ambition far exceeded their concern for the welfare of the country. According to one of King Edward's mistresses, 'the Kaiser chafed at his uncle's association with a financier whose reputation was only too well known', for Willy feared that his uncle's opinions were being swayed by those industrialists and bankers who could benefit from creating friction between London and Berlin.

Despite their mutual dislike, they attempted to display a certain solidarity in public, and there were times when Bertie conceded that Willy behaved very well. He appreciated, for example, Willy's behaviour at the time of his grandmother's death; and he was grateful for the Kaiser's expressed support for the British during the Boer War, even though the majority of Germans were fiercely on the side of the Boers. Such was the strength of feeling that:

> "At every concert, in the course of every theatrical performance and on every possible pretext, opportunity was taken to say hostile things about England and to mock the British generals in Africa."[177]

The Kaiser and the King's attempts to conceal their antagonism, however, were largely unsuccessful and rumours abounded about how much they despised one another. Willy referred to his uncle as 'Satan', and gossips falsely claimed that on one occasion while the Kaiser was visiting Windsor, his remarks so annoyed his uncle that he actually struck him. The story had no foundation whatsoever, but it was used by the press to whip up anti-German feeling in Britain.

At the time of Queen Victoria's death, Willy had been very popular in England but, within a few years of his uncle's accession, opinions were rapidly changing, as to British minds, Willy was coming to symbolise an increasingly bellicose Germany.

The press presented the Kaiser as alternatively a buffoon or a warlord. His fondness for practical jokes was used to demonstrate both his childishness and his cruelty. It was said that, when he shook hands, he turned his sharp rings around on his fingers so that they would dig into the flesh of the one he was greeting. It was also widely– and accurately – reported that he once, for a joke, slapped Ferdinand of Bulgaria on the bottom, which prompted the self-styled Tsar to leave Berlin in disgust. More damaging, however, were the reports of the bellicose statements of his Generals, which created the myth that, like a latter day Napoleon, the ambitious Kaiser, was secretly plotting to conquer the whole of Europe.

Suspicions about Willy's intentions were increased by popular novelists of the day, several of whom portrayed the Kaiser as a megalomaniac, cunningly planning England's downfall. William Le Queux's 1909 novel *Spies of the Kaiser,* for example, contained such inflammatory chapter titles as '*How the Germans are Preparing for Invasion'* and '*The German Plot Against England'*. The mistrust aroused by such stories was mirrored by those Members of Parliament who were watching the development of the German Navy with mounting alarm. Convinced that the 'Kaiserliche Marine' threatened Britain's domination of the seas, the Foreign Secretary, Edward Grey, told Parliament:

"A new situation is created by the German [shipbuilding] programme. When it is completed,

Germany, a great country close to our own shores, will have a fleet of thirty-three Dreadnoughts, and that fleet will be the most powerful which the world has ever yet seen. It imposes upon us the necessity of rebuilding the whole of our fleet. That is the situation."

Willy, however, with some justification, claimed only to want 'a place in the sun' – colonies such as those which Britain, Spain, France and Belgium already possessed. He was inordinately proud of his Imperial Navy but, while he earnestly wanted Germany to be perceived as Britain's equal, he was desperate to assure the British people that his greatest wish was for peace between the two nations.

'I have always felt at home in this lovely country,' he told listeners at the Guildhall in 1891. 'Moreover the same blood runs in English and German veins.'[178]

It was a theme to which he would repeatedly return over the next two decades, frequently reminding his hearers that he was honoured to be Queen Victoria's grandson; but, when the British Parliament and press continued to portray him as a warlord, he became increasingly exasperated, culminating in an explosive interview published by the Daily Telegraph in 1908.

The previous summer, Willy had spent some days at the home of General Stuart Wortley, Highcliffe Castle in Dorset. While there, the two men had chatted informally, and, afterwards, Wortley had informed a journalist named Spender of the content of their conversation. Wortley and Spender decided that what Willy had said could be published in the Daily Telegraph in the form of an interview. They created a manuscript, which they forwarded to the Kaiser, asking if he would consent to its publication. Believing that the interview would help to ameliorate Anglo-German relations, he was very much in favour of the idea, and sent the document to his Chancellor, Prince von Bulow, to seek his opinion. Von Bulow saw no reason why it should not be published, and Willy, therefore, told Wortley to go ahead with his idea. The article appeared in the Daily Telegraph in the autumn of 1908:

"You English are mad, mad, mad as March hares," it reported Willy as saying. "What has come over you that you are so completely given over to suspicions quite unworthy of a great nation? What more can I do than I have done? I declared with all the emphasis at my command that my heart is set upon peace. I am a friend of England, [yet] your press bids the people of England refuse my proffered hand and insinuates that the other holds a dagger."[179]

Rather than assuaging British fears as Willy had hoped, the article created such furore both in Britain and in Germany that Willy came close to suffering a complete nervous breakdown. In a series of heated debates, the Reichstag dragged up every mistake that he had made throughout his twenty-year reign; and the press printed article after article, portraying him as incompetent and dangerous.

Willy returned to Potsdam and took to his bed in a state of utter abjection. His eldest son visited him there, and found him looking aged and weary:

"…he had lost hope and felt himself to be deserted by everybody; he was broken down by the catastrophe, which had snatched the ground from beneath his feet; his self-confidence and his trust were shattered."[180]

Willy never fully recovered from the blow, and those who were closest to him observed that from then on he was far less outspoken and sure of himself, and far more willing to yield to the views of his ministers.

The exasperation which had led him to allow the publication of the interview was, however, understandable. During his grandmother's reign, the bond between Britain and Germany had seemed unbreakable, but, with the accession of Edward VII everything had changed. Deeply hurt that his uncle had given Osborne House to the nation, it appeared to Willy that the new King intended to disregard all that the Queen had wanted, including the fulfilment of Prince Albert's dream of a strong Anglo-German relationship.

As Germany was rapidly becoming the greatest industrial and trading power in Europe, the British were concerned that their own trading interests were being threatened, and the King himself had personally pressed for closer ties with Russia, and Germany's archenemy, France. In 1904, the signing of the *Entente Cordiale* between Britain and France, seemed like a betrayal to the Kaiser, whose own attempts at appeasing the French had backfired when they insisted that relations with Germany could never improve until the Germans left Alsace-Lorraine.

"I have often held out my hand to France;" Willy told friend, "[but] she has only replied with kicks."[181]

In his mind, there was an inescapable connection between Uncle Bertie's penchant for French prostitutes and his love of Parisian society, and the seemingly adulterous relationship between France and Britain. Queen Victoria would, he believed, have been horrified to witness such strained relations between England and Germany.

The political and diplomatic shenanigans aimed at isolating Germany were in many ways the out-picturing of Willy's own sense of isolation. He had often watched with envy as his English and Russian relations holidayed together in Denmark, but, much as he longed to join them, he never received an invitation. Nor could he forget the treatment he received from his aunts when he came to visit his dying grandmother.

For Willy, there seemed little hope of restoring strong bonds between Britain and Germany during his uncle's reign, but King Edward VII, already obese and frequently plagued by bronchitis, could not live forever and Willy had every reason to believe that his successor would be more amenable. His relationship with Cousin George had always been cordial, despite his annoyance that George yielded to his father when he told him to cancel a planned visit to Berlin for Willy's birthday in 1904, on the grounds that he might be insulted. They maintained a casual friendship and it seemed to Willy that, when George eventually succeeded his father, good relations between their two countries would be restored.

In the spring of 1910, while his wife, Queen Alexandra, embarked on a Mediterranean cruise, King Edward VII set out for Biarritz via Paris, accompanied by his latest mistress, Alice Keppel. Already exhausted by a series of political crises, he stopped en route in Paris to visit a theatre, where the lack of ventilation exacerbated his chronic bronchitis. By the time he reached his destination, he felt far from well but he made the most of his holiday, even taking the opportunity to visit the Roman Catholic shrine of Lourdes where, fifty-two years earlier, a peasant girl, Bernadette Soubirous, claimed to have witnessed a vision of the Virgin Mary. If he hoped for a cure in Lourdes, he was to be disappointed; and, by the time he returned to London, observers were struck by how ill he appeared. Determined to continue as though nothing were wrong, he attended a performance of *Rigoletto,* at Covent Garden, and when the opera was complete, a witness noticed that he rose and:

"...opened the door of the box, lingered for a little in the doorway, with a very sad expression on his face...took a last look at the house as if to bid it farewell, and went out."[182]

The first week of May was particularly cold and damp that year, and, over the next couple of days, as his coughing bouts became more frequent, his anxious doctors urged him to rest. When he pointedly ignored their advice, his friends were so worried about him that they telegraphed Queen Alexandra, who had, by then, arrived in Calais on her homeward journey.

Realising the seriousness of the situation, George immediately took charge of the necessary arrangements. Before setting out with his two eldest sons to meet his mother at Victoria Station, he threw the household into confusion by sending an order that the Queen must be allowed to enter the palace quietly through a back door. The King, however, had already sent a contradictory order insisting that everything should continue as usual and therefore the household should gather to welcome her home.

That evening, 5th May, witnesses at the station were perplexed as to why the Prince of Wales had come in place of his father to meet the Queen's train; and as rumours that the King was seriously ill began to spread, George realised it was necessary to issue a bulletin stating that King Edward was suffering from bronchitis which was causing *some* concern.

By the following morning, seeing that his father was obviously deteriorating, George arranged for a further bulletin to be issued, this time stating that there was *grave* concern. For the first time, the public understood the precariousness of the situation and began to gather outside Buckingham Palace, waiting for news.

Waiting, too, with trepidation was George, who spent the afternoon going in and out of the room where his father sat in a chair, gasping for breath and drifting in and out of consciousness. At five o'clock in the evening, a third bulletin announced that King's condition was now critical. He was eventually lifted on to his bed and, at his request, Mrs Keppel was summoned to say her final farewell. With extraordinary grace, Queen Alexandra complied with her husband's wish that she should kiss his mistress, who was then led wailing and screaming from the room. A few hours later, shortly before midnight on 6th May 1910, the sixty-eight-year-old King breathed his last. He had waited almost a lifetime to ascend to the throne but had reigned for only nine years.

So reluctant was Queen Alexandra to part with her husband, that it would be eight days before his body was placed in a coffin, and a further six days before the funeral took place. Throughout that time, George was busily signing proclamations and responding to the countless messages of condolence from all over the world, while liaising with his aides to prepare a dignified funeral.

For the first time, it was agreed that the monarch's body should lie in state, and so, on the morning of May 16th, his coffin was taken to Westminster Hall where a short service was held before the doors were opened to the public. During the next thirty-eight hours, over a hundred-and-fifty-thousand people silently filed past the catafalque, while fellow monarchs and foreign princes arrived from all over the world.

No fewer than nine sovereigns were present at the funeral, and none was accorded greater deference than the German Kaiser. Shortly before nine o'clock on Friday 20th May, he accompanied Bertie's widow, son and daughter, Toria, to Westminster Hall to watch the coffin being placed on the gun-carriage which would take it to the Abbey. In the procession that followed, Willy and George rode alongside the late King's sole surviving brother, the Duke of Connaught, immediately behind Bertie's devoted dog, Caesar, who poignantly followed the coffin. Behind George and Willy, rode the Kings of Norway, Greece, Spain, Bulgaria, Denmark, Portugal and Belgium; and the heirs to the thrones of Turkey, Austria-Hungary, Roumania, Montenegro and Serbia. Participating, too, on horseback were six more of Queen Victoria's grandsons: Henry of Prussia, representing the German navy; Charlie, Duke of Coburg; Ernie, Grand Duke of Hesse; Young Arthur of Connaught; Abbie of Schleswig-Holstein; and Drino Battenberg. Not since Queen Victoria's Jubilee had there been such a gathering of royal relations, and, as virtually every country had sent representatives to pay their respects, for one day, at least, the world appeared to be united.

King George V's accession came at a time of great political turmoil. Parliament was in disarray about the so-called 'People's Budget', and differences of strongly-held opinions about Irish Home Rule. Across the country, too, socialism was gaining ground; and the suffragettes were becoming increasingly militant in their efforts to secure votes for women.

While George struggled to deal with the immense amount of paperwork requiring his attention each day, tension was also brewing within his own household. Contrary to expectation, he allowed his mother and sister to remain in their beloved Sandringham House, while he and his family continued to reside in the cramped York Cottage. It had been difficult enough for his staff to find room to work when he was Prince of Wales, but now that he was King, his household naturally expanded and equerries found themselves struggling for space in nurseries where children were playing. When one member of the household complained that it was 'absurd that a large house like Sandringham should be inhabited by an old lady and her daughter while the tiny York Cottage should have to accommodate a married man with a family of six, more especially when that man happened to be the King', George angrily responded by asking 'what the devil it had to do with him'.[183]

Meanwhile, plans were underway for two coronations – the first as King of Great Britain and her Dominions, and the second as Emperor of India. In June 1911, with due solemnity and pageantry, George was crowned in Westminster Abbey, and during the procession which followed, his cousin Young Arthur of Connaught, a twenty-eight-year-old captain in the Royal Scots Greys played a prominent role, riding beside his father. It was a particular pleasure for Young Arthur to be at his father's side, for shortly afterwards the Duke, together with his wife and younger daughter, Patsy, would leave England for Canada where he was to take over as Governor General.

Present, too, in the coronation procession, was Willy's eldest son, the Crown Prince of Germany, who sensed that already relations between the two countries had improved.

"Everywhere we met with the most friendly personal reception...The reception accorded me and my wife by all classes of the population was exceptionally cordial. The English press also welcomed us warmly."[184]

All was not quite so harmonious, though, for he observed that, as numerous foreign battlecruisers gathered in the Solent to honour the new King, the British sea captains showed an excessive interest in Germany's *Von der Tann*; and, during a conversation with the Foreign Secretary, Edward Grey, when the Crown Prince spoke of his hope of greater co-operation between the two countries, he was somewhat rudely rebuffed.

George, meanwhile, was preparing for his journey to India. Six months after the coronation in Westminster Abbey, he and May set sail for Delhi, where the Durbar – his official coronation as Emperor– was to take place. After five days of audiences with Indian princes, George was crowned on 12th December in a spectacular outdoor ceremony attended by more than a quarter of a million people.

Returning to England, he resumed his rather humdrum routine of rising early, taking a ride with his daughter and attending to his correspondence, before breakfasting with May. Much of the rest of the morning and early afternoons were taken up with meetings with ministers and equerries, followed by a daily visit to his mother, and pursuing his interest in shooting and philately. Since his time in Malta, when his Uncle Affie first introduced him to the subject, George had developed such a passion for stamp collecting that he was widely viewed as an expert, and, when an elderly widow was offered fifty pounds for her late husband's album, she wrote to the King to seek his advice. On seeing the collection, George realised that it was far more valuable than she had been led to believe, and, eager to obtain one particularly rare Bahamian stamp, he advised her to put it up for auction. The widow followed his advice, and George sent an aide to bid on his behalf. Some days later, an equerry phoned him and asked, "Did you happen to see…that some damned fool had given as much as £1,400 for one stamp?"

"I was the damned fool," George replied.

George's passion for stamps contrasted sharply with his late father's love of spectacle and show; and in the early years of his reign, his apparent dullness made him far less popular than his immediate predecessors had been. Unlike his father, he was neither a showman nor prepossessing in appearance; and his domestic life in pokey York Cottage was viewed as so bourgeois that journalists were unable to find any sensational stories with which to fill their newspaper columns. In the absence of scandal, the republican press resorted to invention. George, they said, was 'a man of intemperate habits', or, more dangerously, he had secretly married while stationed in Malta, and consequently his marriage to May was bigamous. George was so incensed by the 'damnable lie' that, on the advice of the Home Secretary, Winston Churchill, he sued the newspaper editor, Edward Mylius for criminal libel, resulting in a guilty verdict and a twelve month imprisonment.

Chapter 22 – The Sport of Kings

Hohenzollerns & Hessians

Willy – Kaiser Wilhelm II; German Emperor; eldest son of Queen Victoria's eldest daughter, Vicky
Dona – Kaiserin Augusta Victoria; Willy's wife
Henry - eldest son of Queen Victoria's eldest daughter, Vicky
Ernie – Grand Duke of Hesse-Darmstadt; son of Queen Victoria's second daughter, Alice

English Princes & Families

Edward VII – (Bertie) Queen Victoria's eldest son
Alexandra – Queen of Britain; wife of Edward VII
George – King George V of Britain; son of Edward VII
May – Queen Mary; wife of George V
Eddy – Duke of Clarence & Avondale; late son of Edward VII
Maurice – Prince of Battenberg
Christle – Christian Victor of Schleswig-Holstein; elder son of Queen Victoria's third daughter, Lenchen
Abbie – Albert of Schleswig-Holstein; younger son of Queen Victoria's third daughter, Lenchen

George was not the only one of Queen Victoria's grandsons to passionately pursue a hobby. Although much of their time was occupied with royal and military duties, several of the princes followed their interests so enthusiastically that they became experts in various fields. In an age of new inventions and rapid advances in medicine, the royal families were also at the forefront of innovation and were often among the first to receive new treatments. As far back as 1721, the Princess of Wales had been the first member of the royal family to have her children inoculated against small pox; and, in 1853, Queen Victoria aroused criticism for accepting chloroform during the birth of her eighth child. Until then, many women heeded the warnings of churchmen who claimed that, according to scripture, women should suffer in childbirth, but the Queen's use of a chloroform gave a royal stamp of approval to anaesthesia.

Five years later, Queen Victoria was at the forefront of communications when she sent the first transatlantic telegram to the United States' President Buchanan; and, in 1876, after meeting the inventor, Alexander Graham Bell, she had a telephone line installed between Buckingham Palace and Osborne House to make the first overseas call.

Queen Victoria was also the first British monarch to travel by train at a time when some doctors feared that the speed of that mode of transport might have a detrimental effect on the body. Her son, Edward VII, was the first to attend an official function by motor car; and the world's first airmail service was employed in celebration of George V's coronation.

Travelling at speed had a particular appeal for Willy and Henry of Prussia. Willy, who had a passion for yacht racing, devised the rules of the Kiel competition, and participated with equal enthusiasm in the Cowes Regatta and other British races, despite the sometimes unsporting response of his English hosts. When, for example, in 1896, his yacht, *Meteor II*, beat the *Britannia* in the Queen's Cup, the English spectators were so disgruntled by the sight of the Prussian ensign that they refused to cheer the winner. The following year, Willy behaved more graciously when the *Britannia* regained the title; and, in 1905, he organised the first transatlantic race for American as well as English and German vessels. So excited was he about the prospect of a German victory in the race between Sandy Hook in New Jersey and the Lizard Peninsular in England, that he personally provided the solid gold Kaiser's Cup, and travelled to New York to see his own vessel, *Hamburg*, some weeks before the contest began. Despite his optimism, the American *Atlantic* won the cup, with the *Hamburg* coming in a close second.

Naturally, Willy's sailor brother, Henry, was a fellow yachting enthusiast but, in 1903, his love of sailing was surpassed by his passion for a new mode of transport.

"It will, I am sure, interest you to hear," he wrote to a friend, "that since two years I have become a most passionate motorist & that I almost prefer motoring to yachting."[185]

Even as a child, Henry had enjoyed dismantling and designing mechanical devices and now he turned his hand to designing automobile accessories. He is credited with having invented the first windscreen wiper, and is said to have also designed the first motor horn. In 1910, he organised a series of trials for the Vauxhall Motor Company, in return for which the owners named one of their most distinctive models in his honour. The following year, he organised a race between Hamburg and London; and, while in England, made a point of visiting the Brooklands motorcycle racetrack in Surrey, where he spoke with the competitors and tested one of the bikes. Willy was also smitten by the motor car, and, in 1907, he established the forerunner of the German Grand Prix – the Kaiserpreis.

Motor racing became such an obsession for wealthy young men that, with or without a racetrack, they competed at every opportunity. In 1914, when Maurice Battenberg was stopped for speeding along Hampton Court Road, he told the arresting officer:

"You fellows are always out trapping on race days!"

Neither his quip nor his royal status protected him from the law, and after receiving a summons, he was given a £3 fine for breaking the twenty-miles-an-hour speed limit.

In the early years of the 20th century, Henry also became a devotee of the new aeroplanes. He had followed with interest the work of the American Wright brothers, and was intrigued to hear of Louis Blériot's first flight across the English Channel. Unsurprisingly, it was not long before he learned to pilot his own plane, impressing fellow enthusiasts by travelling thirty miles in forty minutes before being forced to land due to engine trouble.

As new and faster forms of transport were introduced, it was inevitable that there would also be several disasters. In 1908, Orville Wright was injured and his passenger, Lieutenant Selfridge, was killed, when his plane engine failed; and, in February 1912, crowds of Parisians were horrified to witness the death of a tailor who jumped from the top of the Eiffel Tower to demonstrate the effectiveness of his new parachute, which tragically failed to open. The most famous disaster of the 20th century occurred just two months later when the White Star Line's 'unsinkable' *Titanic* struck an iceberg and sank in the North Atlantic.

News of the sinking reached King George V on the 15th April, and, although it would be some time before the full extent of tragedy was apparent, it was immediately obvious that this was one of the worst sea disasters that the country had ever known. When George was told that over one-thousand-five-hundred lives had been lost, he felt impelled to issue a formal message of condolence:

> "The Queen and I are horrified at the appalling disaster which has happened to the Titanic and at the terrible loss of life. We deeply sympathise with the bereaved relations and feel for them in their great sorrow with all our heart."

Abbie of Schleswig-Holstein and Maurice of Battenberg had a more direct connection with the disaster, since they were acquainted with two of the ship's passengers, the famous couturier, 'Lucille', and her husband, the Scottish landowner and sportsman, Sir Cosmo Duff Gordon. As details of *Titanic's* last moments emerged, it was apparent that the majority of the dead were Third Class passengers, begging the question of how so many women and children could have died when wealthy male passengers survived. Sir Cosmo, like many of his class, was accused of cowardice and of bribing the rescuers to secure a place in the lifeboat, while his wife was accused of ordering the oarsmen to row to safety, disregarding the desperate screams of the drowning women and children. The scandal was so great that the Duff Gordons could not appear in public without being jeered, and, day after day, newspaper headlines described them as callous cowards.

Abbie and Maurice stood by their friends, attending the Board of Trade's official inquiry in early May 1912, during which the Duff Gordons adamantly denied the allegations. Although they were eventually cleared of the charges, their reputations had suffered so badly that the incident would continue to haunt them to the end of their lives.

An unlikely early proponent of motoring at a time when few people believed that 'horseless carriages' had a future, was Ernie of Hesse, whose primary interests were more artistic than technological. Since inheriting the Grand Duchy in 1894, he had modernised the New Palace, gradually redecorating several rooms in the ultra-modern Art Nouveau style, but it was at his quaint hunting lodge, Wolfsgarten, that he gave full vent to his artistic imagination.
"In some of the rooms," wrote one bemused visitor, "the walls were a deep blue with green woodwork and red furniture; in others, gold carved doors and marble walls. The furniture was of the weirdest shape and descriptions."[186]
Ernie's innovations were not solely for his own enjoyment. Like his grandfather, Prince Albert, he recognised the benefits of combining art and technology to prosper industry and trade. In 1899, he founded the Darmstadt Artists' Colony – a community of painters,

sculptors, craftsmen and designers who produced work which would not only improve the quality of life for the Hessians, but also create trade links to the Grand Duchy.

In 1901, the colony produced its first exhibition, consisting primarily of the members' own homes, including those of the famous artists, Peter Behren and Joseph Maria Olbrich, the latter of whom designed a workshop, which was named in Ernie's honour.

Both Queen Victoria and Prince Albert were gifted artists so it is unsurprising that so many of their children and grandchildren inherited their talents. Vicky, herself a proficient watercolourist, encouraged her sons to express themselves through painting, and, by the time of his accession, Willy believed himself to be as competent as any professional. So satisfied was he by his own creations that he decorated a schedule for the Reichstag with pictures of miniature battleships; and to an admiral of the North Sea fleet, he sent two large watercolours which he had painted and hoped would be prominently displayed. Not everyone, however, appreciated his style, as one visitor to the home of the recently deceased Bavarian artist, Lenback, recorded. Alongside Lenbach's paintings was a gift from the Kaiser.

> "Aside from the first canvas of a schoolboy with his first box of paints, you never saw anything like it. It was boldly signed 'Wilhelm' and the august artist had presented it to Lenbach to be exhibited among his own masterpieces."[187]

Nonetheless, following in the footsteps of his hero and ancestor, Frederick the Great, Willy was so eager to support the arts, that he annoyed the Prince Regent of Bavaria by suggesting that his councillors spent insufficient money on acquiring paintings or creating galleries. He personally paid for statues of his ancestors to be erected across the whole of Germany, including no fewer than three-hundred-and-seventy-one of his grandfather, Wilhelm I; and he and Dona frequently visited artists' studios, where, to the amusement of his companions, he never failed to offer advice.

If his paintings were not always appreciated, his musical talents were impressive. He was renowned for his ability to sight-read, and, despite his handicap, became such a skilled pianist that he insisted in taking a piano with him on his travels. Both he and Henry enjoyed composing their own pieces; and Willy especially loved to take the baton to conduct his military bands. He was equally discerning in musical appreciation, and able to express educated opinions about what he did and did not like.

"I don't like Wagner," he is reputed to have said. "He is too noisy. The simple, yet pleasant Gluck is more to my taste."[188]

Cousin George in England was far less discerning, once remarking that he didn't like opera except for *La Bohème* because it was the shortest; but his Battenberg cousins had greater musical appreciation and were also gifted singers and instrumentalists. Drino was known for his fine singing voice; and Leopold was such a proficient violinist that, as Queen Victoria lay on her deathbed too exhausted to speak, she asked that her grandson should play for her instead.

George's lack of interest in opera was matched by his lack of interest in literature and art but, like most of his cousins, was eager to participate in various outdoor pursuits. Most of the princes had learned to swim at Osborne by being tied to rope to prevent them from being washed out to sea. There, too, as in the grounds of their own homes, all became competent horsemen, and several showed great ability on the polo field. Tennis was particularly popular among the Queen's grandsons since most of the palaces had courts where the princes and princesses could compete against each other. While visiting Darmstadt, Willy had enjoyed many matches with his Hessian cousins; and Abbie of Schleswig-

Holstein played with his sister, Thora, on their Aunt Vicky's courts at Krönberg.

Abbie was also a keen golfer who became the first president of the Stoke Park Club, and captained the Sunningdale Club in Berkshire, often travelling overnight from Germany to play a round before lunch with his sister or the renowned cricketer, W.G. Grace. Like his late brother, though, Abbie's particular penchant was for cricket. He was an active member of the Marylebone Cricket Club; and, in 1911, he formed his own team – the Prince Albert of Schleswig-Holstein's First XI – to play against his former school team in the grounds of Cumberland Lodge to celebrate the Prince of Wales' investiture as a Knight of the Garter.

In his youth, Prince Albert had been a successful boxer, and, by the turn of the century, as the sport was enjoying a revival, several of his grandsons became fans. During the 1908 London Olympics, George V was so concerned about the progress of the British featherweight contender, Richard Gunn, that, in the middle of an important Gala Dinner, he sent word that he wished to be told the outcome of a match as soon as it was over. The sport had not attracted so much attention in Germany, but Henry of Prussia, impressed by way it was used in the training of British sea cadets, decided to introduce it to his own young officers.

"I think," he wrote to Lord Napier, "it is good for our 'jack' for the sake of his physical development and am curious to see the result."[189]

His idea was not entirely successful and it would take almost two decades before the sport began to interest German audiences, and not until 1930 did Germany produce a champion.

For the aristocracy and royal families, the English social season revolved around yachting regattas and horse racing. Each year, foreign princes attended the 'sport of kings' at Royal Ascot and the Epsom Derby, as much to see and be seen as to watch the events. An avid race-goer and owner, Edward VII first introduced his sons, Eddy and George, to Royal Ascot in 1877. Their initiation was marred by the sudden illness of a lady-in-waiting, Lady Susan Melville, which led to a delay of half an hour in the Royal Procession, but this did not distract George from the thrill of the race – an interest which he continued to pursue during his reign. Like his father, he became such a renowned punter that it was said that he funded a large part of his stamp collection with his winnings at the race-track; and at Kempton, the Duke of York Stakes was named in his honour. Each year, when possible, he attended the Epsom Derby, entering a horse from his own stable, and it was there, in 1913, that a tragic incident occurred.

Emily Wilding Davison, a well-educated, highly intelligent and deeply religious woman, had abandoned a teaching career to devote herself to the cause of votes for women. She been imprisoned nine times for various offences including setting fire to pillar boxes, smashing windows and disrupting political meetings; and, while in prison, she, like many suffragettes, had adopted a hunger strike in protest at the authorities' refusal to treat her as a political prisoner. Consequently, she had received barbaric treatment such as forcible feeding via a nasal tube, having an ice-cold hose pipe turned on her, and being dragged backwards down a metal staircase, with her head banging on every step.

On 4th June 1913, with the suffragettes' green, white and purple stitched into her coat, she arrived at the Epsom race track, intending to make a protest in front of the King. By chance, another suffragette, Mary Richardson, happened to be standing within view of Miss Davison, and later recorded exactly what she witnessed:

"A minute before the race started, she raised a paper...before her eyes. I was watching her hand. It did not shake. Even when I heard the pounding of the horses' hooves moving closer, I saw she was still smiling. And suddenly she slipped under the rail and ran out in the middle of the racecourse. It was all over so quickly. Emily was under the hooves of one of the horses and seemed to be hurled some distance along the grass…She lay very still."[190]

Miss Davison had attempted to seize the bridle of George's horse, *Anmer,* whose jockey, Herbert Jones, was distinguishable in the King's colours. She was caught by the galloping horse's hooves, kicked and tossed into the air, suffering a fractured skull and various internal injuries. She was taken to Epsom Cottage Hospital, where she died four days later, never having regained consciousness.

George, however was more concerned about the jockey, who had been thrown but, apart from a few bruises, had suffered no serious injuries. Some days later, George's mother wrote to Jones, expressing her son's feelings of sympathy for him at having been involved in this 'accident caused by the abominable conduct of a brutal lunatic woman.' Jones, however, haunted by the face of 'that poor woman' was far more sympathetic and, fifteen years later, he attended the funeral of the suffragette leader, Emmeline Pankhurst, with a wreath to the memory of Emily Wilding Davison.

This was not George's first experience of the suffragettes, nor would it be his last. On several previous occasions, attempts had been made to present him with petitions as he travelled to open Parliament; and, during a visit to Bristol, a woman who attempted to approach him was struck by an equerry with the flat of his sword. Mrs Pankhurst and her two elder daughters, Christabel and Sylvia, wrote to him personally, the latter giving him a detailed account of the horrors of forcible feeding. George agreed that the methods were barbaric but his greatest fear was that, if the public realised what was happening, sympathy would be aroused for the suffragette 'martyrs'.

"His Majesty cannot help feeling that there is something shocking, if not almost cruel, in the operation to which these insensate women are subjected through their refusal to take necessary nourishment. His Majesty concludes that Miss Pankhurst's description of what she endured when forcibly fed is more or less true. If so, her story will horrify people otherwise not in sympathy with the Militant Suffragettes."[191]

The Home Secretary, Reginald McKenna, attempted to solve the problem by introducing – with George's full support – the 'The Prisoners' Temporary Discharge Act' whereby hunger strikers were released when they were too weak to remain in prison, only to be rearrested the moment they recovered. As the attempts at re-arrest led to a series of police hunts and subterfuges, the act was familiarly referred to as the 'Cat and Mouse Act.'

Forcible feeding continued however and, from early 1913, having had little success in their dealings with politicians, the suffragettes more frequently resorted to appealing directly to the King. In December that year, George and May were attending a production of Raymond Roze's opera *Jeanne d'Arc,* when three women secured a box directly opposite the King's and, having barricaded themselves in, waited until the end of the first act before addressing him via a megaphone.

"Calling attention to the impressive scenes on the stage, the speaker told the King that women were today fighting, as Joan of Arc fought centuries ago, for human liberty, and that they, like the maid of Orleans, were being tortured and done to death, in the name of the King, in the name of the Church, and with the full knowledge and responsibility of established Government. At this very hour the leader

271

of these fighters in the army of liberty was being held in prison and tortured by the King's authority."[192]

George did not respond but, as the women were eventually bundled away, forty more suffragettes in an upper gallery scattered leaflets onto the audience below. Soon afterwards, while George and May were attending a matinee at His Majesty's Theatre, a woman chained herself to her seat and accused George of behaving 'like a Russian Tsar', while another climbed onto the stage and called out,

"Your Majesty, stop forcible feeding!"

On 21st May 1914, suffragettes chained themselves to the railings of Buckingham Palace; and, the following month – a year to the day after Emily Wilding Davison's protest at Epsom – George had an even closer encounter with a young suffragette, Mary Blomfield. The daughter of Lady Sarah Louisa Blomfield, co-founder of *Save the Children,* Mary was being presented at court when, as she approached George, she fell to her knees and said boldly:

"For God's sake, Your Majesty, stop forcible..."

She was dragged away before she could complete her sentence. Remarkably, her mother, who claimed to be an ardent supporter of the suffragette movement, let it be known that she was horrified by her daughter's behaviour, causing Sylvia Pankhurst to describe her as 'enthusiastic for militancy of the most extreme kind, as long as it was committed by somebody else's daughter.'

Apart from regular visits to the racetrack, hunting and shooting occupied a good deal of the princes' leisure time. Weekend shooting parties were regular occurrences, and State Visits abroad almost invariably included an opportunity to hunt or shoot. While in India in 1911, George 'bagged' twenty-one tigers – albeit after the prey had been worn down for days and encircled by a ring of elephants. In India he had also participated in the killing of eighteen rhinoceroses; and he was present, too, at the Hall Barn shoot where a record-breaking three-thousand-nine-hundred pheasants were killed in one day. At Sandringham, birds were bred and fattened specifically for the shoot; and George's father set all the clocks half-an-hour fast in order to allow more time for hunting.

Despite his disability, Willy, too was an excellent shot who compensated for his 'useless' left arm by having a stake driven into the ground, on which he could rest the rifle. While in England, he often accompanied his uncle, Christian of Schleswig-Holstein, on shoots in the Windsor Forest, and by 1914 he had bagged a total of 25,372 animals including wolves, boars, foxes, deer, birds and stags.

At Christmas 1891, however, an unfortunate incident put an end to his Uncle Christian's thrill of the shoot. He and his son, Abbie, were staying with the Queen at Osborne, when they and the Duke of Connaught, went out to hunt game. As Abbie took his aim at a pheasant, he suddenly heard his father call out,

"Albert! I am shot!"

Three pellets from the Duke of Connaught's gun had struck a tree and ricocheted into his face. Doctors were called at once and, to Queen Victoria's horror, pronounced the necessity of removing one of his eyes. In spite of the severity of the injury, Christian survived surgery and later obtained a collection of false eyes in various colours to suit his mood!

The Duke of Connaught was not the only member of the family who, despite being a renowned marksman, caused injuries while out shooting. Henry of Prussia not only accidentally wounded a Greek officer in Corfu, but also permanently crippled one of the Grand Duke of Baden's gamekeepers.

By the turn of the century, concern was growing about the welfare of animals, and a number of noteworthy groups were voicing objections to the slaughter of sentient creatures for sport. In 1891, several prominent men, including the author, John Galsworthy, formed the Humanitarian League which was supported by, amongst others, George Bernard Shaw and Christabel Pankhurst. The League produced books and leaflets filled with logical arguments and detailed accounts of the cruelty of hunting and shooting. Among their complaints was the way in which the tigers, which George had shot in India, had been captured by using live bullocks as bait. The group drew attention, too, to the fact that George's cousin, Ena Battenberg, the Queen of Spain, attended bullfights; and that his father, while recovering from appendicitis, had shot, but not killed, a stag which, 'got away to die of such an internal inflammation as his royal murderer had just escaped'. George Bernard Shaw concluded that the princely hunters were not 'cruel monsters' but:

"...conspicuous examples of the power of cruel institutions to compel the support and finally win the tolerance and even the enjoyment of persons of full normal benevolence."[193]

Interestingly, the League drew attention, too, to a meeting between the Kaiser and the Austro-Hungarian Emperor Franz Josef and his heir, Archduke Franz Ferdinand, in December 1913. The purpose of the meeting was to discuss peace in Europe but Willy and Franz Ferdinand also found time to shoot eleven-hundred pheasants.

'A strange way of inaugurating peace,' the League commented, and came to the conclusion that one of the chief purposes of blood-sports was to prepare men for war.

Less than twelve months later, Franz Ferdinand would fall victim to a predator's bullet; and Willy and George would find themselves on opposing sides in a war.

Chapter 23 – An Apostle of Peace

Hohenzollerns (Prussians)

Willy – Kaiser Wilhelm II; eldest son of Queen Victoria's daughter, Vicky
Sissi – Willy's only daughter
Henry – Willy's brother; second son of Queen Victoria's daughter, Vicky

Others

Nicholas (Nicky) – Tsar of Russia; husband of Willy's cousin, Alix of Hesse
George – King of Great Britain; son of Queen Victoria's son, Bertie
May – George's wife
Abbie (Albert) – Prince of Schleswig-Holstein; son of Queen Victoria's daughter, Lenchen
Young Arthur – Prince of Connaught; son of Queen Victoria's son, Arthur, Duke of Connaught
Franz Josef – Emperor of Austria-Hungary
Franz Ferdinand – Archduke; nephew and heir of Emperor Franz Josef
Sophie Chotek – Morganatic wife of Franz Ferdinand
Charlie – Duke of Albany and Coburg; son of Queen Victoria's son, Leopold

The year 1913 began auspiciously for Kaiser Wilhelm. In the 'warm snowless winter with lots of fast gallops each morning', he was preparing for two major events – his daughter's wedding and his own Silver Jubilee – which would not only allow him to display Hohenzollern hospitality to the world, but also to emphasise Germany's peaceful intentions and his desire to remain on good terms with his British and Russian cousins.

Sad as he was at the prospect of his beloved daughter's departure, Willy found comfort in the knowledge that hers was a love-match, which would resolve a longstanding dispute between Prussia and the groom's native Hanover, which, to the Hanoverians chagrin, had been annexed by the Prussians after the Seven Weeks War of 1866.

Willy took pleasure, too, in the knowledge that he would be able to entertain his cousins in Berlin. In March, he wrote to George and May, telling them that a date had been fixed for the wedding; and the same month he told Tsar Nicholas of Russia that:

"The main object of my lines is to convey to you and Alix[hh] our most cordial invitation to the wedding ceremonies. We both would be only too delighted if you could give us the pleasure of your presence and I fervently hope that you will be able to leave Russia for a few days to meet many of your relatives."[194]

By mid-May, visitors to Berlin were struck by the joyful atmosphere pervading the city, where the streets were festooned with garlands, flowers and flags. With meticulous planning, Willy was determined to provide a fine welcome for his royal guests, and, on the day of George's arrival, Union Jacks had been hoisted all along the route from the station to the palace. Dressed in the uniform of a British Field Marshal, Willy went to meet his cousin's train, accompanied by a 'magnificent' Guard of Honour; and George returned the compliment by appearing in the uniform of an honorary Prussian Colonel. Together the King and the Kaiser returned to the palace in a grand procession through streets filled with cheering crowds.

The next day, however, the cordial relations between the cousins temporarily deteriorated when George announced that he intended to go to the station to meet the Tsar. Willy, who had already prepared a great reception for Nicholas,

---

[hh] The Tsarina – Willy's cousin, Alix of Hesse

feared that George's presence would disrupt his plans. Eventually, a compromise was reached when George agreed that, rather than taking part in the procession, he would return to the palace via the backstreets in an unmarked car. The incident, though minor and quickly resolved, was later used by Willy's detractors as an example of his supposed paranoia and desire to keep the King and the Tsar apart for fear that they might start plotting against him.

Over the next few days, Willy played the role of the perfect host, doing everything possible to accommodate his guests and provide them with interesting entertainments. Despite George's boredom during the typical Prussian military displays, relations between the sovereigns were amicable, and the King, the Kaiser and the Tsar were generous in presenting honours to members of each other's suites. To emphasise their shared desire for peace, George gave a poignant address from the British Embassy, to all his British subjects living in Germany:

> "By fostering and maintaining kindly relations and good understanding between yourselves and the people of your adopted home, you are helping to ensure the peace of the world, the preservation of which is my fervent desire."[195]

The wedding, attended by over a thousand guests, took place on what would have been Queen Victoria's ninety-fourth birthday, May 24th 1913. Following a relatively brief and simple Lutheran service, the festivities began with a banquet and the famous Prussian Torch Dance, which involved the bride and groom being led into the darkened ballroom by candle-bearing pages, and gradually inviting more and more guests to join the dance. By tradition, only *Royal* Highnesses were permitted to participate, but such was the Kaiser's fondness for his cousin –a 'mere' Highness – Abbie of Schleswig-Holstein, that he made an exception, and he, too, danced alongside, the Kaiser, the Tsar and the King.

Six months later, George attended a less ostentatious wedding when his niece, Alexandra, Duchess of Fife, married his cousin, Young Arthur of Connaught. The bride, a daughter of George's sister, Louise, and her husband, the immensely wealthy 'Macduff', Duke of Fife, had lived a rather sheltered existence with her younger sister and parents on their Scottish estates. Nonetheless, in 1910, she managed to contract a secret engagement with the visiting Prince Christopher of Greece but, when her father discovered what had happened, he was so enraged that he adamantly refused to sanction their marriage. The unfortunate Christopher escaped to Balmoral to pour out his heart to George, who, amused by the entire incident, advised Christopher to apologise and abandon his suit.

The following year, the Fifes were shipwrecked off the coast of Morocco and, although they survived the ordeal, the stress severely damaged the Duke's health and he died a month later. Since he had no male heir to succeed him, it had already been arranged that Alexandra would become Duchess of Fife in her own right; and, the following year, free of any parental constraints she announced her engagement to the dashing Young Arthur of Connaught.

The wedding took place on 15th October 1913 in the Chapel Royal of St. James' Palace, and although it was not such a grand affair as Sissy's had been, crowds turned out in their thousands to cheer the bride and groom. In the absence of her father, George gave the bride away in a ceremony attended by, amongst others, George's sister, the Queen of Norway; the Crown Prince of Prussia; and the groom's cousin, Ena of Battenberg, Queen of Spain. George's youngest son, John, acted as one of the train bearers; and his eldest son, the future King Edward VIII, was chosen as Arthur's best man. At the time it was falsely rumoured that George intended to confer the title Duke of Kent on Arthur, but, despite much speculation, nothing came of the idea.

Following a reception at Buckingham Palace the couple honeymooned at Rest Harrow in Kent, the home of Arthur's old school friend, Waldorf Astor, before settling into their home in Mayfair. Theirs was to be the last royal wedding at which the guests wore court dress, and the last gathering of the royal German and English cousins. By the time that their only son, Alistair, was born in August 1914, war had been declared and the family ties binding the cousins together would be permanently severed.

Willy, meanwhile, felt his daughter's absence very deeply.

"Now," wrote her English governess, "with the departure of his youngest child, the last one left at home, the private life of the Kaiser's Court has grown in these later days somewhat still and a trifle lonely."[196]

Fortunately, a few weeks after Sissy's wedding, Willy's Silver Jubilee provided a brief distraction from his grief. Visitors from across the globe attended a three-day series of celebrations, including a grand procession through Berlin where two-hundred-and-fifty-thousand people amassed to cheer their Kaiser. Their applause was genuine and Willy had every reason to feel proud of his achievements. During his reign, German industry had prospered, transport had improved, welfare for workers and for the sick had been introduced, and, as he was keen to stress, his country had been at peace.

Despite his increasingly animated assurances that Germany had no desire for war, the press in France, Britain, Russia and even the United States, frequently whipped up fear and mistrust by drawing attention to his naval and military programmes. Those who met the Kaiser face to face, however, gained a very different impression, even going so far as to name him 'an Apostle of peace.'

"He is fine company," wrote the American industrialist, Andrew Carnegie, "and I believe an

279

earnest man, anxious for the peace and progress of the world. Suffice it to say he insists that he is, and always has been, for peace. He cherishes the fact that he has reigned for [twenty-five] years and he has never shed human blood."[197]

'Twenty-five years of peace and we hope for many more!' Willy told Carnegie, leading him to the conclusion that:

"...the peace of the world has little to fear from Germany. Her interests are all favourable to peace, industrial development being her aim; and in this desirable field she is certainly making great strides."[198]

For all his love of uniforms and military parades, Willy had no stomach for war. In 1912, he had helped to avert a conflict between Austria and Serbia, and, like his mother, he dreaded an armed confrontation between Britain and Germany. His emphasis on Germany's pacific intentions, however, was frequently undermined by the belligerent utterances of some of his ministers and generals. In 1913, Charlie, Duke of Coburg, attempted to warn King George V that Admiral Tirpitz, 'the sailor-statesman', had predicted that Germany would declare war as soon as the Kiel Canal was completed in 1915. George dismissed the warning as nonsense but many of his ministers were watching the Kaiser's expanding navy, convinced that Germany intended to replace Britain as 'ruler of the waves.'

As early as 1911, their suspicions appeared to be justified when the Sultan of Morocco sought the help of the French to quell an uprising. The Germans, suspecting that the French had deliberately provoked the unrest as a means to gaining greater influence in Africa, sent a warship to the region, prompting Britain's Chancellor of the Exchequer, David Lloyd George, to make his widely-reported and somewhat inflammatory Mansion House speech. If British interests were threatened, he said, there would be no alternative but to take up arms. It was a statement that was often repeated in the years that followed, and the growing mistrust between the Great Powers was rapidly gaining momentum.

"When the river reaches the waterfall," said the French Empress Eugenie, "no earthly power can stop it."[199] Despite her personal dislike of the Kaiser, the Empress saw him not as a warmonger but rather as a latter day King Canute, trying to hold back the rapidly rising tide of mutual mistrust.

As alliances were formed between Britain, France and Russia, the Germans recognised the dangers of isolation and encirclement, and desperately needed allies of their own. Realising that, during the reign of his uncle, King Edward VII, a formal alliance with Britain was impossible, Willy turned his attention to his friend and cousin-by-marriage, the Tsar. In 1904, he forwarded to Nicholas the draft of a treaty whereby Russia and Germany would agree to come to each other's aid if either one were attacked by another European power. Initially, Nicholas had some reservations and suggested that, since Russia had already signed an agreement with France, the French should be involved in the negotiations. Willy disagreed. It was *impossible,* he said, to take France into their confidence prior to signing the treaty, not least because that would involve dealing with statesmen, rather than princes or kings, and:

> "I am unable to place them – in a question of confidence like this one – on the same footing as you, my equal, my cousin and friend."[200]

The following summer, during his annual cruise, Willy arranged to meet Nicholas aboard his yacht, the *Hohenzollern,* and there, despite his earlier misgivings, the Tsar signed the secret Treaty of Bjorko. Willy was delighted. Not only had he genuinely enjoyed Nicholas' company but he sincerely believed that the treaty was a diplomatic triumph.

"The hours I was allowed to spend in your society will be ever graven on my memory, you were like a dear brother to me," he wrote to the Tsar. "The Alliance…which we concluded will be of great use to Russia, as it will quiet in the minds of people, and great confidence in the maintenance of Peace in Europe."[201]

His joy, though, was short lived. When Nicholas returned to St Petersburg, his ministers were aghast at not having been consulted and pointed out that, due to Russia's prior agreement with France, the treaty could never be ratified.

Germany was not without allies, however. Shunned by Britain and Russia, Willy turned to neighbouring Austria-Hungary – a sprawling empire of various different cultures, many of which were pressing for independence. By 1914, the aged Emperor Franz Josef had ruled for sixty-six years and, although he appeared to be in good health, it was widely believed that it would not be long before he succumbed to one of his recurring bouts of bronchitis.

His nephew and heir, Archduke Franz Ferdinand – a forward-thinking man with a notoriously short temper, exacerbated by the cruel treatment that his wife received in Vienna – was unpopular in the Emperor's court and spurned by the Imperial Family for having committed the unconscionable crime of flouting Habsburg convention to marry a lady-in-waiting rather than a princess 'of the blood'.

It was not only his morganatic marriage, however, which provoked such hostility in the Emperor's court, but also his revolutionary ideas which, his uncle believed, threatened to destroy the Empire. In reality, nothing could have been further from the truth. Frustrated by the outdated Habsburg traditions, Franz Ferdinand was desperate to keep the Empire intact by granting greater autonomy to the different ethnicities – Magyars, Poles, Czechs and Slavs – who resented being ruled from Vienna. In 1908, when the

Austrians annexed Bosnia-Herzegovina, Franz Ferdinand had warned that such a move would enrage the Serbs who dreamed of uniting the southern Slavs into one nation – Yugoslavia. His prediction quickly proved accurate as the annexation aroused such violent resentment that several of the more belligerent Austrian generals recommended an invasion to crush the unruly Serbs once and for all. Franz Ferdinand, to the annoyance of the Generals, was quick to point out the dangers of such an action. Was it worth shedding blood, he asked, to gain only 'a pack of thieves, and a few more murderers and rascals and a few plum trees'; and, more to the point, did the Generals not realise that any attack on Serbia would incur a swift response from the Slavs' protector – the Tsar. Austria-Hungary, Franz Ferdinand said, had neither the means nor the manpower to take on the might of Russia, and war would almost certainly lead to the annihilation of the Empire.

While the Emperor's court and the Imperial Family had little time for Franz Ferdinand, the Kaiser was genuinely fond of the man and was happy to spend time in his company. Apart from a shared interest in hunting and in the navy, they had similar views about how to maintain peace in Europe. While both wished to avoid war, they saw a necessity of maintaining military strength as a deterrent to any would-be attackers. Willy needed a strong ally, and Franz Ferdinand had plans to reorganise Emperor Franz Josef's three armies, which worked independently of one another and comprised so many different ethnicities that often the soldiers spoke a different language from their officers and consequently did not understand their orders. The Archduke was equally enthusiastic about improving the Austrian navy, and had already carried out many inspections and pressed for a more substantial naval budget. All in all, he was a man with whom Willy felt he could do business.

For his part, Franz Ferdinand respected the Kaiser, not least for the gracious manner in which he treated Sophie, his wife. In Vienna, Sophie might be treated with disdain, but Willy appreciated her intelligence and showed her great courtesy and deference, even going so far as to suggest that her eldest son – who, as the child of a morganatic marriage, had been denied any official status in the Imperial Family – might one day be appointed as the Kaiser's regent in Alsace-Lorraine.

In early June 1914, Willy accepted an invitation to Franz Ferdinand's picturesque Konopischt Castle in Bohemia, to enjoy a weekend's hunting and to discuss their plans for peace. Both were content with the terms of the Dual Alliance, whereby each country would come to the other's aid in the event of war, but they were equally keen to approach the Tsar in the hope of creating more peaceful ties with Russia. Despite the failure of the Treaty of Bjorko, Willy was optimistic that his personal relationship with Nicholas would be sufficient to maintain good relations between their countries.

"I am most gratified that you still keep pleasant recollections of the visit you paid us last summer for Sissy's wedding," he wrote to the Tsar in early 1914, "and you may be assured that we all most heartily reciprocate your kind feeling and remembrance."[202]

With such sentiments, he hoped to cement his friendship and, before the weekend with Franz Ferdinand was over, the Kaiser and the Archduke had agreed to approach the Tsar with friendly overtures at the first possible opportunity.

Less than two weeks after Willy's departure from Konopischt, Archduke Franz Ferdinand set out to Bosnia to inspect the troops and attend the Austrian military manoeuvres near Sarajevo. The trip had been planned several months earlier at the invitation of the Austrian military governor of the region, and, although Franz Ferdinand had an ominous sense of foreboding, and realised that his presence might inflame the anger of the Bosnian Serbs, he had decided to undertake the journey for two specific reasons. Firstly, he believed he would have the opportunity to express his intention of granting greater autonomy to the region once he became Emperor; and secondly, the invitation was extended to Sophie, who had, so cruelly been refused any part in his official duties in Vienna. To add to their joy, their reception in Sarajevo was to take place on Sunday 28th June – their fourteenth wedding anniversary.

That day, the crowded streets of Sarajevo were awash with flags, flowers and portraits of Franz Ferdinand and Sophie, and the motorcade moved through the city in an atmosphere of warmth and festivity. Suddenly, though, at the sound of an explosion, Franz Ferdinand's driver accelerated and rush his royal passengers to the City Hall. There, they discovered that a bomb had been thrown at the motorcade and, although it bounced off the bonnet of Franz Ferdinand's car, it had injured several bystanders and members of his suite.

In order to avoid further bloodshed, Franz Ferdinand was persuaded to cancel the rest of the day's engagements, but he insisted on visiting the wounded in hospital before leaving the city. That afternoon, he and Sophie again set out in an open-roofed car with no military escort. Despite warnings that there were other terrorists in the area, the only precaution against further attack was the decision to take a circuitous route to the hospital. Bizarrely, however, the driver was not told of the change of plan and, only when he missed a turning, was he told that the route had been altered. The driver stopped and began to reverse when a young Bosnian Serb, Gavrilo Princip, stepped out of a shop and fired a pistol directly into the car.

Sophie slumped at once to the floor and, while bystanders believed she had fainted, Franz Ferdinand realised that she had been fatally wounded.

"Sophie, little Sophie, you have to live for the children!" he managed to gasp before lapsing into semi-consciousness. He had been shot in the throat and by the time the car reached the hospital he was dead.

Chapter 24 – When the River Reaches the Waterfall

Willy – Kaiser Wilhelm II; eldest son of Queen Victoria's daughter, Vicky
Henry – Willy's brother; second son of Queen Victoria's daughter, Vicky
The Crown Prince – Wilhelm; the Kaiser's eldest son
Max (Maximilian – Prince of Hesse-Kassel; Willy's nephew; son of Willy's sister, Mossy

Nicholas – Tsar of Russia; husband of Willy's cousin, Alix of Hesse

George – King of Great Britain; son of Queen Victoria's son, Bertie
David – Prince of Wales; George's eldest son
Bertie – George's second son

Abbie (Albert) – Prince of Schleswig-Holstein; son of Queen Victoria's daughter, Lenchen

Franz Josef – Emperor of Austria-Hungary

Charlie – Duke of Albany and Coburg; son of Queen Victoria's son, Leopold
Young Arthur – Prince of Connaught; only son of Queen Victoria's son, Arthur, Duke of Connaught

Beatrice – Queen Victoria's youngest child
Drino (Alexander), Leopold & Maurice – Beatrice's sons

News of the Archduke's assassination sent shock-waves through the courts of Europe. Many of Queen Victoria's grandsons had known him personally, for he had regularly visited England in both an official and private capacity. He had represented his uncle, the Emperor, at Queen Victoria's Diamond Jubilee celebrations and King Edward VII's funeral; and he had also made several trips incognito to further his interest in rose breeding. Despite the initial shock, however, and an awareness that the murder could have repercussions, few of the royal cousins appreciated the full significance of what had happened.

A period of mourning was ordered in Russia, Germany and Britain, from where the Tsar, the Kaiser and the King sent personal messages of condolence to Emperor Franz Josef. Willy, abandoning the Kiel Regatta, intended to set out at once to Vienna for the funeral but he was asked not to do so, since his safety could not be guaranteed. The King of Roumania, who was equally keen to pay his respects, had already set out for Austria but was unceremoniously turned back at the border. The late Archduke's detractors were determined to humiliate him even in death. The funeral service was a hurried affair; crowds were prevented from filing past the bier; and, to emphasise Sophie's lowly status as a lady-in-waiting, her coffin was placed far lower than that of her husband.

At the time of the murder, Henry of Prussia, Abbie of Schleswig-Holstein and Charlie of Coburg were holidaying in England. Henry and his wife were staying on the south coast; Charlie was visiting his sister, Alice, at Windsor; and, only two days before the shooting, Abbie, dressed in the uniform of a Prussian Hussar, had ridden beside Cousin George at the Trooping of the Colour. Of the three, only Charlie of Coburg sensed the imminent danger. Henry, who was asked to sound out Cousin George as to what Britain's stance would be if Germany became embroiled in a war, was sufficiently assured by George's reply to tell Berlin that Britain would remain neutral. Abbie, equally optimistic, remained contentedly in England but, when Charlie of Coburg heard of the Archduke's murder, he predicted in horror, 'This means war...' and immediately returned to his duchy.

In Berlin, meanwhile, aghast at the murder of his friend, Willy spontaneously declared that he expected the culprits to be brought to justice with the utmost severity, and he postponed a planned cruise around Norway to await the outcome of the Austrians' investigation. Within a few days, emissaries arrived from Vienna, seeking his assurance that Germany would honour their treaty and stand by her ally in whatever action might be deemed necessary. Clearly, the tubercular Gavrilo Princip had not been acting alone. He had already conveniently confessed to belonging to the 'Black Hand' – a terrorist group, allegedly comprised of Serbian officers and politicians – providing the Austrian war party with a perfect excuse to use the Archduke's death as a pretext for crushing the Serbs once and for all. In guaranteeing them German support, Willy unwittingly 'signed a blank cheque' enabling them to prepare for their long-awaited invasion.

Not wishing to be seen as aggressors, the Austrians created a charade of diplomacy by sending an ultimatum to Belgrade, containing a number of demands which, if met, would prevent a declaration of war. The demands, however, were so extreme that compliance would have required the virtual surrender of Serbia's autonomy. In desperation, the Serb Prince Regent, Alexander, sought the advice and protection of the Russian Tsar.

Though shocked by the harshness of the ultimatum, Tsar Nicholas was convinced that the dispute could be settled through negotiation, and he urged the Serbs to comply with as many demands as were possible without compromising their autonomy. Their response, therefore, was so submissive and amenable that, when Willy read it, he said with relief:

"That is more than one could expect. A great moral victory for Vienna but with it disappears every reason for war."[203]

So confident was he that the matter had been resolved that he embarked on his delayed Norwegian cruise, accompanied by his cousin, Abbie of Schleswig-Holstein, who had recently returned from England.

The Austrian ministers and military leaders, however, were not so willing to let the opportunity of an invasion of Serbia slip through their hands. Emperor Franz Josef had retired to his country estate Bad Ishcl and, during his absence, his ministers continued to plot and prepare for battle. Omitting to mention the extent of Serbs' compliance, they informed him that the demands had not been met in full and therefore he had no option but to sign a declaration of war.

Absent on his cruise, Willy was initially told nothing of these developments and was forced to glean what information he could from the Norwegian newspapers. When he was eventually told of the telegram from Austria to Serbia, he was:

"...terribly upset...but when his agitation had calmed down, he turned to [his cousin] and said, "Abbie, let us go and wash the dogs.' So they retired to the Emperor's cabin, took off their coats and scrubbed the dachshunds."[204]

The horrified Serbs, meanwhile, again appealed to the Tsar, who, bound by his promise to protect them, ordered a partial mobilisation along the Austrian border. As tensions continued to mount, the British Fleet, which had been involved in manoeuvres at Spithead, was ordered to remain in situ on high alert as though Britain, too, were preparing for war. In the days that followed, newspapers printed exaggerated stories, whipping up jingoistic feelings and goading the public to demand immediate military action.

Willy, infuriated by what had happened in his absence, returned at once to Berlin but it was too late. He could not withdraw his promise to support Austria-Hungary, and there was little he could do to prevent 'the river from reaching the waterfall'. His only hope was to persuade the Tsar to back down, and over the next few days Willy and Nicholas exchanged numerous desperate telegrams, each urging the other to show restraint and expressing his desire to find some means of negotiation.

"I beg you," wrote the Tsar to the Kaiser, "in the name of our old friendship, "to do what you can to stop your allies from going too far."

Willy offered to mediate between the Austrians and Serbs, but as the former were already bombarding Belgrade, Nicholas had no option but to order a full mobilisation. At the same time, he suggested that the dispute could be resolved by an international tribunal in The Hague, but the British Foreign Secretary rejected the idea, stating that events had gone beyond arbitration.

To the last moment, the Kaiser and the Tsar made every effort to maintain peace, but by now it seemed that virtually all of Europe was baying for war. As the Tsar's troops continued towards the Austrian border, the Germans issued an ultimatum.

On the evening of July 31st, the Kaiser was joined at Potsdam by his son, the Crown Prince, and his brother, Henry. After dinner, the three men walked in the garden where, according to the Crown Prince, Willy was:

"...excessively serious; he did not conceal from himself the enormous peril of the situation, but he expressed the hope that a European war might be avoided. He himself had sent detailed telegrams to the Tsar and to the King of England and believed he might anticipate success."[205]

The following day, August 1st, Germany declared war on Russia.

Even then, Willy hoped that Britain would remain neutral – a view shared by his optimistic brother, Henry. "Some difference arose between my uncle [Henry] and myself," wrote the Crown Prince, "through my asserting that if it came to war, England would take the side of our adversaries. Prince Henry contested this....His Majesty was in some doubt as to the attitude which England would adopt in the event of a war."[206]

As had been predicted, the French, eager to reclaim the disputed territories of Alsace- Lorraine, rushed to the aid of their Russian ally, leaving Germany at risk of being attacked on two fronts. Fearful of encirclement, the German Generals insisted it was time to implement the Schlieffen Plan, which had been devised decades earlier to deal with such an eventuality. Due to the vastness of his Empire, it would take several weeks for the Tsar to transport his troops to the German border, which, according to the Schlieffen Plan, would give the Kaiser's army time to crush the French before turning to take on the might of Russia on the Eastern Front. The problem was that the border between Germany and France was so heavily fortified that it was barely passable, leaving the Germans no alternative but to approach France through neutral Belgium.

A message was sent to King Albert of the Belgians, requesting access for the German troops. King Albert, unwilling to compromise Belgian neutrality or to allow his country to become a battlefield, responded sharply, 'I rule a kingdom not a road'. Willy accepted the King's refusal and emphatically opposed an invasion, not only because he felt bound by the Treaty of London, which had guaranteed Belgian neutrality, but also because he suspected that a violation of that agreement would bring Britain into the war.

The opinion of the 'All-Highest' Kaiser, however, was completely disregarded by his Generals, who responded to King Albert's refusal with a declaration of war. As Willy had feared, the British government issued an ultimatum, warning that, unless the Germans had left Belgium by midnight on 3rd August, Britain, too, would enter the conflict.

That evening, as had happened for the previous two days, huge crowds amassed outside Buckingham Palace, cheering, waving flags, singing patriotic songs and calling for the King. George appeared on the balcony to immense applause. The newspapers had successfully roused such patriotic fervour that the masses were exhilarated at the prospect of war and, already, young men were hurrying to recruitment offices to enlist in the army. The same was true across much of Europe where crowds welcomed the oncoming slaughter as excitedly as if they were about to attend a great celebration.

By eleven o'clock, British time – midnight in Berlin – no response had been received to the British ultimatum. On 4th August, Britain and Germany were at war.

War was a disaster for the royal cousins, dividing families, turning siblings and cousins into enemies, and destroying friendships which had been formed over many years. Every one of Queen Victoria's surviving grandsons served in one capacity or another, but, tragically, former companions now found themselves on opposing sides.

In Germany, as the Supreme Warlord, Willy ostensibly had overall charge of the army and navy in which all six of his sons would serve. Henry, as an Admiral of the Imperial Navy, would retain his command of the Baltic Fleet – a relatively lowly position since he had often come into conflict with the powerful Secretary of State, Admiral Tirpitz. Henry's two surviving sons, Waldemar and Sigismund also took up naval positions, despite the elder boy being afflicted by haemophilia.

With two sisters in Russia and another in England, Ernie, Grand Duke of Hesse, found the prospect of war abhorrent, but he nonetheless recognised his duty to serve his country, and worked, throughout most of the war, at the Kaiser's headquarters. Charlie, Duke of Coburg, who had been born and raised in England and whose mother and sister still lived there, was equally distressed by the prospect of war but had no option other than to serve in the German army. He let it be known that he believed England had behaved shamefully but, to prevent his having to take up arms against his native country, he was posted to the Eastern Front and promoted to Colonel-in-Chief of the Infantry and a General of the Saxon Cavalry.

Abbie of Schleswig-Holstein was also in a difficult situation since he, too, had been raised in England where all his family lived. Only seven years earlier, he had corrected the French Empress, who mistook his nationality, by telling her:

"I am not a German. I was born at Windsor and my mother is an English woman."

Yet, having received his military training in Prussia and being heir to the Duke of Schleswig-Holstein, as well as being a close friend of the Kaiser, he knew he owed allegiance to Germany. At the age of forty-five, he had long retired from active duty, but he returned to his regiment with the stipulation that he would not fight against the British. Willy accommodated his wishes by appointing him to the staff of General Loewenfeldr – the son of an Englishwoman – in charge of the Berlin defences.

Abbie's refusal to fight against his homeland, did not protect him from accusations of betrayal by the British press. Questions were asked as to why he had been allowed to leave England, rather than being interned as an alien, and even in Parliament he and his family became the subject of several vicious attacks. One Scottish Liberal M.P., William Young, asked whether the Prime Minister, Asquith, would:

"...have the status of this family, evidently of German sympathies, inquired into, and does he consider it either just or expedient that British taxpayers should be called upon to pay for the upkeep of this family to the extent of some £6,000 per annum?"

Fortunately, the slur against Abbie's parents, was swiftly dismissed with a reminder that their elder son, Christle, had fought with the British army and died while on active service.

While the German princes were reporting for duty, their British counterparts were similarly engaged. King George might not have wanted war but, fearing Germany's domination of Europe if Britain failed to participate, he had actively encouraged his Foreign Minister, Edward Grey, to find an excuse for Britain to enter the fray. As Commander-in-Chief of his armies, his participation was confined to inspecting the troops, presenting medals and visiting the wounded, but his two elder sons, David and Bertie, were more directly involved. David, to his great chagrin, was refused permission to fight on the front line lest he should be captured and held as a hostage, and was instead appointed as a Staff Officer and kept out of immediate danger, Nonetheless, he won the respect of the ordinary soldiers for his courage and his concern for their welfare. His younger brother, Bertie, who had just received his commission in the Royal Navy, was directly involved in the fighting, being present in some of the most dramatic sea battles of the war.

The recent birth of a son did not prevent Young Arthur of Connaught from travelling to France as soon as war was declared. He had already seen active service in the Boer War, and was now appointed as an Aide-de-Camp to Field Marshal John French, the commander of the British Expeditionary Force. His cousins, Drino and Maurice Battenberg also set out for France – the former as a Lieutenant in the Grenadier Guards; the latter as a Lieutenant in the 60th King's Rifle Corps. As a haemophiliac, their brother, Leopold, appeared unlikely to see active service, but he, too, served in the King's Rifle Corps, and rose to the rank of Major.

Barely had war broken out when the first royal casualties dispelled the belief that princes and officers were kept out of danger on the battlefield. On 12th October 1914, during a British attack on the German position at the Mont des Cats in Flanders, the Kaiser's nineteen-year-old nephew, Prince Maximilian of Hesse-Kassel, was seriously wounded in the stomach. Three of his retreating countrymen carried him to the hospital of a nearby monastery, informing the monks who he was and asking them to take special care of him due to his being a son of the Kaiser's youngest sister, Mossy. Although he was in great pain, Max survived for seventeen hours, during which time, knowing he was dying, he asked the British doctor who was treating him, to return a medallion to his mother. Tragically, the next day, the doctor, too, died of wounds but by then he had already given the medallion to his wife for safe-keeping. Following the doctor's death, his wife sent the medallion to Queen Mary, who gave it to George, who, in turn, passed on to his cousin, the Crown Princess of neutral Sweden, who was able to return it to Max's mother. Such was the hatred of the Germans in Flanders, however, that the priest who buried the prince refused to reveal the whereabouts of his grave until every one of the Kaiser's soldiers had left Belgian soil. Even after the war, the bitterness was so ingrained that an appeal from the Pope failed to persuade the local people to return Max's body, and it was not until George intervened that his remains were finally released to be interred in Hesse-Kassel in 1926.

Just over a fortnight after Max's death, his British cousin-once-removed, Drino of Battenberg, received a serious wound in his leg. He would make a full recovery and go on to earn further promotions, but his younger brother, Maurice, their mother's favourite child, was not so fortunate.

On 27th October, while leading his battalion in an attack against a German position near Ypres, a shell exploded beside him. As he was hurried away on a stretcher, he was able to bid farewell to his comrades but died before he reached the dressing-station. In spite of her intense sorrow, his mother, Beatrice, who had impressed observers by her stoical response to the death of her husband over a decade earlier, did not allow herself to give way to grief and, as her niece, Marie Louise of Schleswig-Holstein, recalled:

"Her courage never failed and she looked on herself as only one of the thousands of mothers who had given their sons for the safety of England."[207]

Lord Kitchener, the Secretary of State for War, offered to make special arrangements to have Maurice's body brought home for burial, but Beatrice declined, insisting that he would wish to be interred with his comrades in the cemetery at Ypres. She did, however, commission a memorial to him, which was erected three years later near Queen Victoria's mausoleum at Frogmore.

Chapter 25 – Everything Humanly Possible

The Allies

George – King of Great Britain; son of Queen Victoria's son, Bertie (Edward VII)

May – George's wife

Drino – Prince of Battenberg; eldest son of Queen Victoria's youngest daughter, Beatrice

Leopold – Prince of Battenberg; younger son of Queen Victoria's youngest daughter, Beatrice

Maurice – Prince of Battenberg; youngest son of Queen Victoria's youngest daughter, Beatrice

Arthur – Duke of Connaught; son of Queen Victoria

Louise – Duchess of Connaught; Arthur's German wife

Arthur – Prince of Connaught; son of Arthur, Duke of Connaught

Alix – The Tsarina of Russia; daughter Queen Victoria's daughter, Alice; sister of Ernie of Hesse

Nicholas – Tsar of Russia; first cousin of George V

Ella – Grand Duchess of Russia; daughter of Queen Victoria's daughter, Alice; sister of Ernie of Hesse

Lenchen – Queen Victoria's third daughter

Christian – Lenchen's German husband

Sophie – Queen of the Hellenes; Kaiser Wilhelm's younger sister

Alice – Princess of Teck; daughter of Queen Victoria's son, Leopold

Helena Victoria – Princess of Schleswig-Holstein; daughter of Queen Victoria's daughter, Lenchen

Marie Louise – Princess of Schleswig-Holstein; daughter of Queen Victoria's daughter, Lenchen

The Central Powers

Willy – Kaiser Wilhelm II; son of Queen Victoria's daughter, Vicky
Henry – Willy's younger brother
Irene – Henry's wife
Mossy – Willy's younger sister
Friedrich – Prince of Hesse-Kassel; son of Mossy
Ernie – Grand Duke of Hesse-Darmstadt; son of Queen Victoria's daughter, Alice

By the time of Maurice's death, the war had been underway for fewer than three months but already patriotic exhilaration was rapidly turning to horror. The belief that it would all be over by Christmas began to dwindle as trenches were dug along the Western Front, leading to stalemate. Throughout Europe, the royal families devoted themselves to their countries' needs. While princes donned their uniforms and returned to their regiments, their wives and sisters organised ambulances and supplies, trained as nurses, and regularly visited the wounded. In Russia, two of Ernie of Hesse's sisters became nurses, as did Arthur of Connaught's wife, who worked at Paddington hospital. Others ran soup kitchens, knitted socks and gloves, visited the Front, and participated in fund-raising events to provide comforts for the troops and their families.

Initially, there was a sense of camaraderie between the soldiers of opposing sides. Certain Bavarian troops even entertained their French counterparts to supper; and at Christmas 1914, German and British soldiers emerged from their trenches to have a drink together and play a game of football. As the war progressed, though, and the number of casualties increased, friendliness turned to anger, hatred and suspicion. In Greece, Willy's sister, Sophie, was accused of having a secret phone-line to the Kaiser; while, in Russia, Ernie's sisters were vilified as German spies. In Britain, anti-German feeling was so strong that the premises of German businesses, which had prospered happily for decades, were attacked and destroyed; and even innocent dachshunds were kicked in the street. In Belgium, the invading troops had committed so many atrocities that the propaganda posters portraying the Kaiser as an avaricious monster were widely believed.

In truth, however, Willy had little to do with either the conduct of his troops or the progress of the war. His Generals paid scant attention to his opinions, and regularly asked him to inspect battalions or to hand out medals simply to keep him out of their way.

"In the war," wrote his son, "[his] personal modesty led to an almost complete exclusion of his own person from the military and organization measures of the commands of the General Staff."[208]

Contrary to the popular image of a warlord, Willy was more involved with protecting artistic treasures and trying to maintain good relations with his family. As his armies advanced into France, he ordered academics and art connoisseurs to accompany each regiment to catalogue and record items of artistic value, including the stained glass windows of chapels and cathedrals. Where these were at risk of being damaged by bullets and shells, Willy ordered that they should be removed and stored in safety on the understanding that they would be replaced as soon as hostilities ceased. He personally visited the Princess of Poix, whose chateau had first been requisitioned by the British army which had, according to Willy, 'ravaged' the place. When Willy arrived at the chateau he found the entire contents of the princess' wardrobe thrown around the room, her writing desk broken, her letters scattered about, and her silverware buried in the garden.

"I had every garment thoroughly cleaned, hung in the presses, and locked up...All the letters were gathered together, sealed in the writing desk and locked up...I at once ordered that all the silver should be inventoried and deposited in the bank at Aix-La-Chapelle, and returned to the Princess after the war."[209]

On seeing his soldiers dismantling churches, however, witnesses claimed that the German were Philistines, deliberately destroying priceless treasures or stealing French works of art.

Despite his occasional rants about the treachery of the British, Willy, somewhat naively, hoped that the war would not damage his relationship with his extended family. He was shocked and hurt when, in May 1915, George struck the German-based princes – Willy, his brother, Henry, and their cousins Ernie of Hesse, Abbie of Schleswig-Holstein and Charlie of Coburg – from the list of Knights of the Garter, and had their crests removed from St. George's Chapel. The Garter, Willy said, had been presented to him by his beloved grandmother and had nothing to do with the present situation. At times, his naiveté both surprised and touched his British relations. In 1916, when Cousin Abbie's parents, Lenchen and Christian, celebrated their Golden Wedding anniversary, they were deeply moved to receive a message from him via the Crown Princess of Sweden:

"William asks me to transmit to you his loyal and devoted good wishes to dear Uncle Christian and Aunt Helena on the occasion of their golden wedding."[210]

The following year, when Christian died, Willy again made a point of sending sincere condolences to his widow and daughters.

It was not only to princes and family members to whom he showed kindness. On one occasion, he was petitioned by a British prisoner-of-war, seeking permission to return home to visit his dying mother. The Kaiser, to the officer's surprise, granted him two weeks compassionate leave on condition that he gave his word as a gentleman to return later. Equally surprisingly, perhaps, the officer kept his word and returned to the camp, but when a German

301

prisoner presented a similar petition to his British captors, his request was refused.

George, however, did show personal kindness to wounded German prisoners-of-war. While inspecting the troops in France in 1915, he and his equerry, visited a hospital where a prisoner, who had been gassed, lay among the wounded. On discovering that the patient was German, the equerry said he regretted having wasted his pity upon him:

> "...but the King rebuked me and said that after all he was only a poor dying human being and in no way responsible for the German horrors."[211]

Within a couple of days, George himself would be wounded but not by gas or bullets. He was inspecting the troops when his horse, startled by the sudden cheers for the King, reared and threw him before stumbling back on top of him. George was unceremoniously helped to his feet before being bundled into a car and driven back to the chateau where he was staying. Having been examined by the doctors, he was told that he had fractured his pelvis and needed bed-rest but the Commander of British Expeditionary Force, John French, feared that the enemy would discover where he was, and attempt to bomb the chateau. French, therefore, insisted that the King should be returned to England as soon as possible, but when George was told of the plan, he replied angrily:

> "You can tell French from me to go to hell and stay there. I don't intend to move for any bombs!"[212]

It was several days before he was taken by hospital train to Boulogne, and, after a painful Channel crossing on a particularly rough sea, he eventually arrived in London to complete his recuperation, undoubtedly regretting the fact that he had recently taken the pledge to abstain from alcohol for the duration of the war.

Alongside the physical injuries and deprivations wrought by the conflict, the emotional and psychological stress suffered by monarchs and princes was immeasurable. Within three months of the outbreak of war, the German-born King Carol I of Roumania, who had signed a secret agreement with Germany but whose people were overwhelmingly on the side of the Allies[ii], died, exhausted by worry about where his allegiance should lie. Two years later, Emperor Franz Josef of Austria-Hungary finally succumbed to bronchitis; and in 1917 two of Queen Victoria's grandsons lost parents, whose deaths were undoubtedly hastened by the stress of being Germans living in England. In March that year, Young Arthur's mother, Louise, Duchess of Connaught, died of pneumonia and bronchitis at the age of only fifty-six, becoming the first member of the royal family to be cremated. Seven months later, Abbie's father, Prince Christian, died at his home in Pall Mall, and was interred at the Royal Burial Ground at Frogmore.

For George, in the summer of 1917, there was one bright event to ease the pain of the conflict, In July, his thirty-one-year-old cousin, Drino Battenberg, married Lady Irene Denison, the twenty-seven-year-old daughter of the Earl of Londesborough. The wartime wedding was a quiet affair, lacking the glamour of former royal nuptials, for there were neither bridesmaids nor flowers, nor a cake. Nonetheless, the ceremony in the Chapel Royal in St. James' Palace provided the King with a brief respite from the stress of a series of extremely difficult events and decisions.

The previous year, he had faced the Irish Easter Rising, which, it was believed, had been assisted by Germany in the hope that unrest at home would require the transferral of troops from the Western Front. George might have believed that Cousin Willy approved of such seemingly underhand tactics, but, by then, the Kaiser had been virtually side-lined by his new Chief of the General Staff,

---

ii The 'Allies' is used to refer to Britain, Russia, France and their allies; the 'Central Powers' refers to Germany and Austria-Hungary and their allies.

Hindenburg, and his colleague, Luddendorf, both of whom were rapidly turning Germany into a military dictatorship.

Repeatedly, throughout 1916, Willy had vainly attempted to make peace on the understanding that everything would return to the way it had been before the war. His suggestions had been dismissed, not least because the Allies insisted that peace was impossible unless Germany accepted full responsibility for the conflict, and was prepared to make reparation for the damage caused. In despair, Willy frequently retired to his room on the verge of a nervous breakdown.

Meanwhile, the duration and deprivations of the war were leading to unrest in most of the combatant countries. In Britain, food shortages and low wages led to strikes in the dockyards and armament factories; and in Austria-Hungary and Germany, the situation was exacerbated by an illegal British blockade of mines and battleships, which had not only left Willy's beloved Imperial Navy hemmed into the harbours at Wilhelmshaven and Kiel for most of the war but also prevented supply ships from bringing food to the near-starving civilians. Fired by socialist propaganda and promises of peace, workers were becoming increasingly dissatisfied with their leaders, and an air of unrest and dissent threatened not only the production of armaments but also the stability of various governments. Reports of unrest were always troubling but, in March 1917, came the most shocking news of all – revolution had erupted in Russia and the Tsar had been forced to abdicate.

George, horrified that a three-hundred-year-old dynasty could so easily be overthrown, felt nothing but sympathy for his Russian cousin, and wrote to him at once, assuring him of his unfailing friendship. Assuming that the Imperial Family would be sent into exile, he began making arrangements with his ministers to enable them to find refuge in England.

Willy's ministers rejoiced in the Russian Revolution, believing that it would lead to Russia's withdrawal from the war, but Willy himself was aghast at the overthrow of a fellow monarch, and felt nothing but sympathy for the unfortunate Tsar. Believing that he would accept Cousin George's invitation to England, Willy secretly ordered a train to be made available for the Imperial Family to transverse Germany; and he instructed his brother, Henry, to ensure safe passage through the Baltic for any vessel flying the Tsar's ensign.

"I have done everything humanly possible for the unhappy Tsar and his family," he said sincerely, but Cousin George was already having second-thoughts about his original offer. Notwithstanding the fact that his own wife was half-German, he feared that revolution might spread to Britain if he entertained his half-German cousin, the Tsarina, whom he erroneously described 'a Bosch by birth and in sentiment.' Quietly, therefore, to the surprise of even his most liberal ministers, he withdrew the offer and left his 'devoted cousin Nicky' and his family to their fate.

The Russian Revolution had shaken George to the core, and whispers of his pro-German sympathies and numerous German relations were so unnerving for him that, in July 1917, he took the unprecedented step of changing all the Germanic names in his extended family.

"We, out of Our Royal Will and Authority," he proclaimed, "do hereby declare and announce that as from the date of this Our Royal Proclamation Our House and Family shall be styled and known as the House and Family of Windsor, and that all the descendants in the male line of Our said Grandmother Queen Victoria who are subjects of these Realms, other than female descendants who may marry or may have married, shall bear the said Name of Windsor."

Much to his chagrin, George's cousin, Drino, was deprived of his title 'Highness' and created Marquis of Carisbrooke, while his surname, like that of his brother, Leopold, was anglicised from Battenberg to Mountbatten. Charlie of Coburg's sister, Alice – a Princess of Teck – was now to be known as the Countess of Athlone; and, Abbie of Schleswig-Holstein's sisters were to be called Princess Victoria Helena and Princess Marie Louise of...nowhere.

Amused by what he regarded as a petty and pointless exercise, Willy joked that henceforth in Berlin, Shakespeare's *The Merry Wives of Windsor*, should be renamed, *The Merry Wives of Potsdam*.

There was little however for Willy to joke about in 1917. His son, Oskar, who had previously been awarded the Iron Cross for bravery, had collapsed, ostensibly with a heart condition, but probably suffering from shell-shock and exhaustion; a younger son, Joachim, had been wounded in battle; and, the previous year, a second nephew, Frederick, the brother of Maximilian of Hesse-Kassel, was killed in action in Roumania when his throat was cut by a bayonet.

Willy worried, too, about his cousins in Russia, and was furious to discover that his Chiefs of Staff, Hindenburg and Ludendorff, were so eager to force Russia out of the war that they had attempted to ferment civil war by arranging for the exiled Bolshevik, Lenin, to return home via Germany in a sealed train. Funded by international bankers, Lenin arrived to a lukewarm reception, but his promise to broker an immediate peace appealed to the starving civilians and war-weary soldiers, and, within several months of the Tsar's abdication, the Bolsheviks had gained control of much of the country.

Willy's first thoughts were for his captured Russian cousins – the Tsarina, and her sister, Ella, with whom he had once been in love. Lenin's hatred of the Romanovs was so intense that he would not rest while one of them remained on Russian soil, leaving even the saintly Ella, who had devoted

306

the past twelve years of her life to caring for the poor, in great danger. It was widely rumoured that Willy insisted that any peace treaty between Germany and Russia must include a clause guaranteeing the safety of the 'German princesses'; and he sent several messages to Ella via the Crown Princess of neutral Sweden, urging her to leave Russia while there was still time. Ella thanked him for his consideration, but declined his offer on the grounds that she could not abandon the convent of the religious order, which she had founded[ii].

On a wider scale, Willy was desperately worried, too, about the progress of the war. No sooner had the Tsar abdicated than the United States entered the conflict on the side of the Allies. The previous year, the American president, Woodrow Wilson, had been re-elected on the slogan 'he kept us out of the war', but the much-publicised sinking of the passenger ship, *Lusitania*, and Germany's employment of U-boats, led him to an about-turn.

In March 1918, the Bolsheviks signed the Treaty of Brest-Litovsk taking Russia out of the war. The German High Command immediately transferred fifty divisions from the Eastern to the Western Front in the hope that their superior numbers would defeat the Allies before the Americans had time to make an impact. Hindenburg and Ludendorff were confident of success but their offensives were badly-organised; plans were changed from day to day; and, since supplies could not keep up with the stormtroopers' rapid advance, they were frequently forced to halt or even retreat. By the end of April, the hoped-for victory had slipped through German hands, and four months later, the Allies launched a more successful offensive of their own.

Morale among the German troops was sinking rapidly and, as the Foreign Office declared bankruptcy, even the Generals had come to believe that Germany could not

---

[ii] Willy's fears for Ella's safety proved justified. In July 1918, she was murdered by the Bolsheviks by being thrown down a mine shaft and left to die of infected wounds and starvation.

win the war. In August, Hindenburg and Ludendorff met with Willy at his Headquarters in Spa, and agreed that the only solution was to negotiate with the Allies via the neutral European powers. The plans did not materialise, and, a month later, Germany's ally, Bulgaria, concluded a separate peace. At the beginning of October, Willy appointed his cousin, Prince Max of Baden, as Chancellor in the hope that he might be able to broker a fair agreement with Woodrow Wilson. The liberal-minded prince had worked with prisoners-of-war and had a reputation for sincerity, which, it was believed, would give him greater credibility in any ensuing negotiations. Moreover, as the Kaiser's cousin, it was believed he would also do his utmost to protect the dynasty at a time when it was widely reported that the Allies would refuse an armistice until Germany's monarchy had been ousted.

Prince Max forwarded a message to Woodrow Wilson, who responded that the Allies would negotiate if Germany ceased all U-boat attacks, and give an assurance that the autocracy would be replaced by a constitutional monarchy. With Willy's assent, Prince Max agreed to both conditions, but, as they awaited a reply, U-boats continued to attack enemy vessels and when the response eventually arrived, further stipulations had been added.

Sensing that everything was reaching a disastrous conclusion, the German Admiralty decided to launch one final attempt to break to Allied blockade. If Germany were to lose the war, the Admiralty hoped that, through this final operation, they would at least retain a sense dignity and go out in a blaze of glory.

The intention was to launch two separate groups of ships to attack the British and French coasts simultaneously, which would draw out the Royal Navy into a position where it could be attacked by German U-boats and the rest of the Kaiser's fleet. The majority of officers realised that the plan was nothing but a pipe-dream, and knowing that they would be hopelessly outnumbered by the Allied vessels, they saw it as a suicide mission in which they had little desire to participate. On October 27th Ludendorff resigned, and the following day, many of the sailors who were due to take part in the offensive failed to return from shore-leave. Instead they marched through the streets of Kiel, gaining support from workers in the local factories. Within a few hours, more than forty-thousand protestors had left the shipyards and factories and were marching quickly towards Henry's palace, distributing Marxist leaflets. So precarious was the situation that Henry and his wife, Irene, saw no alternative but to flee to the safety of Hemmelmark, and, soon after their departure, protestors entered their home and hoisted a red flag from a tower.

Willy, at his headquarters in Spa, was so shocked by reports of the mutiny that his immediate response was to send troops to Kiel to restore order. To his greater horror, he was informed that such an order was impossible since he no longer commanded the full support of his beloved army. On the same day, news arrived that the Austro-Hungarians had organised a ceasefire and were hoping to arrange a separate peace, leaving Willy to the sad realisation that, with so much unrest at home and no allies left to support him, the only option was to insist on an immediate armistice.

Chapter 26 – A Nice English Cup of Tea

On November 8th 1918, the Kaiser's representative Matthias Erzberger, joined other German and Allied negotiators in the railway carriage of the French Commander-in-Chief, Ferdinand Foch, in Compiegne. Erzberger was presented with a list of demands with which the Germans must comply within seventy-two hours in order to achieve a ceasefire. Alongside the withdrawal of troops from all occupied territories – including Alsace-Lorriane – Germany's armaments were to be surrendered; all prisoners-of-war were to be immediately released; Allied forces must be permitted to occupy the left bank of the Rhine – where, incidentally, most of the thriving chemical industry was located – and Germany, accepting full responsibility for the war, must make reparation payments to France and Belgium. Most devastating of all for Willy was the stipulation that his Imperial Fleet must also be surrendered to the Allies. In return, the Germans would gain only a ceasefire; their own prisoners-of-war would not be released, nor would the blockade be lifted to allow supplies to reach the starving German people.

On receiving a full report of the demands, Willy was so horrified that he stated his intention to return at once to Berlin to rally his troops, but his advisors told him that such a move was impossible since the country was already in the grip of revolution. That evening, he sent an urgent message to his son, the Crown Prince, summoning him to Spa where a meeting of all the Chiefs of Staff had been arranged for the next day.

On the morning of November 9th, following a series of desperate and depressing conversations, the Kaiser's ministers urged him to abdicate but he declared that he would only do so if he were sure that he had lost the support of the army. When the Crown Prince arrived he informed his father that many regiments remained loyal to the Crown, but several of the most vociferous Generals insisted that, without Willy's abdication, the country would be plunged into a bloody civil war. Fraught and depressed, Willy wandered out into the garden to continue his conversation, and, when the Crown Prince had followed him outside, he observed that his father was:

> "...passionately excited and expressing himself to those near to him with violent gestures....Catching sight of me, [he] beckoned me to approach...and now, as I stood opposite him, I saw clearly how distraught were his features – how his emaciated and sallow face twitched and trembled."[213]

In the midst of these discussions, a message arrived from Prince Max of Baden, informing Willy that, since Berlin was now in a state of revolution, he had no option but to abdicate. Under immense pressure, Willy finally agreed that, if it were the only way to avoid civil war, he would abdicate as German Emperor, but under no circumstances was he prepared to step down as King of Prussia.

> "I would," he later stated, "remain, as such, with my troops, since the military leaders had declared that the officers would leave in crowds if I abdicated entirely, and the army would then pour back, without leaders, into the fatherland, damage it, and place it in peril."[214]

No sooner had he reached this decision than further, more devastating news arrived from Berlin. Prince Max, of his own volition, already publically announced that both the Kaiser and the Crown Prince had abdicated. 'Paralysed and dazed', Willy insisted that, no matter what had been said, he remained the King of Prussia and must therefore return to Berlin to conclude arrangements for the armistice. His ministers and Generals were unsupportive, urging him instead to leave the country at once to prevent further bloodshed. For a few arduous hours, he remained in a state of shock and indecision until, at ten o'clock that night, he was told that a band of mutinous soldiers were rapidly approaching his headquarters. Still he insisted that he would not abandon his country, and, clutching desperately at straws, announced that he would go instead to the Front to fight to the death with his armies. Unimpressed, his advisors reminded him that all routes to the Front were blocked by revolutionaries and his only hope of ever saving the monarchy or obtaining fair terms for Germany, was to leave the country while there was still time.

"Since," he wrote later, "in view of the reports made to me, I must needs believe that, by so doing, I should most faithfully serve Germany, make possible better armistice and peace terms for her, and spare her further loss of human lives, distress, and misery."[215]

An urgent telegram was sent to Queen Wilhelmina of neutral Holland, seeking her permission for the Kaiser to enter her country as 'a private gentleman.' At five o'clock the following morning, his train departed for La Reide, and, after a five hour wait at the Dutch border, he received a response from the Queen, who placed at his disposal Castle Amerongen – a fortified structure, surrounded by two moats – which would be guarded by the Dutch police.

En route, news arrived that Erzberger was about to sign the armistice, agreeing to comply in full with the Allies' demands, leaving Willy to hang his head in shame at what had been accepted. Further humiliations were to follow, since Holland was filled with Belgian deserters who, discovering that the Kaiser's train was approaching, gathered at every station and all along the route to the castle.

"It was a most depressing, shameful journey," wrote a member of Willy's entourage. "At every station thousands of people were gathered, greeting us with shouting, whistling, cursing. They threatened us, made signs of choking and hanging us, etc. In such manner was our poor Emperor received on Dutch soil."[216]

312

Willy remained dignified throughout the ordeal and, somewhat ironically, when he eventually reached the castle, his first words were, "And now for a nice English cup of tea."

With the Kaiser's departure, revolution spread rapidly through the German states. King Ludwig of Bavaria had already been forced to renounce his throne; and he was followed by Willy's son-in-law and brother-in-law, Ernst August of Brunswick and Bernhard of Saxe-Meiningen. One after another the Kings, Grand Dukes and Dukes surrendered their authority but, while several fled, Ernie of Hesse sat patiently in Darmstadt, awaiting the arrival of revolutionaries. As the soldiers poured into his palace, he stood up and greeted them courteously as fellow Hessians, and so touched were they by his courage that they permitted him to keep his estates, while relinquishing his power.

His cousin and friend, Charlie of Coburg, remained loyal to the Kaiser to the end, and it was not until 18th November – a week after the armistice had been signed – that he, too, finally yielded to the revolution when the Workers' and Soldiers' Council of Gotha deposed him.

Germany was in chaos, but in Britain there was rejoicing. At eleven o'clock on the 11th November, as the armistice came into effect, George and May, accompanied by George's uncle, the Duke of Connaught, appeared on the balcony of Buckingham Palace as crowds, waving flags and singing the National Anthem, cheered and celebrated the end of hostilities and their country's triumph.

"The scene in London on Armistice Day was a riot I shall always remember," wrote Charlie of Coburg's sister. "We received a telephone message to go to Buckingham Palace to see the King and Queen appear on the balcony, but the streets were so crowded we could not get there."[217]

Once the initial euphoria had subsided, though, the stark reality of the war's effects must have hung almost as heavily on the hearts of the victorious princes, as it did on those of the vanquished. Old friendships and family ties had been shattered; and for George there could only have been regret when he heard of the fate of his cousin and friend, the Tsar, whom he had abandoned in his hour of need.

"One Sunday," wrote his cousin, Princess Marie Louise, "we were all assembled in the corridor waiting for the King and Queen. The King came in slowly and he looked so grave and distressed...and my mother exclaimed, 'Oh George, is the news very bad?' He said: 'Yes...Nicky, Alix and all their five children have been murdered by the Bolsheviks in Ekaterinburg."

That knowledge must surely have haunted George for the rest of his life.

The joy of victory was undoubtedly tinged with sorrow, too, for Drino and Leopold Battenberg, who had lost a brother as well as their royal status. There were no more Battenbergs, Saxe-Coburg-Gothas or Schleswig Holsteins in Britain; the old world order had been destroyed on the battlefields of Belgium and France; and the sun had finally gone down on the halcyon gatherings of Queen Victoria's grandsons in the antebellum days of great European monarchies.

Epilogue

Throughout his exile, Willy dreamed of the restoration of the German monarchy, but, with the passing years he must have come to the sad realisation that he hoped in vain. His first eighteen months in Holland were far from idyllic, for, not only did he face the hostility of his hosts, but also he was accused of war crimes for which the Allies wished him to stand trial. Only Queen Wilhelmina's refusal to extradite him prevented him from appearing before an international tribunal and potentially facing a death sentence. He watched sadly as Germany was humiliated and virtually destroyed by the demands of the Treaty of Versailles, and, alienated from his former friends and cousins in England, he could only reflect on the events of his life and reign, which he recorded in his memoirs.

In 1920, he purchased a country estate in Doorn, and, three months later, he received the tragic news that his youngest son, twenty-nine-year-old Joachim, had committed suicide in Potsdam. Within a year, Joachim's broken-hearted mother, Dona, followed him to the grave.

"My poor father!" wrote the Crown Prince. "Whatever his outward demeanour, I knew that his innermost heart was shaken."

Dona's body was returned to Potsdam for interment but, since Willy was not permitted to set foot on German soil, he could accompany her coffin only as far as the border.

He did, however, find a measure of happiness when, nine months later, he entertained the recently widowed Princess Hermine von Schoenaich-Carolath at his home in Doorn. Despite the fact that, at sixty-three, Willy was almost thirty years her senior, Hermine discovered the two had much in common, and they were married shortly afterwards in November 1922. For the rest of his life, Willy lived as a country gentleman, watching Hitler's rise to power, first with interest and then with horror:

"Of our Germany, which was a nation of poets and musicians and artists and soldiers," he said, "he has made a nation of hysterics and hermits, engulfed in a mob and led by a thousand liars or fanatics."

Willy lived to see the outbreak of the Second World War, before dying of pulmonary embolism on 3rd June 1941, having outlived his younger brother Henry by twelve years. He was buried in the mausoleum at Doorn where, to this day, German monarchists still gather to pay tribute to their former Emperor.

Following the downfall of the monarchy, Henry had resigned his command and had no further association with the navy. Although, he no longer held an official title, he was allowed to retain his estate in Hemmelmarck, where he lived quietly with his wife, Irene, until his death in April 1929.

In Britain, George's fears for his own throne proved unfounded for, despite the rise of socialism, his popularity increased after the war. He was, however, dogged by ill-health and, as he anxiously watched Hitler's rise to power, he predicted that it would not be long before war again erupted in Europe. He worried, too, about his eldest son, David – the future Edward VIII – warning that, 'After I am dead, the boy will ruin himself within 12 months.'

In 1935, he celebrated his Silver Jubilee, but, by then, he was already a sick man and, the following January, he took to his bed in Sandringham, complaining of a cold. For five days his health continued to decline, and on 20th January, his physician issued the famous bulletin:

"The King's life is drawing peacefully to a close."

Since it would be viewed as unseemly to have his death announced in the evening rather than the morning papers, he was given a powerful injection of morphine and cocaine, and died shortly before midnight. According to his doctor, his final words, addressed to a nurse, were, "God damn you!"

Two years after the end of the war, George's cousin, Young Arthur of Connaught, was appointed Governor General of South Africa – a position which he held for four years, before returning to Britain and devoting much of the rest of his life to charitable works and pursuing his interest in homeopathy. He died of stomach cancer in 1938, predeceasing his father by almost three-and-a-half years.

Although deprived of any authority following the downfall of the monarchy, Charlie of Coburg and Ernie of Hesse, were permitted to retain their German estates. Ernie continued his interest in the arts until his death at his beloved Wolfsgarten in October 1937. Charlie, on the other hand, became convinced that Hitler would help to restore Germany's fortunes and, in 1935, he became an official member of the Nazi party. During the Second World War, he was appointed Head of the German Red Cross, and was grieved by the news that his son, Hubertus, had been killed in action. After the conclusion of hostilities, he was placed under house arrest on his estates at Veste Coburg, before being imprisoned in a former Serbian prisoner-of-war camp. By then he was crippled with arthritis, and conditions in the camp were so appalling that, according to his sister, Alice,

"Not having any utensils, he was sent to a rubbish dump to collect a tin, which he cleaned as best he could with gravel. The soup was so thin that they added grass to improve it."[218]

Eventually, he was released on the grounds of ill-health but his property was seized and he was bankrupted by the hefty fines imposed upon him. For the rest of his life, he lived a semi-reclusive existence, dying on 6th March 1954.

Abbie of Schleswig-Holstein also continued to live in Germany, and in 1921, he succeeded Willy's brother-in-law as the official Head of the House of Schleswig-Holstein-Sonderburg-Augustenburg. A few days before his death in April 1931, he admitted to having fathered an illegitimate daughter named Valerie Marie, whom his sisters formally acknowledged as their niece.

The war wrought a dramatic change in the life of Drino Battenberg, 1st Marquis of Carisbrooke, who had grown up in such close proximity to his grandmother, Queen Victoria. With no allowance from the civil list, he had to earn a living and became the first member of the Royal Family to embark on a career in business. He worked first as an ordinary clerk for Lazard Brothers before gaining directorships of several prosperous companies, including Lever Brothers.

In 1922, his younger brother, the haemophiliac Leopold, died during a hip operation at the age of only thirty-two, leaving Drino as the sole surviving son of Queen Victoria's youngest daughter, Beatrice. During the Second World War, he returned to the military, acting as a staff officer in the Royal Air Force, and later became President of the London Branch of 'the Old Contemptibles' – a club for retired members of the First World War British Expeditionary Force, so named because the Kaiser had once referred to them as a 'contemptible little army'. Drino died in Kensington Palace in 1960, the last surviving grandson of Queen Victoria.

Recommended Reading

Alice, Countess of Athlone *For my Grandchildren* (Evans 1979)
Alice, Grand Duchess of Hesse, *Biographical Sketch and Letters* (John Murray 1884)
Aronson, Theo *Crowns in Conflict* (Salem House 1986)
Bennett Daphne *Queen Victoria's Children* (Victor Gollancz 1980)
Croft, Christina *Most Beautiful Princess* (Hilliard & Croft 2008)
Croft, Christina *Shattered Crowns: The Scapegoats* (CreateSpace 2011)
Croft, Christina *Shattered Crowns: The Sacrifice* (CreateSpace 2012)
Croft, Christina *Shattered Crowns: The Betrayal* (CreateSpace 2012)
Croft, Christina *Queen Victoria's Granddaughters 1960-1918* (CreateSpace 2013)
Fulford, Roger (Editor) *Beloved Mama* (Evans 1981)
Fulford, Roger (Editor) *Your Dear Letter* (Evans 1971)
Longford, Elizabeth *Victoria R.I.* Pan 1966
Longford, Elizabeth *Louisa, Lady in Waiting* (Jonathan Cape 1979)
Marie, Queen of Roumania *The Story of My Life* (Cassell 1935)
Marie Louise, Princess *My Memories of Six Reigns* (Evans Brothers 1956)
Mallet, Victor *Life With Queen Victoria – Marie Mallet's letters from court 1887-1901* (John Murray 1968)
Matson, John *Dear Osborne* (Hamish Hamilton 1981)
Nelson, Michael *Queen Victoria & the Discovery of the Riviera* (Tauris Parke 2001)
Nicolson, Harold *King George V, His Life & Reign* (Doubleday 1953)
Packard, Jerrold *Victoria's Daughters* (Sutton 1998)

Pakula, Hannah *An Uncommon Woman* Weidenfeld & Nicolson 1985

Ponsonby, Frederick (editor) *The Letters of the Empress Frederick* (Macmillan 1928)

Ponsonby, Frederick *Recollections of Three Reigns* (Eyre & Spottiswood 1961)

Pope Hennessy, James *Queen Mary* (George Allen & Unwin 1959)

Ramm Agatha *Beloved & Darling Child* (Sutton 1990)

Reid Michaela *Ask Sir James* (Hodder & Stoughton 1987)

St. John-Neville, Barry *Life at the Court of Queen Victoria* (Salem House 1985)

Stanley, Lady Augusta *The Letters of Lady Augusta Stanley – edited by the Dean of Windsor and Hector Bolitho* (Gerald Howe Ltd. 1927)

Topham Alice *A Distant Thunder* (New Chapter Press 1992)

Tyler-Whittle, Michael Sydney *The Last Kaiser: A biography of Wilhelm II, German Emperor & King of Prussia* (Times Books 1977)

Wile, Frederic William *The Men Around the Kaiser* (MacMillan 1913)

Wilhelm II, *My Early Life* (G.H. Doran 1926)

By the Same Author

Biography

Queen Victoria's Granddaughters 1960-1918

Alice, the Enigma – A Biography of Queen Victoria's Daughter

Dear Papa, Beloved Mama – An intimate portrait of Queen Victoria & Prince Albert as parents

Historical Fiction

Most Beautiful Princess – A Novel Based on the Life of Grand Duchess Elizabeth of Russia

Shattered Crowns: The Scapegoats
Shattered Crowns: The Sacrifice
Shattered Crowns: The Betrayal

The Fields Laid Waste

Novels

The Counting House

By Any Other Name

Children's Books

Wonderful Walter

Poetry

Child of the Moon

References

[1] Wilhelm II, *My Early Life* (G.H. Doran 1926)
[2] Fulford, Roger (Editor) *Dearest Child, Letters between Queen Victoria & the Princess Royal 1858-1861* (Evans Brothers 1964)
[3] Wilhelm II, *My Early Life* (G.H. Doran 1926)
[4] Fulford, Roger (Editor) *Dearest Child, Letters between Queen Victoria & the Princess Royal 1858-1861* (Evans Brothers 1964)
[5] Martin, Theodore *The Life of His Royal Highness the Prince Consort Vol IV* (Smith, Elder & Co. 1879)
[6] Fontenoy, La Marquise de *Secret Memories of the Court of Berlin under William II* (DeFau 1909)
[7] Anonymous *The Empress Frederick – A Memoir* (Dodd, Mead & Co. 1914)
[8] Ponsonby, Frederick *Recollections of Three Reigns* (Eyre & Spottiswoode 1951)
[9] Fulford, Roger (Editor) *Your Dear Letter: Private Correspondence of Queen Victoria and the Crown Princess of Prussia, 1865-71* (Evans Brothers 1971)
[10] Fulford, Roger (Editor) *Your Dear Letter: Private Correspondence of Queen Victoria and the Crown Princess of Prussia, 1865-71* (Evans Brothers 1971)
[11] Wilhelm II, *My Early Life* (G.H. Doran 1926)
[12] Wilhelm II, *My Early Life* (G.H. Doran 1926)
[13] Stanley, Lady Augusta *The Letters of Lady Augusta Stanley* – edited by the Dean of Windsor and Hector Bolitho (Gerald Howe Ltd. 1927)
[14] Stanley, Lady Augusta *The Letters of Lady Augusta Stanley* – edited by the Dean of Windsor and Hector Bolitho (Gerald Howe Ltd. 1927)
[15] Trowbridge W.R.H. *Queen Alexandra – A Study in Royalty* (D. Appleton & Co. 1923)
[16] Nicolson, Harold *King George V, His Life & Reign* (Doubleday 1953)
[17] Helena Victoria, Princess (editor) *Alice Grand Duchess of Hesse, Biographical Sketch and Letters* (John Murray 1884)
[18] Fulford, Roger (Editor) *Your Dear Letter: Private Correspondence of Queen Victoria and the Crown Princess of Prussia, 1865-71* (Evans Brothers 1971)
[19] Ponsonby, Frederick (editor) *Letters of the Empress Frederick* (Macmillan & Co. 1928)
[20] Helena Victoria, Princess (editor) *Alice Grand Duchess of Hesse, Biographical Sketch and Letters* (John Murray 1884)
[21] Ponsonby, Frederick (editor) *Letters of the Empress Frederick* (Macmillan & Co. 1928)
[22] Helena Victoria, Princess (editor) *Alice Grand Duchess of Hesse, Biographical Sketch and Letters* (John Murray 1884)
[23] Wilhelm II, *My Early Life* (G.H. Doran 1926)
[24] Fulford, Roger (Editor) *Beloved Mama: Private Correspondence of Queen Victoria and the Crown Princess of Prussia, 1878-85* (Evans 1981)
[25] Wile, Frederic William *The Men Around the Kaiser* (MacMillan 1913)
[26] Helena Victoria, Princess (editor) *Alice Grand Duchess of Hesse, Biographical Sketch and Letters* (John Murray 1884)
[27] Helena Victoria, Princess (editor) *Alice Grand Duchess of Hesse, Biographical Sketch and Letters* (John Murray 1884)
[28] Helena Victoria, Princess (editor) *Alice Grand Duchess of Hesse, Biographical Sketch and Letters* (John Murray 1884)
[29] Helena Victoria, Princess (editor) *Alice Grand Duchess of Hesse, Biographical Sketch and Letters* (John Murray 1884)

[30] Bailey, John (Ed) *The Diary of Lady Frederick Cavendish* (John Murray 1927)
[31] Ponsonby, Frederick *Recollections of Three Reigns* (Eyre & Spottiswoode 1951)
[32] Fulford, Roger (Editor) *Your Dear Letter: Private Correspondence of Queen Victoria and the Crown Princess of Prussia, 1865-71* (Evans Brothers 1971)
[33] Bolitho, Hector *The Reign of Queen Victoria* (Macmillan 1948)
[34] Marie Louise, Princess *My Memories of Six Reigns* (Evan Brothers 1956)
[35] Marie Louise, Princess *My Memories of Six Reigns* (Evan Brothers 1956)
[36] Marie Louise, Princess *My Memories of Six Reigns* (Evan Brothers 1956)
[37] Haig-Brown, Harold *William Haig-Brown of Charterhouse* (Macmillan & Co, 1908)
[38] Haig-Brown, Harold *William Haig-Brown of Charterhouse* (Macmillan & Co, 1908)
[39] Ponsonby, Frederick (editor) *Letters of the Empress Frederick* (Macmillan & Co. 1928)
[40] Ponsonby, Frederick (editor) *Letters of the Empress Frederick* (Macmillan & Co. 1928)
[41] Wilhelm II, *My Early Life* (G.H. Doran 1926)
[42] Helena Victoria, Princess (editor) *Alice Grand Duchess of Hesse, Biographical Sketch and Letters* (John Murray 1884)
[43] Helena Victoria, Princess (editor) *Alice Grand Duchess of Hesse, Biographical Sketch and Letters* (John Murray 1884)
[44] Helena Victoria, Princess (editor) *Alice Grand Duchess of Hesse, Biographical Sketch and Letters* (John Murray 1884)
[45] Gould Lee (Editor) *The Empress Frederick Writes to Sophie* (Faber & Faber)
[46] Fulford, Roger (Editor) *Your Dear Letter: Private Correspondence of Queen Victoria and the Crown Princess of Prussia, 1865-71* (Evans Brothers 1971)
[47] Fulford, Roger (Editor) *Your Dear Letter: Private Correspondence of Queen Victoria and the Crown Princess of Prussia, 1865-71* (Evans Brothers 1971)
[48] *Ladies Treasury* 2 March 1884
[49] Tennyson, Alfred, Lord *A Welcome to the Duke & Duchess of Edinburgh* (1874)
[50] Marie, Queen of Roumania *The Story of My Life* (Charles Scribner & Sons 1934)
[51] Marie, Queen of Roumania *The Story of My Life* (Charles Scribner & Sons 1934)
[52] Marie, Queen of Roumania *The Story of My Life* (Charles Scribner & Sons 1934)
[53] Marie, Queen of Roumania *The Story of My Life* (Charles Scribner & Sons 1934)
[54] Mallet, Victor *Life With Queen Victoria – Marie Mallet's letters from court 1887-1901* (John Murray 1968)
[55] Bailey, John (Ed) *The Diary of Lady Frederick Cavendish* (John Murray 1927)
[56] Stanley, Lady Augusta *The Letters of Lady Augusta Stanley* – edited by the Dean of Windsor and Hector Bolitho (Gerald Howe Ltd. 1927)
[57] Sheppard, Edgar (Editor) *George, Duke of Cambridge – A Memoir of His Prince Life* (Longmans, Green & Co. 1906)
[58] Bailey, John (Ed) *The Diary of Lady Frederick Cavendish* (John Murray 1927)
[59] Bailey, John (Ed) *The Diary of Lady Frederick Cavendish* (John Murray 1927)
[60] Longford, Elizabeth *Darling Loosy – Letters to Princess Louise 1856-1939* (Weidenfeld & Nicholson 1991)
[61] Halsted, Murat, & Munson A. *The Life & Reign of Queen Victoria* (International Publishing Society 1901)
[62] Sheppard, Edgar (Editor) *George, Duke of Cambridge – A Memoir of His Prince Life* (Longmans, Green & Co. 1906)
[63] Sheppard, Edgar (Editor) *George, Duke of Cambridge – A Memoir of His Prince Life* (Longmans, Green & Co. 1906)
[64] Wakeling, Edward, ed. *Lewis Carroll's Diaries: The Private Journals of Chales Lutwidge Dodgson (Lewis Carroll)*, Volume 8 (London: The Lewis Carroll Society, 2004): 596.
[65] Mallet, Victor (Editor) *Life with Queen Victoria. Marie Mallet's Letters from Court 1887-1901* (John Murray 1968)
[66] Gould Lee (Editor) *The Empress Frederick Writes to Sophie* (Faber & Faber)
[67] Gould Lee (Editor) *The Empress Frederick Writes to Sophie* (Faber & Faber)

[68] Gould Lee, Arthur (Editor) *The Empress Frederick Writes to Sophie* (Faber & Faber)
[69] Catling, Thomas *My Life's Pilgrimage* (John Murray 1911)
[70] Liliuokalani, Queen *Hawaii's Story by Hawaii's Queen* (Lothrop, Lee and Shepard 1898)
[71] Williamson, David *Queen Alexandra* (Oliphants 1919)
[72] Nicolson, Harold *King George V, His Life & Reign* (Doubleday 1953)
[73] Albert Victor & George of Wales, with additions by Dalton, John. *The Cruise of Her Majesty's Ship Bacchante 1879-1882 Vol. 1* (Macmillan 1886)
[74] Sheppard, Edgar (Editor) *George, Duke of Cambridge – A Memoir of His Prince Life* (Longmans, Green & Co. 1906)
[75] Sheppard, Edgar (Editor) *George, Duke of Cambridge – A Memoir of His Prince Life* (Longmans, Green & Co. 1906)
[76] Sheppard, Edgar (Editor) *George, Duke of Cambridge – A Memoir of His Prince Life* (Longmans, Green & Co. 1906)
[77] Sheppard, Edgar (Editor) *George, Duke of Cambridge – A Memoir of His Prince Life* (Longmans, Green & Co. 1906)
[78] Wilhelm II, *My Early Life* (G.H. Doran 1926)
[79] Wilhelm II, *My Early Life* (G.H. Doran 1926)
[80] Fulford, Roger (Editor) *Your Dear Letter: Private Correspondence of Queen Victoria and the Crown Princess of Prussia, 1865-71* (Evans Brothers 1971)
[81] Ponsonby, Frederick (editor) *Letters of the Empress Frederick* (Macmillan & Co. 1928)
[82] Wilhelm II, *My Early Life* (G.H. Doran 1926)
[83] Barkeley, Richard *The Empress Frederick* (MacMillan 1956)
[84] Wilhelm II, *My Early Life* (G.H. Doran 1926)
[85] Fulford, Roger (Editor) *Beloved Mama, Private Correspondence of Queen Victoria and the German Crown Princess 1878-1885* (Evans Bros. 1981)
[86] Fontenoy, La Marquise de *Secret Memories of the Court of Berlin under William II* (DeFau 1909)
[87] Legge, Edward *The Public & Private Life of the Kaiser* (E. Nash 1915)
[88] Fulford, Roger (Editor) *Beloved Mama, Private Correspondence of Queen Victoria and the German Crown Princess 1878-1885* (Evans Bros. 1981)
[89] Wile, Frederic William *The Men Around the Kaiser* (MacMillan 1913)
[90] Legge, Edward *King Edward, The Kaiser & The War* (Grant Richards 1917)
[91] Catling, Thomas *My Life's Pilgrimage* (John Murray 1911)
[92] Ponsonby, Frederick (editor) *Letters of the Empress Frederick* (Macmillan & Co. 1928)
[93] Barkeley, Richard *The Empress Frederick* (MacMillan 1956)
[94] Mackenzie, Morell Sir *The Fatal Illness of Frederick the Nobel* (Low, Marston, Searle & Rimmington 1888)
[95] Mackenzie, Morell Sir *The Fatal Illness of Frederick the Nobel* (Low, Marston, Searle & Rimmington 1888)
[96] Ponsonby, Frederick (editor) *Letters of the Empress Frederick* (Macmillan & Co. 1928)
[97] Barkeley, Richard *The Empress Frederick* (MacMillan 1956)
[98] Ponsonby, Frederick (editor) *Letters of the Empress Frederick* (Macmillan & Co. 1928)
[99] Ponsonby, Frederick (editor) *Letters of the Empress Frederick* (Macmillan & Co. 1928)
[100] Gould Lee, Arthur *Empress Frederick Writes to Sophie, Her Daughter, Crown Princess of the Hellenes* (Faber & Faber)
[101] Fontenoy, La Marquise de *Secret Memories of the Court of Berlin under William II* (DeFau 1909)
[102] Layard, Lady Mary *Journal* (reprinted by permission of The Browning Archive Baylor University, Texas)
[103] Fontenoy, La Marquise de *Secret Memories of the Court of Berlin under William II* (DeFau 1909)
[104] Fontenoy, La Marquise de *Secret Memories of the Court of Berlin under William II* (DeFau 1909)

[105] Wile, Frederic William *The Men Around the Kaiser* (MacMillan 1913)
[106] Fontenoy, La Marquise de *Secret Memories of the Court of Berlin under William II* (DeFau 1909)
[107] Louise, Princess of Belgium, (translated by Maude Ffoukes) *My Own Affairs* (Cassell & Co. 1921)
[108] Bismarck, Otto von (translated by Bernard Miall) *The Kaiser vs Bismarck – The Suppressed Letters of the Kaiser & New Chapters of the Autobiography of the Iron Chancellor* (Harper & Bros 1920)
[109] Anon. *The Real Kaiser* (Melrose Ltd. 1914)
[110] Dickinson, A.S.A *The Kaiser* (Doubleday 1914)
[111] Martin, Theodore *The Life of His Royal Highness the Prince Consort, Vol. 4* (Smith, Elder & Co. 1879)
[112] Martin, Theodore *The Life of His Royal Highness the Prince Consort, Vol. 4* (Smith, Elder & Co. 1879)
[113] Martin, Theodore *The Life of His Royal Highness the Prince Consort, Vol. 4* (Smith, Elder & Co. 1879)
[114] Garrett Fawcett, Millicent *Life of Her Majesty Queen Victoria* (Roberts Brothers 1895)
[115] Gould Lee, Arthur (Editor) *The Empress Frederick Writes to Sophie* (Faber & Faber)
[116] Marie Louise, Princess *My Memories of Six Reigns* (Evan Brothers 1956)
[117] Marie Louise, Princess *My Memories of Six Reigns* (Evan Brothers 1956)
[118] Mallet, Victor (Editor) *Life with Queen Victoria. Marie Mallet's Letters from Court 1887-1901* (John Murray 1968)
[119] Gould Lee (Editor) *The Empress Frederick Writes to Sophie* (Faber & Faber)
[120] Marie, Queen of Roumania *The Story of My Life* (Charles Scribner & Sons 1934)
[121] Ponsonby, Frederick (editor) *Letters of the Empress Frederick* (Macmillan & Co. 1928)
[122] Gould Lee, Arthur (Editor) *The Empress Frederick Writes to Sophie* (Faber & Faber)
[123] Legge, Edward *King George & the Royal Family Vol. II* (Grant Richards 1918)
[124] Louise, Princess of Belgium, (translated by Maude Ffoukes) *My Own Affairs* (Cassell & Co. 1921)
[125] Ponsonby, Frederick (editor) *Letters of the Empress Frederick* (Macmillan & Co. 1928)
[126] Fontenoy, La Marquise de *Secret Memories of the Court of Berlin under William II* (DeFau 1909)
[127] Noussane, Henri *The Kaiser as He Is* G.P. (Putnams 1905)
[128] Ponsonby, Frederick (editor) *Letters of the Empress Frederick* (Macmillan & Co. 1928)
[129] William, Crown Prince of Germany *Memoirs of the Crown Prince of Germany* (Charles Scribner's Sons 1922)
[130] William, Crown Prince of Germany *Memoirs of the Crown Prince of Germany* (Charles Scribner's Sons 1922)
[131] Fontenoy, La Marquise de *Secret Memories of the Court of Berlin under William II* (DeFau 1909)
[132] Anon. *The Real Kaiser* (Melrose Ltd. 1914)
[133] William, Crown Prince of Germany *Memoirs of the Crown Prince of Germany* (Charles Scribner's Sons 1922)
[134] Noussane, Henri *The Kaiser as He Is* (Putnams 1905)
[135] Dehn, Lili *The Real Tsaritsa* (1922)
[136] Ramm Agatha (Editor) *Beloved & Darling Child – Last Letters Between Queen Victoria and Her Eldest Daughter 1886-1901* (Alan Sutton Ltd. 1990)
[137] Ramm Agatha (Editor) *Beloved & Darling Child – Last Letters Between Queen Victoria and Her Eldest Daughter 1886-1901* (Alan Sutton Ltd. 1990)
[138] Gould Lee, Arthur *Empress Frederick Writes to Sophie, Her Daughter, Crown Princess of the Hellenes* (Faber & Faber)
[139] Sheppard, Edgar (Editor) *George, Duke of Cambridge – A Memoir of His Prince Life* (Longmans, Green & Co. 1906)

[140] Gould Lee, Arthur *Empress Frederick Writes to Sophie, Her Daughter, Crown Princess of the Hellenes* (Faber & Faber)

[141] Trowbridge W.R.H. *Queen Alexandra – A Study in Royalty* (D. Appleton & Co. 1923)

[142] Sheppard, Edgar (Editor) *George, Duke of Cambridge – A Memoir of His Prince Life* (Longmans, Green & Co. 1906)

[143] Hudson, Robert *George, Our Sailor King* (Collins Press 1914)

[144] Reid, Michaela *Ask Sir James* (Eland 1987)

[145] Trowbridge W.R.H. *Queen Alexandra – A Study in Royalty* (D. Appleton & Co. 1923)

[146] Nicolson, Harold *King George V, His Life & Reign* (Doubleday 1953)

[147] Ponsonby, Frederick *Recollections of Three Reigns* (Eyre & Spottiswoode 1951)

[148] Nicolson, Harold *King George V, His Life & Reign* (Doubleday 1953)

[149] Pope-Hennessey, James *Queen Mary* (George Allen & Unwin 1959)

[150] Marie, Queen of Roumania *The Story of My Life* (Charles Scribner & Sons 1934)

[151] Woodward, Kathleen *Queen Mary A Life & Intimate Study* (Hutchinson & Co. 1928)

[152] Nicolson, Harold *King George V, His Life & Reign* (Doubleday 1953)

[153] Gore, John *Queen Mary* (Illustrated London News 1941)

[154] Vyrubova, Anna *Memories of the Russian Court* (Macmillan 1923)

[155] Fontenoy, La Marquise de *Secret Memories of the Court of Berlin under William II* (DeFau 1909)

[156] Gould Lee, Arthur *Empress Frederick Writes to Sophie, Her Daughter, Crown Princess of the Hellenes* (Faber & Faber)

[157] Sheppard, Edgar (Editor) *George, Duke of Cambridge – A Memoir of His Prince Life* (Longmans, Green & Co. 1906)

[158] Buxheoveden, Sophie *The Life And Tragedy Of Alexandra Feodorovna Empress Of Russia* (Longmans Green & Co. 1928)

[159] Buchanan, George *My Mission to Russia* (Cassell & Company 1923)

[160] Gould Lee, Arthur *Empress Frederick Writes to Sophie, Her Daughter, Crown Princess of the Hellenes* (Faber & Faber)

[161] Reid, Michaela *Ask Sir James* (Eland 1987)

[162] Louise, Princess of Belgium (translated by Maude FFoukes) *My Own Affairs* (Cassell & Co. 1921)

[163] Marie, Queen of Roumania *The Story of My Life* (Charles Scribner & Sons 1934)

[164] Mallet, Victor *Life With Queen Victoria – Marie Mallet's letters from court 1887-1901* (John Murray 1968)

[165] Buchanan, George *My Mission to Russia* (Cassell & Company 1923)

[166] Ponsonby, Frederick *Recollections of Three Reigns* (Eyre & Spottiswoode 1951)

[167] Eager, Margaret *Six Years at the Russian Court* (1906)

[168] Eager, Margaret *Six Years at the Russian Court* (1906)

[169] Levine, Isaac (editor) *Letters from the Kaiser to the Tsar* (Frederick A. Stokes 1920)

[170] Gould Lee, Arthur *Empress Frederick Writes to Sophie, Her Daughter, Crown Princess of the Hellenes* (Faber & Faber)

[171] Reid, Michaela *Ask Sir James* (Eland 1987)

[172] Ponsonby, Frederick *Recollections of Three Reigns* (Eyre & Spottiswoode 1951)

[173] Anonymous *The Empress Frederick – A Memoir* (Dodd, Mead & Co. 1914)

[174] Wilhelm II, *My Early Life* (G.H. Doran 1926)

[175] Collier, William Miller *At The Court of His Catholic Majesty* (A.C. McClug & Co. 1912)

[176] Durland, Kellogg *Royal Romances of Today* (Duffield & Co. 1911)

[177] Alice, Princess, Countess of Athlone *For My Grandchildren* (Evans Bros 1966)

[178] Legge, Edward *King Edward, The Kaiser, and the War* (Grant Richards Ltd 1917)

[179] *Daily Telegraph* 19th October 1908

[180] William, Crown Prince of Germany *Memoirs of the Crown Prince of Germany* (Charles Scribner's Sons 1922)

[181] Legge, Edward *King Edward, The Kaiser, and the War* (Grant Richards Ltd 1917)
[182] Wortham H.E. *Edward VII, Man & King* (Little Brown 1931)
[183] Ponsonby, Frederick *Recollections of Three Reigns* (Eyre & Spottiswoode 1951)
[184] William, Crown Prince of Germany *Memoirs of the Crown Prince of Germany* (Charles Scribner's Sons 1922)
[185] Legge, Edward *King Edward, The Kaiser, and the War* (Grant Richards Ltd 1917)
[186] Ponsonby, Frederick *Recollections of Three Reigns* (Eyre & Spottiswoode 1951)
[187] Hamilton, Allan Maclean *The Kaiser's Psychosis* (The North American Review)
[188] Noussane, Henri *The Kaiser as He Is* (Putnams 1905)
[189] Legge, Edward *King Edward, The Kaiser, and the War* (Grant Richards Ltd 1917)
[190] Richardson, Mary *Laugh a Defiance* (Weidenfeld & Nicholson 1953)
[191] Nicolson, Harold *King George V, His Life & Reign* (Doubleday 1953)
[192] Pankhurst, Emmeline *My Own Story* (Everleigh Nash 1914)
[193] Salt, Henry S. (Editor) *Killing for Sport* G. Bell & Sons 1915)
[194] Levine, Isaac (editor) *Letters from the Kaiser to the Tsar* (Frederick A. Stokes 1920)
[195] Legge, Edward *King George & the Royal Family Vol. I* (Grant Richards 1918)
[196] Topham, Alice *Memories of the Kaiser's Court* (Methuen & Co. 1914)
[197] Carnegie, Andrew *Autobiography of Andrew Carnegie* (Constable & Co. 1920)
[198] Carnegie, Andrew *Autobiography of Andrew Carnegie* (Constable & Co. 1920)
[199] Alice, Princess, Countess of Athlone *For My Grandchildren* (Evans Bros 1966)
[200] Levine, Isaac (editor) *Letters from the Kaiser to the Tsar* (Frederick A. Stokes 1920)
[201] Levine, Isaac (editor) *Letters from the Kaiser to the Tsar* (Frederick A. Stokes 1920)
[202] Levine, Isaac (editor) *Letters from the Kaiser to the Tsar* (Frederick A. Stokes 1920)
[203] William, Crown Prince of Germany *Memoirs of the Crown Prince of Germany* (Charles Scribner's Sons 1922)
[204] Marie Louise, Princess *My Memories of Six Reigns* (Evan Brothers 1956)
[205] William, Crown Prince of Germany *Memoirs of the Crown Prince of Germany* (Charles Scribner's Sons 1922)
[206] William, Crown Prince of Germany *Memoirs of the Crown Prince of Germany* (Charles Scribner's Sons 1922)
[207] Marie Louise, Princess *My Memories of Six Reigns* (Evan Brothers 1956)
[208] William, Crown Prince of Germany *Memoirs of the Crown Prince of Germany* (Charles Scribner's Sons 1922)
[209] Wilhelm II (translated by Thomas Ybarra) *The Kaiser's Memoirs* (Harper and Bros. 1922)
[210] Marie Louise, Princess *My Memories of Six Reigns* (Evan Brothers 1956)
[211] Ponsonby, Frederick *Recollections of Three Reigns* (Eyre & Spottiswoode 1951)
[212] Ponsonby, Frederick *Recollections of Three Reigns* (Eyre & Spottiswoode 1951)
[213] William, Crown Prince of Germany *Memoirs of the Crown Prince of Germany* (Charles Scribner's Sons 1922)
[214] Wilhelm II (translated by Thomas Ybarra) *The Kaiser's Memoirs* (Harper and Bros. 1922)
[215] Wilhelm II (translated by Thomas Ybarra) *The Kaiser's Memoirs* (Harper and Bros. 1922)
[216] William, Crown Prince of Germany *Memoirs of the Crown Prince of Germany* (Charles Scribner's Sons 1922)
[217] Alice, Princess, Countess of Athlone *For My Grandchildren* (Evans Bros 1966)
[218] Alice, Princess, Countess of Athlone *For My Grandchildren* (Evans Bros 1966)